THE TWENTY-FIRST CENTURY WILL BE AMERICAN

◆

ALFREDO G.A. VALLADÃO

Translated by John Howe

VERSO

London • New York

First published by Verso 1996
This edition © Verso 1996
Translation © John Howe 1996
First published as *Le XXIe siècle sera américain*
© La Découverte/Essais
All rights reserved

Verso
UK: 6 Meard Street, London W1V 3HR
USA: 180 Varick Street, New York NY 10014–4606

Verso is the imprint of New Left Books

ISBN 1–85984–939–3

British Library Cataloguing in Publication Data
A catalogue record for this book is available from the British Library

Library of Congress Cataloging-in-Publication Data
A catalog record for this book is available from the Library of Congress

Typeset by Keystroke, Jacaranda Lodge, Wolverhampton, UK
Manufactured in the USA by The Courier Companies

For Gobinha

CONTENTS

CONTENTS

FOREWORD

The twenty-first century will be American for the simple reason that America alone possesses the three pillars of power: military, economic and cultural. As a result of the final collapse of the Soviet Union, the United States has become the coordinator of planetary security. The US must now decide where and when an international "police operation" is needed; and Washington alone has the privilege of being able to intervene anywhere in the world. America also comprises the world's largest, wealthiest homogeneous market; the combination of advanced technology with control of the great flows of petroleum, finance and audio-visual images produces economic hegemony. American culture is not shy about its universal vocation. It is proud of its capacity to integrate all other cultures, and has diffused across the entire planet to be incorporated into all other societies.

It should be fairly clear by now that this work is opposed to all theories positing an American "decline". But it is not just an ode to the obvious power of the United States. Abroad, the debate has all too often been undermined by the dreary predictability of ideological passions: the anti-Americans eager for evidence of their great bogey-man's relentless decline, the fans wanting to be reassured as to the permanence of their protective model. In Washington itself the "declinists" at least share one common concern with their adversaries: the wish to perpetuate and strengthen the primacy of the United States. The first group, generally to be found in the opposition, bewails the nation's decrepitude the better to present itself as the alternative capable of restoring the lost grandeur. The second group – generally in power – defends its record, positive by definition, and maintains that it alone can guarantee continuing prosperity. It is high time people gave up skating on the thin ice of short-term politically motivated prophecies.

Academics espousing the decline theory often have the good taste to base their predictions on the histories of the great empires of the past, Rome in particular. The United States, like the Roman empire in the fourth century AD, is said to be on the point of collapsing under the weight of military expenditure, economic stagnation and "barbarian" pressure. But what if the declinists are four or five hundred years out? If we must have a great historical parallel, it may be more appropriate to use the first century BC when the Roman Republic, after a definitive triumph over its mortal enemy Carthage, embarked in pain, war and disorder on its profound mutation into a "universal" empire. Then as now, the uncertainty of the times inspired all sorts of Cassandras. The literature of Rome's decadence, of which Sallust remains the strongest exponent, was at its most vigorous during the last few decades before the victory of Augustus and the establishment of the imperial institution.

This book is intended to chronicle the fall of the American Republic and its transformation into a vast "World-America" – a democratic empire with a vocation to merge with the entire planet, even at the expense of American domestic interests. In seeking to decipher the most recent manifestations of this extraordinary historical process, these pages will keep their distance from the transitory surges of euphoria and pessimism that form a nation's political life. The ups and downs of America's political, economic and cultural existence have to be evaluated in terms of the subterranean forces pushing towards an American-centred global civilization.

It is only natural that the triumph of World-America should worry those who remain attached to local or national particularisms, American or other. But it is pointless to fret over the inexorable march towards a planetary empire. The metamorphosis of civilizations is not subject to individual volition. The era of sovereign nation-states jealously guarding their own economies, cultures and political identities, which began with the American and French revolutions, is now drawing to a close. It will not survive the accelerated integration of the world. It is futile to complain about mounting "barbarity" and withdraw into a nostalgic cult of the national past. Of course there is nothing undignified about defending old values which have proved their worth. But the dignity is that of the chief of a small tribe of Amazonian Indians who, faced with disintegration of his community due to the pressures of modern society, tells the women to stop having babies so that the tribe will die out of its own accord: if death is inevitable, it is always better to die on your feet. But life goes on.

Throughout history, humanity has been forced to adapt to new forms of social organization. Every time this happens there are enormous losses, but there are gains as well. This book is intended to be resolutely optimistic. Instead of mourning for the lost Republic, let us restore contact with the dynamism of its beginnings. In these closing years of the twentieth century, five hundred years after explorers' caravels opened up the universe for the European heirs of the Roman empire, all the peoples of the earth can at last share the dream of those navigators and aspire to their great adventure. A World-America awaits their discovery and conquest.

This work is divided into three parts. The first deals with the great cultural mutations that will enable the new democratic empire to manage the biggest challenge of the twenty-first century: the amalgamation of all human communities. Chapters 1 and 2 address the religious implications of the American political system, tracing its evolution from the Calvinism of the first colonists to the current religious revolution and the appearance of a new universal cult. The eclipse of white, Anglo-Saxon, Protestant America and the birth of a new multiculturalism occupy chapters 3 and 4; the resulting movement from American provincialism to a world culture that flourishes alongside all existing particularisms is described in chapter 5.

The second part describes the decline of the American Republic and the birth of World-America. The increase in the influence of the White House, the neutralization of the power of Congress, the decline of the political parties and the establishment of a vast client system managed by a new imperial nobility are covered in chapters 6 and 7. The internationalization and gradual dislocation of the United States and the emergence of Washington as the political capital of the planet are addressed in chapter 8.

The third part describes the construction of the new universal democratic empire. Chapter 9 seeks to expose the analyses that cite conjunctural accidents to conclude that America is in economic decline: in reality, America possesses the largest, most productive and most innovative economy in the world, and its bosses make no secret of their intention to manage the world economy. Chapters 10 and 11 deal with the nuts and bolts of this economic power: mastery of computer technology and telecommunications, and control of oil, capital and audio-visual images. The organization of planetary trade around the NAFTA pole, the struggle against protectionism and the establishment of new criteria for development aid are detailed in chapters 12 and 13. The politico-military angle is the subject of the last chapter; quickly digesting the lessons of the end of the Cold War, the United States has succeeded in building a new worldwide security pact in which its status is that of *primus inter pares*.

Just a word, finally, to express my gratitude to José Garçon, without whom this book would never have been written; and my thanks to Richard Boidin and Marc Perrin de Brichambault for their encouragement, their invaluable advice and their friendship. I would also like to thank my friend Michèle Carteron, of the press service of the US Embassy in Paris, for making the task of research so easy, as well as Marguerite Le Roy, head of the Benjamin Franklin documentation centre, for her help in guiding me through the unbelievable undergrowth of the Library of Congress.

PREFACE TO THE

ENGLISH-LANGUAGE EDITION

This book was first published in France in the spring of 1993, just a few months after President Bill Clinton's arrival in the White House. As might be expected, therefore, it goes into some detail on the deeds and attitudes of his predecessor George Bush, along with the stated *intentions* of the young president-elect. This English edition contains a number of minor amendments covering the first three years of the Clinton administration, in particular the election to Congress of a Republican majority, led by Newt Gingrich, promising a "Contract with America".

I have deliberately kept these changes to a minimum, even in the economic chapters, whose figures and examples refer mainly to the first two years of the present decade. It had never been my intention in any case to provide an exhaustive record of contemporary American political and economic events. And I am vain enough to believe that the three years since the book's publication in French have merely confirmed and underlined what I was trying to describe: a new and very forceful dynamic of history. America today is effectively the centre and driving force of one of the greatest social, economic, political and cultural revolutions the modern world has seen. It is the first revolution in history to have reached the entire planet, casting doubt on established certainties and undermining ancient institutions, even the sovereignty of nation states; including the United States of America.

The end of the Cold War was not the starting point of this new metamorphosis of human history, but the collapse of the Soviet bloc certainly cleared the way for it. Events are accelerating, and the scale and complexity of the social forces in play compel statesmen, even the most powerful, to fly (so to speak) "by the seat of the pants". An increasingly disoriented public would very much like to be given a guiding light, what George Bush would call a "vision thing". And once again, the presidential elections of November 1996 are going to be conducted around this unfulfillable demand.

But although politicians cannot control or even foresee the future, some of them possess enough intuition to blaze valid new trails. Despite the handicap of a clamorous and fickle public opinion, George Bush and Bill Clinton both managed, each in his own way and in accordance with his own ideas, to steer America through the tempests of "globalization" and give it a decisive impact on the post-Cold War reorganization of the world. Washington today is no longer simply the capital of the United States, but a sort of planetary capital. Bill Clinton knows what he is talking about when he repeats that the distinction between internal and foreign policy is becoming increasingly blurred. America is being integrated with the rest of the world and the world with America. A "World-America" is being born, and imposing itself – for better or worse – on all the nations of the planet, including the American nation.

Paris, 14 April 1996

PART I

FABRICATING A NEW

AMERICAN DREAM

1

THE OLD GODS OF AMERICA

"The key to America's growth, expansion and innovation has always been our openness to trade, investment, ideas, and people. As this openness is at last being reciprocated around the world, we find ourselves at a special advantage,"[1] stated George Bush. In a variation on this theme, Bill Clinton elaborated, "For the new world toward which we are moving actually favours us. We are better equipped than any other people on Earth by reason of our history, our culture, and our disposition to change, to lead and to prosper."[2]

Both presidents seem in little doubt of the role the United States will play in the twenty-first century. As they see it, the traditions of innovation and dynamism that are entrenched in American history will serve the United States well in this changing world. If they are right, during the twenty-first century the American Republic will be transformed into a vast World-America, a democratic empire with a vocation to encompass the entire planet: the final frontier.

In this evolutionary process there are distinct echoes of the religiosity that played a central part in the foundation of the United States. The American Republic was built on the conviction that it was divinely ordained; this faith in a sacred mission originally gave strength and cohesion to a diverse collection of émigrés of disparate confessions and origins. A similar belief in a kind of divine protection for American endeavours still exists today.

Piety has always been a virtue in America. It is not simply a private matter; frequent public references to the glory of the Almighty form the essence of what amounts to a civic creed. The Bible is omnipresent, statesmen and ordinary citizens alike punctuating their everyday discourse and marking their important decisions with allusions to Holy Writ. This religiosity buttresses the conviction that America is on a divinely inspired mission, and shows that in the United States, religion and politics are one.

But success becomes impious when it is the fruit of pride. The old Calvinist inheritance, which had become no more than an external badge of membership, was incapable of resisting Mammon: the Republic, at its peak, worshipped at the altar of Wealth. Business is a pretty ecumenical divinity as long as everyone is making money and the country believes its power is growing. But the terrible crisis of the 1930s left America an orphan. Bereft of both God and devil, it turned in desperation to a very human Saviour: the president. The cooling of relations between the Americans and Heaven gave President Franklin D. Roosevelt a free hand to begin the slow strangulation of the old oligarchic republic. And to turn the White House into the embryo of an imperial government.

CALVINISM AND REPUBLICAN VIRTUE

The Constitution of the United States, written in 1787 – the oldest still in force in the world today – is venerated as the cornerstone of the whole American democratic edifice. So much so that it has become virtually sacrosanct, and its survival is identified with the survival of the American Republic itself. The Constitution established the subtle combination of veneration for the law and mistrust of all political power that – at least until Roosevelt's "New Deal" and the Second World War – characterized relations between citizens and the state.

The Law of the Pastors

This highly specific attitude to the public domain has its roots in the strong religious tradition of the United States. The Calvinism of the Pilgrim Fathers is one of the fundamental influences – ancient Rome is the other – for the development of American constitutional government.[3] The social organization of the Puritans' first New England colonies was broadly modelled on Jean Calvin's Geneva. Convinced that they were a chosen people entrusted by Providence with the task of purifying and reviving religion, the colonists saw their community as a sort of holy experiment, a New Jerusalem where people would live by the Gospel.

The community and the religious congregation were thus one and the same. The civil magistrates (known as Nursing Fathers in some of the colonies) did not really represent a government, since as they saw it power belongs to the Lord alone. They were simply believers, chosen for their integrity and virtue, responsible for settling disputes and enforcing the moral code laid down by the ministers.

The conditions under which the colonists lived also left their mark on the way these church-dominated towns worked. Most of the towns were isolated in vast tracts of land, enjoying a very large measure of autonomy and self-sufficiency. This enabled them to develop a robust local democracy, with free choice of ministers and magistrates. The system was based on the *covenant*, a form of contractual obligation to the community by each of its members and a direct religious ancestor of the Constitution. But this social egalitarianism excluded recidivist sinners and anyone declining to make a profession of faith. Religious homogeneity, the idea that God's will should be done in both public and private matters, observance of established moral rules, were essential to the very survival of the civic community.

There were no powerful established authorities to enforce the harsh Calvinist code of discipline in the new colonies. Respect for the rules was ensured by strong group pressure: everyone's life was subject to scrutiny by everyone else. Great emphasis was placed on individual fervour: forceful sermons made the congregation tremble; psalms and liturgies chanted in unison encouraged group emotion and physical involvement (still a prominent feature of American evangelism). The values and practices of this colonial Calvinism became so deeply rooted in the New World that they can be found at the centre of the great social debates at every turning-point in United States history. They also lie behind the revival of religious fundamentalism over the past three decades.

By the time of its independence, America had become a far more complex entity than that first handful of New England colonies. The state institutions were now faced with a multitude of different religious congregations, and the colonies had outgrown the entirely localized management of power; so it had become difficult to maintain a solid connection between magistrates and pastors. Nevertheless the Fathers of the Constitution retained the original Puritan emphasis on individual responsibility, moral duty, local democracy and defying political power. The system defined by the American Constitution thus gives precedence to the legislature and to regional and local government at the expense of federal executive power. The principle of separation between executive, legislature and judiciary was clearly included to prevent the emergence of a strong central government. Perhaps this is the moment to recall that the apolitical, managerial word "administration" is widely used by Americans in preference to "government".

Distrust of politicians who were no longer directly supervised by the clergy resulted in the attribution to the Supreme Court of its essential role as guardian of the Law. Under the leadership of John Marshall (1801–35), it even awarded itself the power to assess the constitutionality of decisions taken by Congress or the president. In a sense, on a symbolic level, the Supreme Court inherited the authority held by ministers in the early Calvinist congregations.

The framers of the Constitution, still worried by the threat federal power might pose to the freedom of the citizen, guaranteed wide autonomy to the states by reserving for them all powers not explicitly allocated to the Union (in the Tenth Amendment, included in the Bill of Rights, voted in 1791).[4] So broad was this allocation that it was not until 1925 that the Supreme Court (in a judgement concerning freedom and equality of religious worship) declared that the States were also bound by the Bill of Rights. The presidency itself, armed with a right to veto legislative acts, was clearly conceived as a counterweight to the extensive powers of Congress. Anticipating every possible risk, the Fathers conferred the title of commander-in-chief on the president but placed actual control of the armed forces in the hands of the legislature, enshrined the right of every citizen to bear arms in the Second Amendment and gave the states the right to raise their own militias.[5]

Government of the "Chosen People"

The American Republic thus rests on three axioms:

1. The idea of strong local autonomies in which the individual, free and responsible, is answerable in the first instance to his or her own community. Since this community is supposedly based largely on religion, there must be total freedom of worship and association, and all religions must be equal before the law. This is covered in the First Amendment, at the top of the Bill of Rights. All matters that are not specifically covered by the Constitution are thus exempt from state control (hence the defensive flurry that arises when the federal government seeks to act in the social or economic sphere).

2. A central administration that is supposed to limit itself to keeping order and acting as mediator in a society conceived as a mass of competing private interests. Any hint that the federal government wants more autonomy or is considering taking the initiative on some issue is to be viewed with the deepest suspicion.

3. A sacralized Constitution, protected by a court of senior judges that defines the powers of all the governmental institutions and is itself independent of them.

To accommodate the break between political and religious power, which was already apparent by 1787, the United States thus transposed the local practice of the religious covenant to the national civic level. Ambiguity remained, however, as the proliferation of diverse cultural communities rendered obsolete the whole idea of a civil government supervised by a religious moral authority. On one level, the constitutional law was considered the product of strictly secular human deliberation, and thus imperfect by definition. But it still had to be written into the divine plan somehow; its purpose after all was to guarantee the unity and happiness of people living by the Gospel and regenerating Christianity in the American New Jerusalem. The great deeds in the history of God's new chosen people could only be directly inspired by the Almighty.

The state may not be able to identify itself with a particular religious denomination, but it is still expected to show some piety: the national motto is "One Nation under God"; the banknotes bear the famous slogan "In God We Trust". On 30 April 1789 George Washington, in his inaugural address to Congress, affirmed without beating about the bush: "No people can be bound to acknowledge and adore the invisible hand which conducts the affairs of men, more than the people of the United States. Every step by which they have advanced to the character of an independent nation seems to have been distinguished by some token of providential agency."[6] The corollary of this close link between the country's destiny and the heavenly plan is that whenever the nation strays from the true path, exposing itself to divine retribution, it is threatened with ruin.

This tension between secular and sacred at the heart of the Constitution condemned the federal government to a sort of purgatory. When in power, the statesman was enjoined to show both authority and humility, to be ambitious to serve, but also to possess a spirit of sacrifice. The need was felt, however, for at least one historical reference that might serve as an example of this idyllic conception of political life. The first rulers of the young republic chose the classical Roman ideal of stoic virtue:[7] moral austerity, honesty, fidelity, strong will and devotion to the mother country untainted by desire for personal gain. In practice, this paradigm has been attained no more often in the United States than it was in Rome. But the identification with the Romans – another people that believed itself to be "chosen" – had a strong formative influence on the attitudes of future holders of federal power in the United States.

FROM THE REPUBLIC TO THE
"GOSPEL OF WEALTH"

Thus the central power was supposed to be left voluntarily "unoccupied", and kept that way by the classical virtues and the reciprocal surveillance exercised by its three components: the White House, Capitol Hill and the Supreme Court. But its survival in that form was far from certain, given the appetites of bankers and merchants in the North-East, farmers in the West and the southern planters. Whatever the intentions of the framers of the Constitution, the federal government was capable of enormous extension. The main influence groups – the landed and money aristocracies – could hardly be expected to ignore this fact.

The Virtues of Money

Having no vocation of its own, the central government quickly became the tool of private interests. So complete was this process that President Andrew Jackson (1828–36), who claimed to be acting in defence of democracy, torpedoed all possibility of establishing a permanent corps of senior civil servants to ensure continuity (and some measure of autonomy) for the state. The spoils system was thus established, with the victor in elections acquiring automatic patronage rights. The federal administration came to be seen as a dispenser of posts and revenues to interest groups, which gained and lost control of central government democratically, as the result of elections.

Nevertheless the original constitutional philosophy was maintained, for what it was worth, at least until the Civil War. America was then still largely a country of isolated agricultural communities, whose considerable de facto independence from Washington was kept alive by sketchy communications. The country's most powerful forces were still at the formative stage, with the first industrialists arriving on the scene to complicate the political game still further. But the dominant groups cancelled each other out, and this gave them a common interest in keeping the state fairly neutral.

The war between the North and the South was to shatter this equilibrium. Quite apart from its moral implications, the abolition of slavery embodied a decisive choice on the part of society. Was America going to be a land of exporting planters, or of industrialists? Should it retain the essentially rural character and values of the America that existed at the time of the framing of the Constitution, or should it evolve into an industrial, urban nation? The split was so deep that it was bound to

8

fracture all existing institutions: the parties, the churches and, of course, the federal and local governments.

The defeat of the South thus called into question most of the social mechanisms that formed the bedrock of the Republic's values. The biggest winners were the captains of industry, who had been very active even before the conflict and who not only gained entry to the old oligarchy, but took control of it. Reinforcing the central government and partially eroding traditional local powers, the hostilities had created an immense field of anarchic freedom, very favourable for the investment of fabulous war profits.

The door was open for the Rockefellers, Armours, Harrimans, Carnegies and Morgans, adventurers and robber barons in control of colossal fortunes and enormous steel, railroad, cannery or petroleum conglomerates. Their advent paved the way for state corruption: the government of Ulysses S. Grant (1869–77) was undoubtedly the dirtiest in American history. Throughout this Gilded Age the power of money made – and unmade – federal officials, state governors and legislators. The central administration showered gifts on industry: loans, fiscal aid, tariff concessions. A like-minded Supreme Court rubber-stamped a virtually unlimited economic *laissez faire*.

This inversion of values inevitably cast doubt on an institutional system symbolically based on the Roman and Calvinist virtues. The churches, divided and disoriented by the Civil War, no longer functioned as solid landmarks. But more importantly, the Gilded Age denied the sanctity of labour, a fundamental Puritan social ethic. In the early days, work had been seen as a moral duty. Wealth and success represented, at most, a rather precarious sign of divine approval (in which it would be sinful to take too much pleasure): an encouragement to persist on the path of virtue. Now the time had come for the big captains of industry, men like the steel magnate Andrew Carnegie, to start preaching a "gospel of wealth".

The accumulation of capital, the formation of great holding companies, total freedom of production and distribution of wealth, were all defended as manifestations of divine providence. Transposing Darwin's theories on the evolution of animal species to the economic field, Carnegie became the defender of a form of social Darwinism: " . . . the man of wealth thus becoming the mere agent and trustee for his poorer brethren, bringing to their service his superior wisdom, experience, and ability to administer, doing for them better than they would or could do for themselves."[8] Individual salvation – never taken for granted in the

Calvinist doctrine of predestination – was thus replaced by a sort of calculable collective salvation, administered by the financier.

Virtuous individualism in the setting of an independent religious congregation, one of the pillars of the American soul, was not under attack by this gospel of wealth alone. The rapid growth of the industrial working class, fuelled by heavy – and largely Catholic – immigration, represented another challenge to the Puritan foundations of the state. In response to the triumphant arrogance of big business the first trade unions and mass protest movements started to appear. They owed a good deal to the organizing abilities of Jewish immigrants, and even more to the Irish Catholics who dominated the union movement. Pope Leo XIII effectively authorized the faithful to become militants by addressing the question of the workers directly, in the encyclical *Rerum novarum* published in 1891. But in America, with its Calvinist traditions, a Christian denomination that preached social responsibility and even state intervention was something altogether new. The principle of individual responsibility had always been maintained in the strictest sense, slightly attenuated by the duty to help others in the community: "The Lord helps those who help themselves." Moreover, the Catholics had always been regarded as the enemy.

Profane Power and the Cult of Business

What with the oligarchy's gospel of wealth and the basically Catholic militancy of the urban "plebs", where could the Puritan tradition find a home? Especially as it was now embodied in a nascent middle class: a disparate collection of indebted farmers, small businessmen crushed by the great monopolies, liberal professionals worried about social polarization and an intellectual and academic elite shocked by the decline of moral values. The social gospel evolved by "enlightened" East-Coast Protestantism was the theological response to this disarray. The new gospel rejected the classical Calvinist view that every human being is a sinner by nature. It even went so far as to claim that the sin is not necessarily an individual human act, but may also be attributed to social injustice in an over-secularized world.

The social gospel may not have received unanimous support from the Protestant communities, but it did at least cause a powerful upsurge of social activism, especially among the less dogmatic denominations, like the Congregationalists and the Methodists. By the same token, however, it weakened the Puritan religious bedrock and threatened to confuse religious practice with political or trade-union activity. The middle class had already opted for more energetic state action against the monopolies and some kind of minimal social justice. In this context the social gospel served as a useful framework for the necessary political commitment. But the progressives, as subscribers to this vast body of ideas were called, were divided. Some of them accepted the development of big industry and the attendant changes as inevitable; others went on fighting for a return to the *status quo ante*.

The first of these groups believed that the prosperity of the middle classes would henceforth depend on rapid industrialization. They therefore favoured a strong central government with the means to force conglomerates to observe the rules of competition and guarantee a just peace on the factory floor: big government versus big business. Their champion was President Theodore Roosevelt (1901–09), who also contributed his own taste for foreign intervention and expansion. The second group, along with President Woodrow Wilson (1913–21), dreamed of restoring the original American values: a federal executive that would be strong enough to restrict the conglomerates and encourage small businessmen, but weak enough to pose no threat to individual liberties.

Wilson, whose ideas were deeply rooted in Presbyterian theological culture, was the very stereotype of a Protestant believer in the Calvinist ascent of the American nation. His fall – due in large part to the United States's entry to the First World War in 1917, which he had tried desperately to avoid – coincided with the collapse of the Republic's original institutional framework. For the First World War had strengthened executive power, but had also been immensely profitable for the monopolies; the result was that after the Armistice, the country found itself saddled with both big business *and* big government. This posthumous victory for Theodore Roosevelt's ideas also destroyed the bond between politics and its moral and religious setting, the symbolic link at the heart of American culture. From that time on, until Jimmy Carter's election in 1976, political debate in the United States was to be strictly secular.

The delicate balance of power instituted by the Founding Fathers had been suddenly deprived of the solid foundation provided by a myth of origin. The late-nineteenth-century gospel of wealth, with its residual traces of moral justification, was unceremoniously dumped in favour of business pure and simple. "The business of America is business," proclaimed President Calvin Coolidge (1923–29).[9] Having re-established control of the government, the oligarchy used it as a source of financial and administrative support for business. There was no question of accepting an autonomous executive that might be tempted to mediate in social conflicts or try to regulate the economy. Its wings were to be clipped through the rapid demobilization of the armed forces and the adoption of a strictly neutral foreign policy. International action was recognized as a tempting way for the White House to retrieve its independence.

CONSECRATION OF THE WHITE HOUSE

The first great metamorphosis of the American Republic was thus complete. The federal institutions were now in the service of the dominant interest groups, but a democratic mode of operation ensured their continuing balance. The wage increases and trade union concessions obtained, through hard struggle, during the war years guaranteed the regime's legitimacy in the eyes of the working "plebs". And the middle class – especially the small businessmen, those emblematic figures of the American republic – shared the general postwar prosperity.

1929: Failure of the God of Business

This secularization of politics, including the dropping of references to America's providential destiny, was further reinforced by a first cultural revolution among the younger generation in urban areas and large tracts of countryside.[10] In Europe during the Great War, soldiers and nurses had been exposed to societies far less puritanical than their own – a "danger" that had worried General John Joseph Pershing, commander of the American expeditionary force in France. This "lost generation", better educated and informed than its predecessors, returned home determined to get the best out of life. And life, by the 1920s, had little in common with the austerity of earlier times.

For the first time, the automobile became widely available. In 1923 some two million examples of the Model T Ford, designed fifteen years earlier, had already been sold. By 1927 sales of the Model T had reached the stupendous level, for that period, of fifteen million.[11] The privately owned car brought a hitherto unknown level of mobility, multiplying opportunities for going out on picnics or drives, and escaping family surveillance. Cinemas showing increasingly "daring" films were opening everywhere. Nightclubs and dance halls were springing up like mushrooms. Girls were throwing away their whalebone corsets and dancing with abandon to wicked new tango and foxtrot rhythms.

This "dissipated" conduct inevitably elicited a strong reaction from the religious communities. The Puritan fundamentalism which, in the name of the Bible, had been fighting a rearguard action against Darwin and the theory of evolution for the past decade added its muscle to the "legions of decency". In 1919 this movement managed to obtain a constitutional amendment banning alcoholic drinks throughout the nation. But this was a token victory for a form of religiosity that was being swept away by the spirit of the times. In the end, prohibition actually encouraged people to drink by supplying the extra frisson of illegality. This too was a first: a whole generation of men and women sprinkling their lives liberally with whisky. And the first tangible result of this profound revolution in manners and morals was the victory of the suffragettes (many of whom were in fact very straitlaced individuals): in 1920, the Nineteenth Amendment to the Constitution at last gave women the right to vote.

But the most fundamental change was probably caused by that extraordinary invention, radio. In 1922 there were only 30 radio stations in the whole country, with 100,000 sets installed in 60,000 households. In 1930, with 13.7 million households already equipped, there were 618 broadcasting stations, and nearly 4 million new sets were produced. By 1946, at the dawn of commercial television, the market was saturated, with 1,750 stations and 16 million sets produced.[12] For the first time, the great majority of Americans could be informed almost instantly about the important events occurring in the country. People listened to the same programmes and heard the same music; fashions arrived and departed at lightning speed. A mass culture was born. And the politicians at last had a means of speaking directly and simultaneously to a multitude of electors. President Franklin Delano Roosevelt, with his fireside chats broadcast coast-to-coast, was the first to exploit radio's potential.

This great festival of American "rugged individualism", to use the term coined by President Herbert Hoover (1929–33),[13] came to a sudden end on the day of the stock market crash in 1929. The carefree, apolitical "lost generation" was totally unprepared for the Great Depression of the 1930s. So, too, was the entire system of the oligarchic Republic: betrayed by the economy – its sole justification since the abandonment of its traditional moral and religious landmarks – it was utterly helpless before the scale of the crisis. The time was ripe for a strong central government, for the appearance on the scene of a man of providence, a saviour.

Franklin Roosevelt, elected in 1932, was being called a dictator by some of his opponents after just a few months in the White House. The term seems unduly harsh, given the robust nature of the American democratic system. But it is true that the new president was breaking

13

with all the *laissez-faire* traditions of the past. His programme during the election campaign had been notably succinct. Without going into detail he affirmed the principle of a "permanent government responsibility" for human well-being. Franklin Roosevelt, who inherited some ideas from his cousin and predecessor Theodore, openly favoured big government and even economic planning. He believed that only a strong presidency, with autonomy of thought ensured by his establishment of a "brain trust" around the president, could hope to deal with the problems of fourteen million unemployed and 85,000 bankrupt businesses, or with the effects of a 50 per cent drop in national income.

A Saviour for America

Franklin Roosevelt spent the first hundred days of his administration getting his New Deal programme rushed through. Congress passed a series of acts enlarging the federal bureaucracy in spectacular fashion and extending the powers of the president, who was authorized to act by decree in certain cases. From 1933 onwards Congress even accepted a de facto restriction of its own prerogatives: henceforth the White House would propose and administer new programmes. In this way, the executive became the real initiator of new laws for the first time, and Congress fell into the habit of waiting for the presidency to submit its plans for the future. Soon, at an almost revolutionary speed, the federal government was intervening in every area of the country's social and economic life.

Obviously the White House was going to come into conflict with the oligarchy, which had hitherto reigned supreme and was still entrenched in the Supreme Court. The emergence of an increasingly independent presidency posed a direct threat to the system that enabled the various dominant groups to share power in a democratic and equitable manner. But the Great Depression had left supporters of big business rather on the sidelines.

Franklin Roosevelt had no difficulty in playing off the pressing demands of the "plebs" against this somewhat weakened "business nobility". The president was an adept politician who – thanks to radio – was able to speak directly to the masses, bypassing Congress and the Supreme Court. Although he was by no means a socialist activist, Roosevelt handed a series of victories to the trade union organizations with the National Industrial Recovery Act (NIRA) of 1933, the National Labor Relations Act of 1935 and the Fair Labor Standards Act of 1938. One of these concessions, the legalization of collective bargaining, was a crucial move in his struggle to overcome the resistance of the business community. By deliberately promoting union power – "Big Labor" – Roosevelt-style big government acquired the weaponry to intervene in big business (banking in particular), which was soon forced to accept strong regulation supervised by the executive.

The tactic of seeking the support of public opinion was especially successful during the decisive confrontation with the oligarchy in 1937. The Supreme Court declared that the main acts of the New Deal were unconstitutional, and attempted to deprive the White House of a good proportion of its new power. Roosevelt, who had just been triumphantly re-elected, decided to cross the Rubicon: he accused the Supreme Court of abandoning its constitutional role to play politics, and went so far as to propose a reorganization which would enable him to appoint his own nominees to the Supreme Court and gain control of it. This mini-putsch was seen as too audacious to be acceptable, even to a Rooseveltian Congress. But the president achieved his object anyway: the last bastion of the oligarchy took fright and capitulated. The Court overturned its decisions and made no further difficulties about the presidency's new initiatives. But now the Supreme Court too had become irremediably politicized.

The popular "dictator" had manoeuvred adroitly to consolidate his power in domestic politics. But he also needed a foothold in the crucial terrain of foreign affairs, where executive authority is most legitimate, and can act with the greatest autonomy. In his battle with big business, Roosevelt had already declared himself in favour of free trade and against adopting high customs tariffs to protect American industries. In 1934, the Trade Agreements Act gave the president the power to negotiate reciprocal reduction of tariffs with foreign governments, without first obtaining the consent of Congress.

This victory by the executive, astonishing though it was in a constitutional system like that of the United States, would have been incomplete if it had not been backed by military success. The situation in Europe and the Far East was looking increasingly dangerous and Roosevelt, who was openly interventionist, found himself confronting conservative lobbies that favoured neutrality. By 1940 the White House had prevailed: Congress approved war loans and, for the first time in American history, peacetime conscription was established with the Selective Training and Service Act. The presidency had at last got its hands on a large, permanent military machine. It was never going to let go.

Elected four times in succession, haloed with victory after the Second World War, Roosevelt still did not manage – did he even try? – to transform the White House into a seat of personal power. At the time of his death on 12 April 1945, his prestige was equal to that of the ancient Roman heroes so admired in America: "A prestigious leader who, in contrast to a weakened and diminished *nobilitas* . . . appears swathed in a victor's aura from battlefields abroad, and is presented at home as a benefactor of the *populus romanus*."[14]

His successor and former vice-president, Harry S. Truman, further consolidated the administration's military influence. In 1947 the United States for the first time acquired a Department of Defense, institutionalizing the Pentagon. In 1950 the Korean war, and the creation of the North Atlantic Treaty Organization (NATO) integrating western armed forces under American command, involved the United States definitively in world affairs. A return to the isolationist tradition was now impossible. Henceforth, the White House wielded both domestic and international power, with political and military repercussions extending beyond the American national context. Slowly, the federal head was becoming independent of its original civic body.

The growing autonomy of the White House did not pass unnoticed. Congress, which acquired a Republican majority in 1946, asked the oligarchy's pre-New Deal hero, Herbert Hoover, to set up a commission with the aim of curtailing the influence of the executive. To exorcize the fear of personal power, Congress adopted the Twenty-Second Amendment, banning the election of the same president for more than two successive terms. But it was too late to undo all the consequences of Roosevelt's rise to power. Politics were going to be centred on the White House from now on. The only thing missing from the new structure was a new kind of legitimacy, a mission able to unite America behind its commander-in-chief and reaffirm its role in the divine plan. What was needed was a state religion to reconcile the nation with the Almighty.

2

A CULT FOR THE UNIVERSE

Being an adolescent during the postwar era was a great adventure. This generation in the United States could look forward to three decades of uninterrupted prosperity, freedom, intellectual boldness and radical experimentation both in private life and in politics. But it also had to cope with the fear of a nuclear apocalypse, racial tensions, the great campaign for civil rights, the risk of conscription for a war widely regarded as immoral and a sense of responsibility for a motherland turned world power. A strange generation, permissive but also thirsty for ethical values, that shifted all the country's social and political balances.

Of this generation, those coming of age in the 1960s had a unique experience, being free for the first time – thanks to the discovery of antibiotics and contraceptive pills – to make love undeterred by worries about disease or unwanted children. In the sexual domain, women suddenly acquired the same freedom of choice and the same responsibilities as men. It was a historic revolution in manners and morals, and one that spread very rapidly to the rest of the planet. The moral and social values underlying American family relations, communal bonds and even political institutions could hardly survive unaffected.

But this unique sexual liberation should not be confused with carelessness or frivolity. This generation is *grave* in the classical sense of the word. Confronted with all the responsibilities that accompany freedom, rejecting the values of the past, it was inevitably hungry for meaning. This triggered a new religious quest that was taken up by the whole American nation.

A GOVERNMENT WITHOUT ETHICS?

The increased power of the White House posed a challenge to the whole American republican tradition. The nuclear age concentrated the supreme power of collective life and death in the hands of the head of state, subject to his sole judgement. His character, his experience and his behaviour under pressure had become the crucial elements of a system in which the balance between the different power centres had tilted in the direction of the Oval Office.

At the same time, the old party structures were steadily relinquishing control over their own candidates. The electoral process was increasingly dominated by audio-visual communications, so presidential campaigns could reach a wider audience directly; this also accounts for the candidature of populists, adventurers and unknowns. No doubt the choice had become wider. But during the Cold War, with the fate of the whole planet at stake, presidential elections in the United States were periods of expectation, and sometimes apprehension, for Americans and foreigners alike.

Nuclear Apocalypse and the Reign of Competence

The republican spirit underlying America's eighteenth-century Constitution had been completely abandoned. The magistrates had not only escaped from the ministers, they had handed much of their authority to one of their number. Now this individual was assuming the airs of a supreme pontiff. Fear of nuclear war – especially after the Soviet Union launched Sputnik in 1957 – generated a strange fascination with the apocalypse. The hypothesis that the destruction of humanity was now possible gave birth to a sort of nuclear eschatology: God's omnipotence had been expropriated by the president of the United States and the first secretary of the Communist party of the Soviet Union.

This radical secularization of the Day of Judgement flattened all moral values and left the religious field a charred ruin. Survival became, in effect, the supreme value to which all others must be subordinated. The doctrine of national security, with the president as its guardian and high priest, could now stand in place of a code of ethics: the community must accommodate itself to a form of discipline imposed by a strategic vision focused on ensuring the group's continued existence. The biblical Armageddon had become a simple matter of technological, economic and political management. The end of the world had been reduced to the unthinkable failure – unceasingly guarded against by the White House – of nuclear deterrence.[1]

This sort of atomic religion, which took on substance during the second half of the 1950s, encouraged a technocratic conception of the presidency. The main qualification for governing the country became "competence" – military of course, but competence in all the other fields as well. The president was not just responsible for protecting America against nuclear obliteration, but also for personally ensuring the "happiness" of the people (a responsibility originally assigned by the Constitution to the government as a whole, and still appearing in the Declaration of Independence). This cult of competence was adopted by the generation that gained power in 1960. Around their cold concept of politics – a huge planetary chess game, playable by anyone who could master the rules – President John F. Kennedy formed his "ministry of talent" incorporating "the best and the brightest".

The men and women of that generation had been marked in childhood and adolescence by the Great Depression and the Second World War. On being demobilized in 1945 they behaved rather like the veterans of the Great War: they enjoyed their recovered peace and prosperity to the full, and drowned childhood memories of penury in a deluge of consumption. The only government they knew was the strong Rooseveltian administration. The powers appropriated by the White House seemed to them wholly natural, a fact of life. Avid for comfort and material goods, practising religion largely for show, without falling into transports of faith, they dreamed of steady scientific, technical and social progress steered by an executive that comprised the best experts in the country.

Kennedy's assassination in 1963 was a terrible blow to this whole generation. Lyndon Baines Johnson – although he continued the murdered president's work, perhaps with greater concrete success – was too slick and wily a politician to revive the enthusiasm of Kennedy's admirers. Already inclined to view politics as a game of efficient manipulation, this technocratic generation succumbed to the prevailing weakness for "reasons of state", soon to be luridly reflected in the cynicism of the Nixon-Kissinger tandem.

Rebels without a Cause

The idea of a government liberated from all moral rules was nevertheless something too strange for America to stomach. The triumph of realpolitik brought in its wake a radical split with the next generation, the "baby boomers". The launching of the Free Speech Movement in 1964, at the University of California, Berkeley (in the middle of the most prosperous and dynamic region of the globe), signalled a youth revolt which quickly spread to the rest of the world. As we have said, the baby boomers enjoyed the hitherto unknown privilege of sexuality without anxiety. So it is not surprising that their first break with the preceding generation should have arisen from their rejection of "hypocritical" family and social conventions. Especially as their own parents had hardly been paragons of virtue.

This denunciation of hypocrisy quickly extended to all parental values and views regarded as hollow or cynical. The critical spirit of young people who had never experienced hard times, who took individual freedom for granted, thus amplified the general disaffection with a way of life that seemed to be leading to a society of material abundance wholly lacking in soul. Two works by the philosopher Herbert Marcuse – *Eros and Civilization*, published in the United States in 1955, and *One-Dimensional Man*, in 1964 – served as a theoretical basis for this revolt against the "consumer society". The problem of non-communication between parents and children of the baby-boom generation had come to be seen as a fact of life since the appearance of the cult film *Rebel without a Cause* (1955). In the James Dean character America had discovered the archetype of a sensitive, generous young rebel totally misunderstood by his family.

The new generation was going to fight for a world that would be more transparent, more honest, more just: in a word, more "moral". The student movement accordingly lent its support to the Rev. Martin Luther King Jr's struggle to gain recognition for the black community's civil rights. At the same time, an increasingly powerful feminist movement was overturning traditional morals in the United States. In 1966, woman activists formed the National Organization for Women (NOW), whose programme was "true equality for all women in America, and . . . fully equal partnership of the sexes, as part of the worldwide revolution on human rights".[2] The culmination of this initiative, in 1972, was the proposed Twenty-Seventh Amendment to the Constitution, or the Equal Rights Amendment (ERA), guaranteeing equal rights for the sexes.

This mobilization was not restricted to the problems of American society alone. The United States's entry to the Vietnam war, justified in terms of an abstract strategic imperative (preventing the fall of a "domino" which might start a Communist landslide in South-East Asia), seemed to this generation a perfect example of the immoral use of power. People were actually being asked to die in the Vietnamese paddy fields for these "reasons of state"! "Hey, hey, LBJ," yelled the pacifist demonstrators in Washington, "How many kids did you kill today?" The White House was accused of imperialism. A large segment of American youth came out in support of "oppressed peoples".

For the first time in American history conscription radically divided a whole generation. On one side were those who went, believing that it was their duty or that they had no choice. On the other were deserters, draft dodgers and those astute enough to find legal ways of avoiding the draft. Also for the first time, morale sank very low at the front: discipline decayed, officers were killed or maimed by their own men, drug abuse became widespread. Vietnam was first and foremost an internal American debacle, a moral dislocation.

Lyndon Johnson understood this when he announced after the Vietnamese Tet offensive, in the summer of 1968, that he would not be contesting the presidential elections. Richard Nixon, elected later that year, managed to extract the United States from the quagmire by using every means, dignified and otherwise, available to the "imperial presidency". But he too was swept away by the groundswell of discontent, a whole society insisting that American power must have some sort of ethical foundation once again.

THE BABY BOOMERS: A MORAL COUNTERCULTURE

The quest for a new politics, taken up by the baby boomers, might have changed America deeply, but was largely unsuccessful. The ideal of civil rights foundered in the rioting and repression of the black ghettoes at the end of the 1960s; and the slogan "Black Power!" was deeply disturbing to white youth, with its pacifist and universalist leanings. The women's movement did succeed in getting the Supreme Court to legalize abortion in 1973, but failed to obtain approval for the Equal Rights Amendment.

The American withdrawal from Vietnam, which did not take place until 1973, left Indo-China utterly devastated. Fifty-seven thousand Americans were killed and 154,000 were wounded in the course of the war. The disillusioned war veterans, a large proportion of whom were young blacks from poor backgrounds, came back from Asia imbued with a culture of drugs and violence that exacerbated misery and insecurity in the big-city black ghettoes. Political activists lost their followers and the "moral generation" of the baby boomers dropped politics to take up the quest for a new spirituality.

Peace and Love: The New Epicureans

Since the early 1970s the United States has witnessed an extraordinary religious expansion. Over the preceding decade, young people from middle-class backgrounds made the trip to Katmandu or visited ashrams in India; oriental forms of wisdom and religion spread to America and mingled with local Protestant traditions. New religious communities and lay phalansteries based on one "life discipline" or another sprang up everywhere. Cults ranged from black magic to television evangelism via shamanism, spiritualism, mind-expansion through the use of drugs, transcendental meditation, the proliferation of gurus of variable honesty and spiritual quality, Buddhism, Christian charismatic groups and Jewish and Muslim fundamentalisms. But two main tendencies seem to have had the strongest impact on this strange American spiritual Great Awakening: a neo-Epicurean, neo-Pythagorian, "lay-religious" movement, and a Christian movement embracing the two biggest American denominations, Catholics and Baptists, as well as fundamentalist evangelicals.

From the end of the 1960s thousands of young people were abandoning active politics to live communally; many left the cities for the perceived simplicity and freedom of country life. Disillusioned by the sterility (and the many failures) of political militancy, they were now trying to carve out an autonomous space in which to be self-sufficient. Large abstract categories – Justice, Goodness, Truth – were regarded with mistrust. Better, the young believed, to live in the present, giving priority to tangible experiences, than to try to follow a political agenda that could quickly lose touch with reality and become meaningless. They were attracted by autarchic utopianism, the free establishment of a collective way of life independent of the laws governing conventional society. This experimental counterculture believed that the only valid standards were those established personally by the individual in balance with nature.

But this movement, echoing the Garden of Epicurus, also sought to live virtuously by establishing (often in a dogmatic manner) a borderline between "natural" pleasures and the "vain" pleasures of consumer society. The ideal was to find a balance that would make the individual self-sufficient. The communities advocated a healthy and simple diet, "natural" medicine (they tended to characterize illness as the result of an imbalance between the physical and the psychic) and perpetual friendly discussion to resolve internal conflicts. These groups also tended to reject all forms of hierarchy and expected women – and children – to be treated on a strictly equal footing with men. In effect, these neo-Epicureans were seeking something the ancient world called "ataraxia", the conquest of happiness by refusing to be troubled by the outside world: Peace and Love.

Despite their rejection of politics these groups had a profound impact on America. They were certainly instrumental in raising public awareness of environmental problems, and have always been prominent in the hard core, fundamentalist wing of the ecology movement. And they embodied aspects of the moral counterculture by launching non-violent attacks on every taboo of American society. The conservatives, especially the new evangelical sects, aimed their thunderbolts at this "marginal" culture, which they caricatured as consisting essentially of sex, drugs and rock'n'roll.

New Age: The Return of Pythagoras

The truth is that the neo-Epicureans, moralistic rather than religious, were too indifferent to the question of faith not to be perceived as a foreign body in the United States. Faced with the unremitting hostility of the rest of the country, the communities eventually broke up, their ageing members forced, one by one, to reintegrate with conventional society. They had some impact on American attitudes, but failed to satisfy the need for spirituality. It is hardly surprising, then, that many baby-boomers returned to the fold of traditional Christianity; some of them even enlisted in the ranks of their most virulent former adversaries, the fundamentalist evangelical sects.

But this return to tradition did not affect the people who had been planning to establish a new American spirituality since the 1960s. The New Age family gradually formed out of thousands of small groups, a nebulous phenomenon emerging little by little from the vast reservoir of the "psychic" movement: groups practising spiritualism, occultism and clairvoyance, researching into parapsychology and ESP or trying to make contact with extraterrestrial beings, all strongly influenced by Eastern philosophies and religions. Around 1971, large numbers of these groups organized into a huge network called the New Age movement.[3]

Quite unlike the withdrawn and self-sufficient neo-Epicurean communities, this movement aspires to a radical transformation of the individual and of society. Its adepts seek to achieve universal harmony through individual and collective disciplines centred on the Divinity. But this New Age god is a rational principle of unity, bringing humanity together with nature – like the Pythagorean monad – rather than founding a particular religion: a universalist, optimistic, peaceful messianism aiming to reconcile faith with science and progress. The imperfections of human nature are not thought to be intrinsic like original sin; they are flaws correctable through moral disciplines based on a scientific awareness of humanity's place in the universe. And in the pure tradition of Pythagoras's disciples, the individual soul is regarded as part of the world's soul: hence the belief in reincarnation and past lives.

New Ageism thus provided an outlet for a whole fringe of baby boomers seeking a spirituality capable of giving meaning to their involvement in social struggles and satisfying their need for the universal. But it also attracted a segment of the next generation of fifteen- to twenty-year-olds, along with people from academic and scientific circles and some followers of spiritualist disciplines. From its centre in California, the movement spread rapidly to all the other states and even overseas.

In a country where freedom of worship is total, the neo-Epicureans and neo-Pythagoreans would only have been two of the many different religious denominations if they had remained private cults. But in becoming vehicles for an alternative culture, they were questioning the *social* values held sacred by America – a somewhat decayed tradition of Christian morality – and were thus challenging the authority of the country's institutions. Their "liberated" morals and equal treatment of women, children, the descendants of black slaves and newly-arrived immigrants gave permanent proof of their rejection of the community's established rules. They could thus be perceived as a threat – not religious but political – to the nation's cohesion. This threat was compounded by the dissatisfaction with the established social hierarchy being shown by members of major religious denominations. These included the Baptists and the Catholics who traditionally express the religiosity of the American "plebs".

A NEW STATE RELIGION

The path leading to the "imperial presidency", inaugurated by Franklin D. Roosevelt, greatly weakened the representative congregations of the old American elite, the Episcopalians and Presbyterians in particular. For the sixty million Catholics and fifteen million Southern Baptists who represent almost half the American religious corpus, the effect was very different.[4] Between 1940 and 1990, while the population of the United States grew by 88 per cent, the numbers of Catholics and Baptists increased by 160 per cent and 152 per cent respectively. The number of Episcopalians, Presbyterians and Methodists all increased by less than 65 per cent over the same period.[5]

The Power of the Catholics

The vitality of the Baptist religion is largely due to the piety of black and poor white communities in the southern states, the Bible Belt. The deep religiosity of Afro-Americans – many of whose political leaders are also clergymen – and the convivial character of their liturgy eventually influenced a generation of whites who were looking for a "born-again" Christianity. The Catholic Church, by contrast, benefited from the arrival of new immigrants of Hispanic, Polish, Baltic, Filipino and Vietnamese origins.

Both of these religious denominations – owing partly to the social background of their believers – found themselves involved in the great social movements of the 1960s. Both churches had traditions of activism – the Catholic Church in the trade unions and the Baptist Church in local communities – but they had not yet risked themselves openly in great national debates. This was a considerable leap for the Baptist congregations, traditionally jealous of their autonomy and distrustful of all hierarchy and political authority. But how could they remain silent when the whole black community was mobilizing behind Martin Luther King Jr and a multitude of other clergymen?

Catholics had more political experience. In the United States, however, they had been outcast for so long that they had acquired the habit of trying to pass unnoticed, so much so that they consistently occupied the patriotic high ground. It used to be said in jest that in wartime Catholic bishops advised their flocks to praise the Lord and pass the ammunition. But the Catholics were no longer a minority subject to discrimination. Nearly 30 per cent of Americans were Catholics, and the decline of Protestant political domination had left a very tempting vacuum.

The new power of Catholicism was not only apparent in the election of John F. Kennedy, or in the high concentrations of Catholics in the most dynamic and important parts of the country. In Congress, which despite everything is still a bastion of white Protestant America, the Catholics have gained a lot of ground. In 1963 11 per cent of Senators and 20 per cent of Representatives were Catholic. By 1991 these percentages had increased to 20 and 28 respectively.[6]

Thus, the Catholic Church began to intervene in American politics, not only in the field of manners and morals, but also – shockingly for America – in foreign policy and even military affairs. For example, on 3 May 1983, in the middle of the Reaganite Cold War, the USCC (the American Catholic bishops' conference) published a pastoral letter attacking the sacred cows of nuclear deterrence and the monopoly of strategic knowledge exercised by military and civilian experts.[7] Two years later, it encouraged Congress to defeat proposals for funding the new MX intercontinental nuclear missiles. The USCC also spoke out against military aid to the Nicaraguan *contras* and supported a negotiated peace in the region. It joined the campaign against American investment in South Africa. The Catholics in the south-eastern states showed what they thought of Ronald Reagan's political asylum policy by trying to protect refugees fleeing from Central America.

The USCC also launched a broad national debate on economic policy, starting in November 1984 with the themes of the papal encyclical *Laborem exercens* and going on to question the morality of capitalism itself. This provoked such an uproar that a number of leading Catholic business-men felt obliged to come out publicly in defence of the American economic system. During the 1984 presidential election, some bishops crossed a decisive symbolic line by openly campaigning against candidates who favoured legal abortion. The White House recognized the amount of influence wielded by this new religious power: on 10 January 1984, Ronald Reagan restored diplomatic relations with the Vatican after an interruption lasting 117 years.

The Rise and Fall of Protestant Fundamentalism

In traditional circles, the upsurge of countercultural "superstitions" and the obvious determination of a "plebeian" religion to play a more impor-tant role in the country's life were perceived as mortal threats to American social cohesion. Extremist groups, with or without the consent of their parent religious congregations, began tapping the new thirst for spiritual-ity to fuel the revival of a great Protestant fundamentalist movement. In 1979, Rev. Jerry Falwell, judging that this movement was weakened by internal divisions, founded the Moral Majority, a religious federation mandated to intervene directly in politics in favour of "traditional values" and against the ravages of secular humanism. The Moral Majority used the new mass medium of television with great skill and perspicacity. Its frontline clergy appeared as the high priests of an electronic religion whose liturgy consisted exclusively of inflamed sermons delivered via the small screen to twenty million spectators at a time. In the early 1980s the politico-religious strategy of televangelists like Jerry Falwell, Pat Robertson, Jimmy Swaggart and Oral Roberts worked very well. Their sermons attacked moral decline, the counterculture, social security (claimed to encourage "laziness and irresponsibility") and the frivolity and cosmopolitanism of the ruling classes. All of this sounded eminently reasonable to members of the white middle class who had stayed on the sidelines during the great upheavals of the 1960s and 1970s.

The fundamentalists' influence was extensive enough to revive the arguments over abortion, religious worship in schools, pornography and the tedious creationist rearguard struggle against Darwinism. They can even claim to have played an important role in securing the elections of Ronald Reagan and George Bush. And they played a decisive part in ensuring the defeat of the proposed Equal Rights Amendment in 1982.

These few successes apart, however, the record of the new evangelists is pretty thin. True, the themes of their sermons were discussed nationally, and the majority of politicians – both Republican and Democrat, including President Clinton himself – espoused their idea of a struggle to revive American "values". But few of their demands for the institution-alization of morality were adopted by Congress. Worse still, a number of leading clerics were caught with their pants down in various forms of sexual and financial misconduct. By the early 1990s the fundamentalist movement had become a shadow of its former self. In 1992 it was still able to exert some influence over the Republican party platform. But electoral concern had shifted to other problems; and Bush, facing Bill Clinton, swiftly and discreetly abandoned his crusade for American "family values". After the big Republican party gains in the 1994 Congressional elections the fundamentalists started another assault. But they were forced to give up the frontal ideological offensives that had alienated the sympathies of most Americans and fall back on a more political approach. These days the movement uses indirect means: the promotion of constitutional amend-ments or technical modifications to certain laws and regulations.

What could possibly explain this meteoric rise and fall? First and foremost, these religious integralists are out of step with the Puritan tradition they claim to represent. In the early days, this tradition had no need to play politics for the simple reason that the social bond was itself religious: with a Calvinist background common to most of the communities, close collaboration between ministers and magistrates went without saying. In today's America, not only has this unifying bond disappeared, but there is also a proliferation of new cults, many of them non-Christian, all clamouring for their place in the sun.

This places the Protestant fundamentalists in an opposite situation to their illustrious forebears: they have to try to impose their values on a largely resistant society. It leaves them no choice but to call on the state for support, making themselves dependent on the government and running the risk of being used by it. It is the sort of opportunity politicians always seize: conservative candidates start paying lip service to the evangelical agenda a few months before an election, then swiftly revert to normality as soon as the votes are in. Thus, the ministers have submitted to the magistrates, or, in any case, to the president, and their loss of credibility becomes inevitable. In the end the American Protestant integralist adventure will have served only as a further boost for presidential authority.

The White House has thus become the only institution in the country able to embody the symbolic social bond and the common interest. In the multitude of ethnic groups, religions and lobbies, the only sentiments shared unanimously by all Americans are love and respect for the supreme magistrate, guardian of the honour of the star-spangled banner and commander-in-chief of the armies that protect the United States. Individuals may be opposed, sometimes violently, to one president or another. But they remain aware that the office itself involves the only choice in which all of the citizens can participate.

This symbol of the nation's unity, which from some angles has a quasi-religious aspect, is of course something that cannot be questioned. But Kennedy's assassination, Johnson's defeat, the humiliating dishonour of Nixon's departure and the undistinguished stop-gap presidency of Gerald Ford, somewhat eroded civic faith in the presidency. The succession of catastrophes felt like a sort of divine punishment for America's sins. Had Providence deserted the United States?

This question approached the very core of American identity: America's idea of itself and its mission in the world. It had become necessary to restore the link with the Almighty; and to that end, at all costs, to recast the presidency in closer alignment with a moral vision. That in fact is the meaning of the election of Jimmy Carter, a peanut farmer whose political baggage consisted of a single term as governor of Georgia, a man not ashamed to present himself as a born-again Christian whose politics would be based on strict moral principles.

Carter was very unlucky, though. His defeat stemmed from his inability to give Fortune a discreet nudge in the right direction. In American historical mythology, Providence shows its hand during great ordeals from which the United States emerges victorious, especially the wars which have been so frequent in the nation's life. The president's failure to deal decisively with the episode of the American diplomatic hostages in Teheran seemed to prove that he did not know how to win divine favour. So that by its very failure, the Baptist Jimmy Carter's adventure pointed the way to a sort of new state religion, of which Ronald Reagan was to be the first high priest. Mediation between God and America was beginning to be seen not as a function of the presidency itself, but of its current occupant.

The Triumphal Cult of the President

The symbolic bond linking Americans is now embodied in the person of the president. But the tenant of the White House must also demonstrate, through military and economic successes, that he is chosen by Providence to lead the nation and that he is thus an exceptional being. Mistakes are not permitted. He represents the main factor of cohesion in a heterogeneous country, and holds in his hands a power of decision stretching across much of the planet. A sort of lay religion has begun to form around this emblematic figure, fed by the ubiquitous television images used so skilfully by Ronald Reagan.

The old Hollywood trouper made many appearances before his legions dressed in the jacket and cap of commander-in-chief. The invasion of Grenada supplied a bargain-basement military triumph. And the bicentenary of the Constitution provided an opportunity for a world network television spectacular that extolled the glories of America and its providential mission. The Reagan years also saw an extraordinary economic boom (on credit perhaps, but real enough for the elite and large segments of the middle class). Ronald Reagan was so obviously favoured by the gods that he was even forgiven for setbacks like the marine withdrawal from Lebanon and the secret funding of the Nicaraguan *contras* (illegal, but in the cause of freedom, after all).

The election of a president every four years thus became a rite of cyclical refoundation. The candidate starts as a simple citizen, perhaps even a complete unknown, but that is unimportant. Every four years, thanks to "the great mystery of democracy" (Bill Clinton's phrase), he is transformed into the mediator between the City and the Divinity. The original Puritan foundations have been definitively reshaped: all authority, both profane *and* sacred, is now concentrated in the supreme magistrate. The success of a president used to be synonymous with that of the American Republic. The happy victor would be cheered and toasted; then later, like a good servant of the nation, he would step back into the ranks. But since Ronald Reagan's presidency, it is the man himself who is honoured; for it is he who is the instrument of Providence.

The president has thus, in relations with the Almighty, substituted himself for the body of the Republic. The new state religion is based on the celebration of triumphs achieved by the holder of supreme power. The Reagan revolution was of crucial importance. It recycled all the founding myths of the United States, this time in the service of the presidency and the president himself. Reagan, in effect, was enthroned as the "great communicator": for the Americans, for foreign peoples and for the Almighty. The American Republic, the state of the Founding Fathers, has been eroded in favour of a new system, still embryonic but already distinct enough to have its own name. For want of a better title, let us call it the "democratic empire".

This empire seems particularly well adapted to the central place America will occupy in the world of the twenty-first century. Based on religious celebration of the president's triumph and his role as mediator between the City and the Divine, the new system offers two major advantages. First, it allows a radical separation between public religion and private religions. Virtually all of the plethora of cults in the United States can recognize themselves fairly easily in a triumphalist ideology that does not favour any one of them, not even the WASP tradition. The presidential cult thus comes into its own as a sacred, federalizing symbol: a crucial role now that the nation has become a mosaic of beliefs and ethnic communities, each demanding respect for its own authenticity. While it may not prevent serious new tensions from arising, it can only strengthen the coherence and unity of American society. The only real challenge on the horizon is the growing influence of the Catholic Church and its demand – officially advanced by the Pope – to be recognized as a public moral authority.

Second, it supplies an ideological platform and a televisual liturgy perfectly adapted to the internationalization of the modern world and the ambition to establish an American universal leadership. The triumph of the White House is a ritual accessible to everyone in the world. The November 1992 presidential election was exhaustively covered by the media world-wide, including "global" networks like the quintessentially American CNN. There were even local opinion surveys to measure the putative "vote" of the French, the British, the Germans and the Japanese. People were aware of the growing importance of the White House in their own lives and in the affairs of their countries. Never before had the "democratic emperor" seemed so naturally the leader of the post- Cold War world.

In 1988 George Bush took over and consolidated the Reagan heritage. The televised Gulf War carried the triumphal cult of the presidency to new heights, the tenant of the White House materializing in Iraq as the thundering Jove of the new world order. He even held a military triumph in Washington, completing the symbolic identification with a victorious Roman emperor. However, he dispensed with the Roman custom of employing a slave to hold the victor's laurel wreath and murmur in his ear the republican sentiment: "Remember that you are only a man."

Despite his extraordinary popularity as commander-in-chief, Bush suffered from the same defect as Carter: an inability to persuade Providence to smile on the American economy. Worse still, he kept saying that there was no point in any government action, that God would provide. When nothing happened people began doubting the president's auguries. And apart from all this, the conqueror of Saddam Hussein made a mistake typical of the Second World War generation: he was impious, careless about governmental morality.

Bush made it perfectly clear both in 1988 and in 1992 that he was ready to use any means, even immoral ones, to win the elections. Later, the scandal of his murky relations with the Baghdad regime, and his use of doubletalk when referring to repression in China and conflicts in former Yugoslavia, exposed his taste for secret action and political manipulation at the expense of ethics. But a president who takes the place of the Republic in the role of mediator with the Almighty has to appear every bit as pious as the rest of society; an impious prince cannot be acceptable to Heaven. His government takes on the appearance of a blasphemy that has to be exorcized as quickly as possible. At the polls.

Even at the height of the political scandal over secret backing for the *contras*, Reagan always tried to preserve his image as an upright and pious man. Bush, by contrast, did not seem to understand the need to follow suit, and was beaten by an almost unknown baby boomer. The postwar "moral generation" – white, suburban, fortysomething – had at last gained supreme power. It had experienced the counterculture. It had travelled abroad. Its tastes and values were more eclectic, more open to the outside world. Now it had inherited the planet's only superpower, and with it the heavy responsibility for extending and stabilizing the new American democratic empire. It had at least one formidable asset: the ability to fabricate a universal culture.

3

AMERICA YIELDED TO

THE IMMIGRANTS

The evolution of the American democratic empire is a phenomenon of unprecedented scale. It affects the very foundations of society, its values and religious sentiments, the meaning of citizenship and the political institutions established by the Constitution. The stimulus for this change was provided by war, as is so often the case with great nations. Before the Second World War the American Republic developed separately, independent of Europe, Asia and Africa. Of course, it occasionally used force to open foreign markets to its trade, ensure free passage for its shipping or counter European ambitions in the Americas and the Pacific. And in 1917 it had been obliged to make an extraordinary effort to separate the belligerents in the Old World, whose quarrels were threatening to engulf the entire planet.

But suspicion of the Old World, perceived as obscurantist and backward, irretrievably doomed to armed conflict and social injustice, had never been wholly eliminated. America had always retreated into itself, into its dream of building an ideal society of freedom and progress, at a safe distance from these "medieval countries". The victory of 1945, by making the United States responsible for the political management of the non-Communist world, dissolved this splendid isolation for ever.

THE PEAKING OF WASP AMERICA

The United States started changing radically during the 1950s. Over the subsequent four decades the American population increased from 150 to 250 million. Following the 1965 Immigration and Nationality Act, immigration – both official and clandestine – reached the record levels of the great influx between 1900 and 1920. And for the first time the great majority of migrants was not European, but Latin American and Asian. Over the same period rural areas emptied rapidly, to the advantage of gigantic megalopolitan clusters. The population became concentrated in the coastal regions at the expense of the continental interior, and in the South and the West, to the detriment of the traditional political and economic centres of the Midwest and the Northeast. All the American nation's familiar balances – geographic, ethnic, linguistic, religious, cultural and institutional – were turned upside down.[1]

Closing the Door to Immigrants

Until the end of the First World War immigration to America – except by "Orientals" – was unrestricted. Labour was always needed, and a point was made of giving an honourable welcome to anyone who had been persecuted in his or her country of origin or was simply looking for a better life. In the early 1920s, however, a coalition of trade unionists and xenophobic nativist movements managed to impose very restrictive new legislation.[2] The unions feared that the flood of new arrivals would threaten the high wages won during the period of war economy. The nativists, who were rabidly anti-Catholic and anti-Semitic, opposed the massive influx of new immigrants from southern and central Europe, whom they accused of being unassimilable in an America which had to remain white, Anglo-Saxon and Protestant.

The National Origins Act, adopted by Congress in 1924, established country quotas that openly favoured migrants from northern Europe, especially the British; Asian immigrants, just as blatantly, were barred. The Great Depression of the 1930s reduced the flow of immigrants to a symbolic trickle; indeed a fair number of Italians, Greeks, Poles and Czechs even chose to return to Europe. Thus between the wars, for the first time in the country's history and despite opposition from the White House, immigration was practically halted.

But this virulent rejection of foreigners perceived as undesirable had important repercussions. It encouraged the import of labour from Mexico (the American hemisphere being quota-exempt at that time) and the Philippines (until the 1934 law of independence), and the migration of black farmers from the South to work in the northern factories. Yet another effect was the accelerated Americanization of the European "new immigrants" who had opted to remain. Fewer in number and more isolated than their predecessors, they made greater efforts to integrate, helped by the American tradition of social mobility. The white ghettoes emptied as some of these émigrés joined the middle class and dispersed into the landscape. The ethnic associations and journals were threatened with oblivion. For a time the WASP ideal of the melting pot – the symbolic crucible in which new arrivals are Americanized – was given a new vitality.

The Republican Hierarchy

The America of the Founding Fathers – Protestant, white, oligarchic, republican, powerful and isolationist – was at its peak. It rested on a social pyramid based on a delicate ethnic and religious hierarchy. Federal executive power, reinforced by Roosevelt's New Deal, was in the hands of the (generally Anglican or Episcopalian) East-Coast Anglo-Saxon money aristocracy. It was balanced by a Congress whose members represented a provincial elite which was also Anglo-Saxon but included people from the second wave of immigrants from northern Europe, mainly Lutheran Germans and Scandinavians. These Nordic, Protestant whites were the bedrock of a rapidly expanding middle class. But this class was also open to other whites – Catholics from Ireland and southern Europe, Jews and Orthodox Christians from Eastern Europe – who were to make the Democrats a major political force.

This group supplied the bulk of industrial workers. The trade unions were effectively controlled by the Catholic Irish, who thus gained influence in the local politics of big urban centres and in the Democratic Party. After the founding of the Congress of Industrial Organizations (CIO) in 1934, the American workers' movement also sought to integrate the black workers who had been moving northwards since the turn of the century.

At the bottom of the scale were all the have-nots, the urban and rural "plebs": poor whites scratching a living in the back country, the urban lumpenproletariat, the millions of freed slaves and "aliens". This category included black sharecroppers, free for half a century, but subject to a system more exploitative than slavery; Mexicans working in the most precarious conditions as platelayers, industrial strikebreakers or farm labourers in the South; and Asians on the West Coast, subjected to violent racial discrimination.

BLACKS AND HISPANICS:
THE NEW CITIZENS

The great crisis of the 1930s and the New Deal institutions had started to unravel the fabric of the American Republic. The United States's entry to the war in 1941 was going to throw everything into doubt. Political and ethnic balances, ways of life, the great metropolitan centres were all going to be changed forever by the accession to citizenship of a new wave of immigrants.

The Great Internal Migration

The war needed labour to keep military industry rolling and expand the armed forces. Since European immigration was practically prevented by the conflict, it was necessary at first to fall back on national resources. Small farmers – blacks, whites and Mexican-Americans – poured into the industrial centres in the North and the West of the country. The southern countryside emptied, especially as the initial migration caused a shortage of labour which led to the increased mechanization of agriculture. It was the start of one of the biggest movements of a single population group in American history: twenty million farmers (sixteen million whites, four million blacks) eventually left their land for the towns of the East and West Coasts.[3]

Another great reservoir of labour – women – was tapped at the same time. Millions of women began to work in the armaments industries and in all the logistical services of the armed forces. Appreciable numbers of women had taken part in the war effort in 1917–18, overseas as well as at home, and this experience had played a determining role in the change of attitudes during the 1920s and 1930s. Their mass participation in the Second World War was the trigger for a cultural revolution which over-turned relations between the sexes in the United States.

This vast internal migration was augmented by the arrival of a new category of immigrants: the Hispanics from Latin America, mainly from Mexico and the Caribbean. The Mexican presence in the United States dates from the conquest of Texas and California in the nineteenth century. It was consolidated by a further wave of immigrants early in the twentieth century: the Mexican revolution caused nearly a tenth of the population to migrate northwards. The 1929 crisis led to the repatriation, voluntary or forced, of a fair proportion of these immigrants. By the eve of Pearl Harbor they had dwindled to a small minority without much

political or cultural influence on the country. They were scattered throughout the territory but remained relatively numerous in the southern border
regions.

From 1942 onwards, with the war effort in full swing, American
agriculture started running short of labour. President Franklin Roosevelt
negotiated an agreement with Mexico for the import of agricultural
workers (known as *braceros*) on a temporary basis. But on the heels of
these short-term "legal" immigrants there followed millions of illegal
"wetbacks", so called because they were believed to swim in across the Rio
Grande. The *Bracero* programme, periodically interrupted and renewed
until the early 1960s, enabled some ten million Mexican *peones* – half of
them illegal entrants – to work in the United States. And their wages, well
below American norms, led to spectacular agricultural development in the
southwestern states.[4]

Paradoxically, this massive influx of agricultural workers accelerated
the urbanization of the Mexican population already settled in the United
States. The existing Mexican-American farmers could not survive the
competition from their ex-compatriots. Following the example of the
small black and white sharecroppers from the South, they decamped to try
their luck in the arms industry, then in construction, textiles, automobile
assembly and the public sector. American towns, especially in the West
and in Texas, started to acquire the Latino flavour they have today.

The Whites and the New Plebs

This Hispanic wave was not limited to Mexicans alone, nor was it
restricted to the West Coast. Starting in the 1940s, aided by the new
facility of air transport, hundreds of thousands of Puerto Ricans headed for
New York. Most were virtually destitute and gravitated to the lowest paid
jobs. They had, however, the great advantage of already being American
citizens. But, even more than the chicanos, they brought a disturbing
element into the rigid ethnic hierarchy. The Puerto Rican population is
largely mulatto and includes every shade of skin colour and racial nuance.
Now this mixed population was gradually occupying whole quarters of the
greatest city in the United States. Were these people white or black?

Those of the newcomers who had light skins were accepted as whites
and had a better chance of achieving prosperity. But the other New
York communities could see that Puerto Ricans constituted a single,
identifiable, culturally homogeneous group, entirely distinct from the
Europeans. This ambiguity echoed the status of the Caribbean island

itself, a free state associated with the United States. These first visible divisions between culture and race, between American citizenship and retention of a foreign connection, were the early signs of an approaching upheaval. The massive arrival of Hispanics and blacks – formerly farmers and migrant workers – in the American megalopolitan clusters destroyed the existing social structure. A sizeable nucleus of lower "plebs" – the "underclass" – took root at the very heart of the country's great urban centres of economic and political power.

This new demographic reality was guaranteed to upset isolationists, patriotic groups and other partisans of a melting pot reserved exclusively for Americans of European origin. Meanwhile, the huge mass of refugees seeking to leave Europe for the United States after 1945 revived the question of renewing large-scale immigration. President Harry S. Truman, citing the American tradition of asylum and the duties accompanying the United States's assumption of international leadership, battled for the expansion of immigration quotas. Part of Congress was hostile to this, afraid of the invasion of foreign "subversives"; the veterans' associations feared new competition on the labour market. Nevertheless the White House finally got the Displaced Persons Act passed in 1948, followed by the Refugee Relief Act in 1953.

These two laws opened America's doors to some 700,000 European refugees: first displaced Germans (mainly Catholics), then Balts, Poles and East-European Jews fleeing from Communist regimes, then Hungarians in 1956. A year later the Refugee Escape Act, based on the idea of solidarity with victims of communism, legalized the waves of refugees that arrived over the next two decades: 900,000 Cubans, 800,000 Indochinese and 600,000 East Europeans.[5]

The executive's traditional support for the welcoming of immigrants was insufficient to silence xenophobic lobbies still dreaming of a return to the prewar situation. In principle the new refugees were supposed to be registered by nationality in future quotas, as stipulated by the National Origins Act of 1924. The Immigration and Naturalization Act, passed by Congress in 1952, established an even more restrictive interpretation of this system of national quotas. While it is true that the law gave Asians some access to citizenship, it also instituted an overall annual ceiling of 250,000 immigrants, 85 per cent of whom were supposed to be from northern and western Europe. As for the Mexicans, the *Bracero* programme ended and a remorseless hunt for illegal immigrants began.

THE WHITE HOUSE KICKS IN THE DOORS

The 1952 act was the swansong of the old America. It was not only opposed by every subsequent occupant of the White House, but made no difference whatsoever to the influx of foreigners. Its limitations became apparent in 1960, when Fidel Castro took power in Havana and a tenth of the Cuban population decamped to Miami. To appreciate the scale of this change, consider that in the 140 years between 1820 and 1960 the United States received forty-one million immigrants, while over the next thirty years, 1960–90, another twenty million arrived, illegals included. At the same time, the composition of the immigrants changed radically: until 1960, 84 per cent of new arrivals were from Europe, 13 per cent from the Americas and 3 per cent from Asia. By the 1980s only 10 per cent were from Europe while 45 per cent came from the Americas and 41 per cent from Asia.[6]

Muscle for Economic Growth

The partisans of frontier closure could not prevail during the postwar economic boom. Economists and federal administrations explained endlessly that there had to be cheap labour to keep the factories going, there had to be consumers to lead growth. Thus, from the early 1960s, immigration policy looked like an effort to channel the flow of migrants rationally, rather than a barrier to stop them entering. The White House continued to maintain that restrictions were contrary to American ideals and economic interests. It still had to negotiate with Congress, but had now seized the initiative on this matter.

After Lyndon Johnson's 1964 electoral triumph, the Immigration and Nationality Act of 1965 definitively abandoned the system of quotas by national origin. Between the world wars the old ethnic and religious criteria had maintained the balance of power and a sort of social stability in the United States. But the new America, engaged militarily and economically throughout the globe, could no longer use a policy inherited from its isolationist past. The American presidency, already the incarnation of world leadership, wanted a new system of control based on humanitarian responsibility (to the family group and to refugees) and the country's economic needs (the professional skills of applicants for entry). The 1965 act is in fact a compromise between the executive's vision and Congress's desire to restrict the entry of foreigners: the new criteria were adopted, but an overall quota for Asians was retained and, for the first time, a quota was fixed for the Americas.

History often stutters. The Immigration and Nationality Act of 1965, like the 1924 act, produced results unforeseen by its promoters. First, the measures in favour of preserving the family unit resulted in the swamping of legal quotas: extensive Hispanic and Asian families created a siphoning effect, with new arrivals sucking large numbers of close relations into the United States after them. Second, the criteria concerning professional skills caused an explosion of immigration from Asia, where the applicants were better educated and qualified. And third, given the new difficulty in getting visas, the act stimulated illegal immigration from Central America and Mexico.

Three and a half million immigrants between 1960 and 1970, four and a half million over the following decade and six million between 1980 and 1990 (without counting between five and eight million "illegals"):[7] by the early 1980s it was clear that this massive influx was out of control. But the American authorities showed no sign of panic; on the contrary, they stood firm and continued to stamp papers. In 1986, during Ronald Reagan's presidency, a new Immigration and Control Act granted amnesty, and the chance of legalization, to all illegals who had arrived in the United States before January 1982. It even (in a special concession to the powerful Californian agricultural lobbies) legalized some temporary workers who had been taken on much more recently.

A New Latino-Asian America

This Nth attempt to bring the phenomenon under legal control was practically ignored. The penalties stipulated for employers of illegal immigrants made little difference to the behaviour of the parties concerned. As for the illegals themselves, only a quarter, or at most a third, bothered to get legal papers. Never mind: the 1986 act was extended in 1988 to give them another chance. Meanwhile their numbers continued to increase, apparently unhampered by all the police patrols and barriers along the Rio Grande. Better still, a new Immigration Reform Act, adopted in 1990, raised the overall ceiling for immigration applicants other than refugees. The figure increased from 490,000 to 700,000 between 1992 and 1994 and 675,000 for 1995.[8]

So the United States at the end of the twentieth century has a very different face – and skin colour – from the United States of the 1930s, and the change is still accelerating. In 1980, one American in five was of Hispanic, Asian, African or Native American descent. Ten years later the proportion was one in four. Over the same period the Hispanic population increased from 14.6 to 22.4 million and today represents 9 per cent of the total population (12 per cent if illegals are counted).[9] The number of Asians – Chinese, Filipinos, Japanese, Indians, Koreans and Vietnamese – has increased by 108 per cent over the last decade to reach 7.3 million.[10]

Not only is immigration by Latinos and Asians being maintained at high volumes, but both, especially the Latinos, are groups whose birthrate is still high. The number of Mexicans, for example, has increased by 30 per cent every ten years since 1960 *without counting immigration*. The American Census Bureau estimates that the population of the United States in 2050 will be 383 million, a 50 per cent increase on the 1990 figure, attributed largely to immigration.

Projections for the year 2010 forecast a "legal" Hispanic community of more than thirty million, displacing blacks as the country's largest ethnic minority.[11] But these statistics give a poor impression of the real impact of Latinos, most of whom are concentrated in a small number of the country's more dynamic states: California, Texas, Florida, New York and Illinois. They are 40 per cent of New Mexico's population, a quarter of California's and a fifth of Arizona's: a peaceful *reconquista* of the territories lost in the nineteenth century.[12]

Are the freed blacks and the new immigrants – Latinos and Asians – following the path marked out by their predecessors, the Germans, Scandinavians, Irish, Italians, Russians, Greeks and Jews? Will they become Americanized bit by bit, like the Europeans before them? Will the famous melting pot be extended to include them? Half a century after the demographic turning point of the Second World War it is apparent that things are changing. Opening its doors to new citizens from all over the world has made the WASP Republic come apart at the seams. American power – henceforth planetary both inside and outside its domestic frontiers – needs a universal model for the management of ethnic diversity.

4

MANAGING THE WORLD MOSAIC

It was inevitable that the American ethnic cauldron would boil over sooner or later. The delicate mechanisms of white Anglo-Saxon Protestant power were too fragile to cope with the sudden arrival of a mass of new citizens foreign to these values. The subtle balances between regional oligarchies and between the different communities of European origin excluded by definition the "lower plebs", made up of the descendants of black slaves and recent non-white immigrants, Hispanics in particular. Established in the hearts of the great cities, the coal hands and stokers of the American economic boom, they were inevitably going to demand their share of citizenship.

In their struggle for integration these outsiders could count on one faithful, if self-interested, ally: the White House. The ethnic and religious networks of the old WASP Republic declined as these new actors occupied the political arena. The executive seemed to be the only institution capable either of managing intercommunal tensions or of protecting the achievements of civil rights movements. Thus the successes as well as the failures of the plebeian insurrections of the 1960s and 1970s reinforced federal power at the expense of Congress and the states. Between Kennedy and Reagan the whole of American political life changed out of all recognition.

THE BLACKS CAMPAIGN FOR CITIZENSHIP

The black population of the United States has the distinction of being the only one not to have arrived of its own free will. It is also the most significant group left out of the American dream. The liberation of the southern slaves after the Civil War was effectively negated by their exclusion from voting rights and the establishment of segregationist Jim Crow laws. The laws in the North were less oppressive, but in most communities racial discrimination remained a feature of social life. At the beginning of this century the blacks, who were American citizens de jure, tried to gain recognition for their most basic rights, but met with little success.

From Civil Rights to Black Power

Here, too, war was a decisive element. The first great political victory of the black movement – symbolically important although its practical effects were limited – was won during the Second World War against racial discrimination in the military industries. The influx of black farmers to the big cities revived the ghettoes, abandoned by white minorities, and the mass of newcomers gave added strength to those already fighting for civil rights. During the 1950s and until the historic 1964 Civil Rights Act, the black population, under the leadership of the Rev. Martin Luther King Jr, mobilized as never before to have its full citizenship recognized. In the process it brought a significant change into the history of ethnic relations in the United States: for the first time, a racial minority consciously and deliberately appealed to the federal government to help it gain acceptance among other ethnic groups. The blacks – not without reason – no longer regarded the melting pot as a natural mechanism of American civil society, but as the product of a voluntarist policy that ought to be entrusted to the central executive. The latter profited by strengthening its control over local governments and Congress, as it was frequently called on to intervene to uphold the equality of citizens before the law.

The federal administration – impelled by the Korean and Vietnam wars – imposed anti-discriminatory practices on the armed forces; President Lyndon Johnson forced Congress to swallow the civil rights acts of 1964 and 1965, guaranteeing every American citizen the right to vote and abolishing all segregation in public places. These acts also set up a federal agency to promote non-discrimination in the workplace, and gave the federal government the power to cut off funding from recalcitrant local public bodies. At the same time, the White House radically enlarged the American social security programme, created during the Great Depression of the 1930s, and launched the War on Poverty, mainly benefiting the black population. So the rise of the black civil rights movement and the extension of federal government powers went, so to speak, hand in hand.

But although the descendants of the slaves were now backed by the authority of the administration against the prejudices of American society, that society was still not ready to give them equal treatment. A more or less veiled discrimination persisted in daily life. It is true that a small number of blacks – sportsmen, media professionals, civil servants, soldiers, politicians, business lawyers and small and medium businessmen – were gradually finding their way into the national elite, with a larger minority joining the middle class. But the majority was still outcast, rejected, foundering slowly in the misery and delinquency of immense urban ghettoes. In 1965, ignited by a huge riot in Watts, a district of Los Angeles, black America burst into flames. Stokely Carmichael coined a slogan that combined all the community's passions and frustrations: "Black Power!"[1]

The Impossible Afro-American Nation

No community in the United States – apart from the Native Americans, a special case – had ever before demanded a separate government of its own. On the contrary, they had all striven to increase their influence in the existing institutional framework, to the point of dissolving in the common political pot. But the demand for Black Power represented a deliberate rejection of integration and even desegregation in the name of specifically black culture and values.

This was not the first time that blacks, publicly excluded from civil life, had sought refuge in a non-American identity. The best-known earlier examples are the creation of Liberia during the nineteenth century and the Jamaican Marcus Garvey's "Back to Africa" movement during the First World War. By the end of the 1960s, however, their African roots seemed more remote; the new project was to establish an identity that would be clearly Afro-American. But this task soon began to look almost impossible.

Slavery in the United States had virtually destroyed all meaningful references to the origins, which in any case were extremely diverse, of the blacks taken from Africa by force. Tribal, ethnic, even clan and family links had been almost totally erased by the organization of menial labour and by repression. In such a context, weak and disparate oral traditions were not sufficient to create a strong common culture. Only a particular form of religious syncretism, combining the choral tradition of Protestant communities with that of African cults, managed to serve as a cement for Afro-American identities.

43

The destruction of original black cultures is common to the whole American hemisphere. But in Latin America and the Caribbean, racial mixing meant that the blacks had made an important, sometimes central contribution to the nascent personality of their country of misfortune. In the United States, though, the Afro-American community had been placed in a wholly untenable situation: its identity was thoroughly massacred, and at the same time it was denied any real participation in the mainstream of the nation's cultural life. It is well known that music – the most universal and least "material" art, and thus the most easily accepted by a "foreign" ear – had been the main black contribution to American culture; and that this black music was despised by the "white" culture until the end of the 1950s.

The movement that arose from Black Power tried hard to recreate lost roots: Islam, a mythic Ethiopia, the Marxism of African liberation movements, the renewal of academic interest in African history and, more recently, the radicalism of "black anthropologies" and other "politically correct" sciences. These researches certainly gave a measure of pride to a community whose past had been obliterated by force. But progress was blocked by the limitations of an artificially constructed identity, and by the stubborn refusal of white society to accept any form of mixing with its former slaves.

Of course some Afro-Americans have managed, bit by bit, to work themselves into important administrative and political posts. Some black businessmen have become super-rich. The chairman of the joint chiefs of staff during the Gulf War was black. A black judge sits on the Supreme Court, and four members of President Bill Clinton's first cabinet were black. Forms of discrimination have become subtler, less visible; nowadays the black lower middle class can live in reasonable harmony with its white neighbours. The Rev. Jesse Jackson's presidential campaigns in 1984 and 1988, and the election of black mayors in the country's biggest metropolitan centres – Los Angeles, Detroit, Chicago, Philadelphia, New York, Atlanta, Washington D.C., New Orleans, San Francisco, Baltimore, Seattle – have done much for the self-esteem of the Afro-American community.

But blacks remain the poorest ethnic group in the United States, with incomes 45 per cent below those of whites and 20 per cent below those of Hispanics. And the gap is still growing.[2] So that at the dawn of the twenty-first century, the bulk of the black population seems doomed to remain a "nation" isolated in urban ghettoes: "reservations" that are often tougher and more miserable than those allotted to the Native

44

Americans. Neither separate Black Power nor real integration, but a sort of social no man's land, subject to sudden explosions of self-destructive violence.

LATINOS AND ASIANS:
THE SUCCESS OF THE "ALIENS"

The struggle by the descendants of the slaves for integration into American society has thus ended for the time being in semi-failure. But it has opened the way to more subtle action by other minorities, the Hispanics in particular. The fight for civil rights taught a few simple lessons to the non-Europeans. First, they learned not to place excessive faith in white civil society or its representatives in Congress, but to exploit their own electoral strength and the power of the executive. Second, they learned to cling firmly to their cultural roots, while refusing to be imprisoned in a ghetto. And third, instead of dreaming of a mythical separate nation or waiting for America to change, they now understand that they must change America themselves.

An Open Community versus Segregation in Ghettoes

Traditionally, European immigration to the United States was an experience both exhilarating and traumatic. The new arrivals landed with dreams of fortune and happiness, but also without familiar cultural reference points. The migrants – for the most part young single men – found themselves in an unknown and dangerous land. To have any chance of being accepted they had to shed their former identities and, in many cases, learn a new language and anglicize their names.

It is hardly surprising then that these would-be Americans initially sought the reassuring company of their former compatriots. But the various ethnic associations, while keeping alive a few snippets of original culture and promoting a measure of solidarity with the old country, were just stepping stones into American melting pot. Without family landmarks, without the social constraints of the home village, with the supporting and restraining role of religion weakened, the immigrant had no choice but to make himself a new life as an American.

Like the free European immigrants before them, and unlike the blacks, the new immigrants from Latin America and Asia are close to their traditions. What is altogether new in their case is that they have been able to maintain close family, clan and even national links with their countries of origin.[3] The European Catholic populations – Irish, Italian, Polish and Portuguese – had tried to resist integration in their day, aided by their traditionally disciplined and powerful Church. Yet the Anglo-Saxon crucible melted them down in the end. What is so different about the Hispanics and Asians today?

First and foremost, the migrants of the second half of the twentieth century have benefited from the vast revolution in transport and communications. The telephone and relatively cheap and rapid air travel make it possible to maintain permanent contact with friends and relations living on the other side of the planet, something particularly useful to the new Asian immigrants. Incidentally, it is perhaps a little early to assess the impact of Asian immigration on the United States. The Asian population is concentrated in the West and the South, especially in Los Angeles, San Francisco and Honolulu. Asian-Americans are the richest minority (the average household income is 10 per cent higher than that of non-Hispanic whites) and the fastest growing (108 per cent between 1980 and 1990). Even so, in 1990 they represented only 2.9 per cent of the total American population.[4] They are better educated, with much higher levels of academic achievement, than other Americans. And they have a mode of family life that links the social rise of individuals with that of the whole clan.

This strong collective organization, based on extended and extensive families, the powerful aid networks that link the communities and the maintenance of social ties and allegiances with people who have stayed in the country of origin, all serve as barriers to fuller integration. But it is also true that the rapid rise of Asians to high-level jobs in administration and the universities encourages individualism and tends to erode traditional clan solidarities. And the Chinese, Japanese, Koreans, Filipinos and Vietnamese are not all bound together (as the Hispanics are) by a common language and religion, although emigrants from both the Philippines and Vietnam are largely Catholic. The Asian-Americans undoubtedly help to blur the frontier between the United States and Asia, and they are a challenge to the Anglo-Saxon melting pot. But there is nothing to suggest that as their integration into the middle class proceeds, the Asians will not follow in the footsteps of their European predecessors.

This could not be more different from the situation of the Latinos, who are moving into position to impose a new culture on the United States for the first time since 1797.[5] The effects of the communications revolution are strengthened in their case by geographical proximity, and the fact that the border states already contain a large, stable population of chicanos. Since the time of the *braceros*, Mexicans have adopted the habit of moving back and forth across the frontier as though it did not exist. Between the Mexican provinces of Tamaulipas, Coahuila, Chihuahua, Sonora and Baja California, and the states of Texas, California, Arizona, New Mexico and Colorado, there is more integration than separation. The Rio Grande and the Florida Straits today are much less formidable as barriers than the Atlantic Ocean of eighty or a hundred years ago.

For the Hispanics, this proximity has greatly reduced the pain of separation from the native soil. The immigrants no longer consist over-whelmingly of young single men, but are often couples or whole families. Also for the first time, significant numbers of young single women are setting out on the great adventure, encouraged by the solidarity they know they will find in their own communities (this phenomenon is also found among the Asian migrants). This family-based cultural continuity provides far closer psychological and moral supervision, made more effective by the structured nature of the Catholic religion common to most of the community. All of these elements help strengthen and maintain awareness of a strong cultural specificity. And, unlike that of the black ghettoes, this specificity is based on living roots rather than a reaction against discrimination by white society.

The Hispanicization of the United States

The first sizeable political action by the Hispanics took place in the mid-1960s, when the civil rights movement was in the ascendant. Led by the charismatic Cesar Chavez, the chicano agricultural workers went on strike in the California fruit fields. But their objective was not so much integration into American society as a simple demand for economic and social justice. While Black Power and the dream of a separate nation held the attention of a part of the Afro-American community, José Angel Gutiérrez was founding a party called *La Raza Unida* in Texas; it aimed to play the electoral game and win control of counties in which there was a Hispanic majority. The term *La Raza* has subsequently come to symbolize the wish of Mexican Americans – and soon of their Puerto Rican and Cuban cousins – to promote their own values, culture and way of life on an equal footing with the Anglo-Saxons.

By the early 1990s the Latinos' ethnic strategy had borne fruit. Despite the constant arrival of new immigrants who statistically depress the average level of incomes in the community, the number of Hispanic households classified as rich (annual income over $50,000) has increased by 240 per cent over the last two decades to include some 2.6 million people. And even though 40 per cent of Hispanics are still classified as poor, the average household income quickly rose above that of the black minority.[6] The number of Latino elected representatives on local and regional levels is increasing rapidly in the South and West of the country. Since the 1970s there have been Latino Governors of Arizona, New Mexico and Florida; more recently, Latinos have become the mayors of several large cities (Miami, Denver, San Antonio, Santa Fe and Tampa). Despite their penchant for local activity, no less than nineteen Hispanics were elected to Congress in November 1992, and there were two in Bill Clinton's first cabinet.

But their economic and electoral successes pale before their extraordinary cultural influence. Tex-Mex cuisine and Afro-Cuban rhythms rapidly became integral to the American way of life, to the point of becoming all-American export products. But the scale of the Latino revolution is best measured by its linguistic impact. Hispanics are the first group of immigrants who have sought to have their own language officially recognized. The 1965 Voting Rights Act which, in the name of broadening democracy, instituted bilingual voting slips, provided a toehold. Taking advantage of the very liberal climate at the end of the 1960s, the Hispanics formed an alliance with educational reformers who were trying to help children with English-language difficulties. Thus, when the 1968 Bilingual Education Act released funds for the establishment of bilingual courses in schools, Latinos were the first to benefit. Confirmed in 1974 by a Supreme Court decision stipulating that a child had a right to be taught in a language he or she could understand, bilingual education has become the main weapon in the campaign to preserve a Hispanic identity.

The danger this posed to the Anglo-Saxon melting pot was very quickly apparent to the non-Hispanic white communities, which from the early 1980s campaigned vigorously against a mechanism that hampered integration and favoured the development of a separate culture. Led by the US English movement, they not only persuaded the Reagan administration to cut funds allocated to bilingualism, but also managed to persuade more than a third of the states to adopt laws establishing English as the official language.

But it was too late; bilingual education was able to survive and develop even without public funding. The administrations in several of the states that adopted pro-English measures continue in practice to accept other languages. Nowadays, in certain areas of big towns like Miami, shops feel that they need to put up a sign specifying *Se habla Inglés*. And the powerful Spanish-language media – press, television and advertising – have gone from strength to strength in the South and the Southwest of the United States. Spanish-language television networks watched by the bulk of Latinos on both sides of the Rio Grande and as far east as Florida underline the established presence of Spanish in the United States.

A NEW MULTICULTURAL ELITE

The sudden arrival of this mass of new citizens – people who were not only non-white but intended to remain so – had the effect of virtually eliminating prejudice between population groups of European origin. Compared to these "outsiders" an Italian, Pole or Greek suddenly took on the appearance of a long-lost WASP cousin. At the same time, during the late 1960s, these non-WASP whites – or rather the remnants of the ethnic associations that used to represent them – succumbed in their turn to the attractions of community-based references.

Merging of the White Communities

The combined pressure of all ethnic groups, whites included, produced the Ethnic Heritage Act of 1973, allocating facilities for the preservation and promotion of the various identities present on American soil. The Hispanics, of course, were well prepared to derive every possible advantage from legislation of this sort. But the associations representing the groups of European descent were mere shadows of their former selves: they had no means of countering the desire for integration among their potential members. So that in the final analysis the 1973 Act only served further to undermine the legitimacy of the Anglo-Saxon model.

The traditional barrier separating white, Protestant, Anglo-Saxon and Nordic America from southern and eastern Europeans had started to dissolve in the camaraderie forged on the battlefields of Europe during the Second World War. When they returned home in 1945, the GIs benefited from a special law – the GI Bill of Rights – giving them easy access to further education and promoting social mobility. The war had broken a number of taboos. Congress had no choice but to agree to adopt specific laws giving admission to the United States to the 150,000 wives or fiancées and the 25,000 children brought home by the returning troops from all over the Old World.[7]

The first consequence of the rapid social assimilation of people who before 1940 had been new immigrants was the dropping of all specific ethnic references apart from a few snippets of folklore. This helped dilute the WASP monopoly of the predominant cultural norm. The values of the American Republic had been tied, symbolically at least, to a specific religious posture – "classic" Puritan Protestantism – and the celebration of Anglo-Saxon customs and usages. Now a place had to be made for a culture of social advancement that rewarded merit or political skill, something which, among whites, is largely independent of any religious or ethnic particularism.

In 1960 the United States elected its first Catholic and "Irish" president, who appointed a "Pole" to his first cabinet. A "Greek", Spiro Agnew, became Richard M. Nixon's vice-president; one of his "compatriots", Michael Dukakis, was the Democratic candidate in the 1988 presidential election. An "Italian" woman, Geraldine Ferraro, tried her luck as vice-presidential candidate on the 1984 Democratic ticket. A "German Jew" and first-generation immigrant, Henry Kissinger, was the country's real strongman throughout the first half of the 1970s. His successor was a "Pole", Zbigniew Brzezinski, who headed the National Security Council under Jimmy Carter. Many other such examples could be found among members of Congress and state governors, and in the state assemblies.

The other result of this more agnostic version of the melting pot for Europeans was a geographical upheaval. Better educated, richer, more individualist and mobile, the non-Hispanic whites abandoned the city centres – henceforth occupied by the non-white "lower plebs" – to settle in the more convivial suburbs. But these districts did not generate the strong sense of collective attachment the ethnic communities felt for their original areas. Suburban life did provide a sort of substitute for trusting neighbourly relations, but left people much more dependent on their own resources. And as the suburbs expanded (more than half the American population now lives in suburban areas) this European mobility, combined with the movement of the new non-white immigrants, shifted the demographic balance of the country: over the last thirty years the numbers of inhabitants in the South and West have increased by 47.7 per cent and 70.4 per cent respectively; whereas the populations of the Northeast and Midwest have increased by only 13.4 and 15 per cent. The South and the West, which generate 55 per cent of the gross national product, housed 55.6 per cent of the American population in 1990, compared to only 45.6 per cent in 1960.[8]

Ethnic Populism and Multiracial Centralism

The demographic revolution of the last half century has thus played a key role in the great mutation of the American Republic. The Anglo-Saxon melting pot has practically disappeared, to be replaced by a more or less peaceful coexistence between three cultural references. The first of these, and clearly the one that still predominates, is the "white" mass culture promoted essentially by the omnipresent television. The obligation to address the largest possible audience has made this culture relinquish all specific attachments to a religion or the values of a particular ethnic group. Thus sanitized and rendered neutral, it projects a residual and very general expression of the American dream: the celebration of individual success and happiness.

The second reference consists of a culture of exclusion: that of the black ghettoes, plunged in an endemic revolt against the prevailing norm but without much hope of changing the situation. This culture is thus becoming established as a permanent source of violence and counter-violence in the heart of the great American metropolitan clusters.

The third reference is Hispanic, buttressed by the Spanish language; it has a universal vocation based not on neutrality but on strong traditions: Catholicism, allegiance to social hierarchies, rejection of individualism, Iberian racial mixing in the New World and respect (as well as a taste) for authority. Having done much to dissolve the ethnic and religious model of Anglo-Saxon America, it is now goading the United States to behave more openly towards Latin America and tolerate ethnic mixing. But it is also opening the way to acceptance of more centralized and hierarchical political institutions.

So what is left of the social pyramid that ensured the greatness of the American Republic until the 1940s? The tilting of the country towards the South and the West, and the erosion of traditional "white" values, have dispossessed the East-Coast money aristocracy of its dominant role in the central administration. In 1964 a Texan, Lyndon Johnson, became the first southerner to be elected president since the Civil War (the Virginian Woodrow Wilson does not really count, being an exemplary Puritan Presbyterian whose whole career had been in the North). The South and West have monopolized the White House ever since, in the persons of Nixon, Carter, Reagan, Bush (a northerner but a naturalized Texan) and Clinton. For the last thirty years, moreover, presidential cabinets have included members from the Sunbelt, born into all the white ethnic minorities. Even non-whites have been appointed to important government posts; Bill Clinton's first cabinet was deliberately multiracial.

The executive, which has become extremely powerful through its role as great social mediator and its increased military responsibilities abroad, is thus gradually losing its regional and ethnic attachments. It is now open to anyone's ambitions; its mushrooming institutions are soaking up brilliant, careerist young people from all corners of the country. The nucleus of a sort of new "federal aristocracy" is starting to take shape; its *cursus honorum* typically passes through the staff of a member of Congress, a senior post in a government department, a stint in a fashionable private think tank, a top academic job, a column in a prestigious daily paper. The jackpot is appointment to the National Security Council at the White House.

This deterritorialization extends to the legislature. Demographic upheavals and the new balances between cities and suburbs, towns and districts have greatly reduced the power of the pre-1940 local elites. Congress, which mirrors the American regional balance in Washington, is inevitably affected. Since the Second World War the balance of power between the White House and the Congress has altered radically in the White House's favour. The rise of the executive, as we shall see, has practically reduced Congress to an overseer of initiatives taken by the presidency.

The old Protestant northern European elites are gradually having to make room for newcomers. For these last, their community of origin matters less than their ability to cope with electoral behaviour that is far more capricious than it used to be, and to manage delicate negotiations between ethnic groups. Given the unstable and shifting nature of much local political life, these "new senators" and representatives depend for their survival on their capacity to attract federal funding for their constituencies. In this way, willingly or unwillingly, they become clients of the central administration.

On the level of the states, the powers of governors and representatives in the state assemblies have been eroded in a similar way to those of the national institutions. The big cities are gradually coming under the political control of whichever non-white ethnic minority is the local majority; but this group has to reach an accommodation with the other groups in the area. The life of the metropolitan centres thus hangs to a large extent on the mood swings of the "plebs", a factor that encourages populist practices. And because of the demographic, economic and symbolic weight of the great cities, this populism has also become endemic in battles for political power in many states.

This profound upheaval of political life illustrates the great vitality of American institutions. The fact is that they have succeeded in adapting very quickly to a society that now metaphorically resembles a *mosaic* of juxtaposed communities rather than a melting pot. In a very real sense, this institutional mutation is a measure of stability. It indicates an increased flexibility, enabling the Americans to absorb any culture or belief from any ethnic community or interest group. In a world that is being rapidly internationalized, there is no need to wonder whether this or that cultural specificity is assimilable or not: it always is.

There is another advantage in all this for the government in Washington; it puts the United States several lengths ahead in the job of managing the globalization of the planet's political and economic structures. Through their family and cultural connections, using their linguistic skills, the minorities present in the United States open all the regions and markets of the world to American influence. And America itself is perceived as a place that could belong to all, since all are represented there.

This ethno-cultural revolution is a precondition for the extension of American leadership to the whole world. But the white middle class, squeezed between the plebeian populism of ethnic balance and the universalist centralism of the federal elite, still needs to be convinced. Now perceived as broadly homogeneous, embracing the better paid sectors of the working class and open to non-whites, it is the middle class that has paid, in numerical terms, for the new social polarization. In 1969, 71.2 per cent of all households were classified as middle income. Today the figure has dropped to 63.3 per cent; over the same period the high-income figure has grown from 10.9 per cent to 14.7 per cent and the low-income category has also increased, from 17.9 to 22.1 per cent.[9]

Middle class, suburban America is in fact disoriented. Torn between the tenacious dream of social mobility and the rejection of politicians who no longer seem to represent its interests, the middle class is seeking a new place amid the gigantic mutation of the Republic's human balances and institutions. Its anxiety stems precisely from the loss, in a remarkably short time, of all its landmarks, most of all the traditional Anglo-Saxon, Protestant values which used to serve – well or badly, consciously or otherwise – as a handbook for its integration and participation in the construction of a New World.

The power of the White House is thus going to depend to some extent on its ability to restore the confidence of this white core of American citizens. The responsibility falls on the generation of the post-1945 baby boom, now in its forties, which is represented by President Bill Clinton or Newt Gingrich, Speaker of the House of Representatives. This age group – moralistic and tolerant, realistic and naive, made up of explorers rather than architects – is perhaps not really prepared for the task. But it has one advantage over its predecessors: it has been the promoter of the most extraordinary cultural revolution in the history of the United States.

5

THE FACTORY OF WORLD CULTURE

As a new Jerusalem awaiting its golden age, America used to be a place where culture in the European sense was a luxury enjoyed by a minority of rich idlers; religion was the mainstay of the social bond, and the only book in most American homes was the Bible. Art, beauty and even education were associated with privilege and simultaneously despised and envied. Culture was seen primarily as a commodity imported from the Old World by big businessmen hoping to acquire respectability. American artists with enough means or determination would go to Europe to learn the rudiments of their craft.

Of course there were some bright stars in the American firmament: Nathaniel Hawthorne, Herman Melville, Walt Whitman, Mark Twain, Henry James. There was the energy of the Hudson River school of painters, the delicacy of landscapists adapting techniques picked up in France or England. It is true, too, that purposeful settler pragmatism and the shortage of trained architects gave birth to America's most original contribution to the history of architecture: the skyscraper, a vast steel frame clothed in stone. All the same, most of the time, people were content to follow the Europeans.[1]

The First World War caused a few tremors. The "lost generation" spent the roaring twenties roistering in Paris, its artists sniping at an America they regarded (with a touch of arrogance) as a cultural desert. But apart from a tiny minority of individuals, America at large remained obstinately withdrawn into its shell. Definitive change came after the Second World War, when the country's new international responsibilities swept away the last vestiges of provincialism. Or perhaps it was that the rest of the planet had suddenly acquired a provincial air.

FROM PROVINCE TO HUB OF THE UNIVERSE

Intellectuals (especially critical ones) have never had a good press in the United States. In the early 1920s they were accused, by President Coolidge himself, of undermining the "national conscience" and fomenting sedition. In the late 1960s Vice-President Spiro Agnew dubbed them the "nattering nabobs of negativism". But although Americans have little esteem for their intellectuals, they have always been avid for knowledge.

Cosmopolitanism between the Wars

This aspiration to learning and good taste is what drove captains of industry – Rockefellers, Carnegies and Guggenheims keen to dress up their robber-baron images – to found their museums, galleries and cultural foundations. Where art was concerned, these institutions had clear pedagogic aims; the generous donors had more regard for chronology and the encyclopedia than for artistic merit. As with the Soviet museums a few years later, the primary task was to educate the public. The promotion of mass culture by a private arts establishment has been a central characteristic of American intellectual life ever since.

The first break with American provincialism was a consequence of the Great War. Millions of soldiers had been exposed to European fire and the European way of life. A new generation, rebellious and restless, started to debunk received ideas. For the first time, American intellectuals attacked their national cultural life with real rage and passion. Their critical enterprise was so radical that it amounted to little more than outright rejection. From the Paris cafés to Greenwich Village, nobody doubted that American culture was dead.

This withdrawal by a more cultivated and cosmopolitan generation led, paradoxically, to a flowering of literary talent. Looking at their country through new eyes, these angry young writers produced original poetry and novels: Ezra Pound, Ernest Hemingway and Gertrude Stein left the United States and participated in the lively expatriate community in Europe; John Steinbeck, Sinclair Lewis, Eugene O'Neill and William Faulkner dealt more directly with American social problems. Through them, the United States acquired new literary traditions that remained clearly marked by their openness to the outside world, even when using American settings.

In other areas of artistic endeavour the United States was still provincial, with some luminous exceptions, notably the dancers Isadora Duncan and Martha Graham, the painters Edward Hopper and Man Ray and the sculptor Alexander Calder. But the province suddenly became a refuge for a pleiad of European artists and intellectuals fleeing from the advancing Nazi jackboot. American cinema acquired new master practitioners like the German Fritz Lang, music was enriched by a range of new talents including Kurt Weill, Stravinsky, Bartok and Schönberg. Science welcomed (among others) Enrico Fermi and Albert Einstein; philosophy, Adorno and Hoeckheimer; architecture, Walter Gropius and Marcel Breuer. In every domain, America opened its arms. Without prejudices, excluding no one, resolutely eclectic, it profited from every contribution, from every source. And its culture began to acquire the universal flavour that was to give it such strength thirty years later.

Universal Jazz

The construction of an original mode of expression from a wide range of foreign sources had certainly given a dynamic stimulus to intellectual life. Yet it had not created a specifically American art form. Moreover, this process still affected only a small minority. But while this intellectual culture was blossoming, a different and more potent phenomenon was developing in America, evolving in an endless orgy of creativity: jazz, a universal music. A fusion of black and white source material, rooted in African polyphonic traditions of rhythm and song, the religious psalms of the Calvinist liturgy and Anglo-Irish folk ballads, with a light dusting of European classical music, jazz is hybrid art *par excellence*. It may be the only true syncretism so far produced by a nation that has trouble accepting the mixing of ethnic communities. Such a proclamation of universality could only conquer the planet. With its totally open structure, jazz can make room for any and every new contribution. It is the main stem from which all the great musical phenomena of the second half of the twentieth century have sprung: rock'n'roll and its variants, salsa, world music, and so on.

Jazz and its offspring may thus be said to constitute the archetype of a World America. This music – now a planetary phenomenon – was perfectly adapted to the technological power of the new media, most of which were developed and first used in the United States. We have already noted the importance of radio in consolidating the power of Roosevelt's White House. But music radio, due largely to the existence of jazz, also played a decisive role in transforming American society and morals. Music and dance did not simply launch the first sexual revolution in America; they were also responsible for a radio craze that swept the entire nation. The foxtrot and the charleston, swing, blues and bebop persuaded Americans to tune in to the vast amalgam of news, sentiment, advertising and practical advice that radio had become by the late 1930s.

This music was of course crucial to the success of the big Hollywood musicals, which, in turn, helped pave the way for the new televisual civilization, the triumph of the moving image. It is worth recalling that America between the world wars already represented the biggest cinema audience in the world; and that in 1960, when television was taking its first steps in Europe, 76 million TV sets had already been produced in the United States,[2] and nearly nine out of ten American households had one.[3] But if a good fairy hovered over the cradle of mass culture in America, then globally, it must have been the universal art of Afro-American jazz.

THE DISCOVERY OF POLITENESS

An eclectic fine arts culture and a mass culture open to absolutely any influence thus provided the foundation of American cultural internationalization from the 1950s onward. In the absence of norms defended by a traditional intelligentsia or by the state, American intellectual and artistic life is relatively free from the tendency to hierarchize its products. The important thing is the suitability of a given work to its public, whether that public is a minority or not. So the first criterion has always been the ability of a work to reach an audience big enough to guarantee its survival.

The Art of Market Shares

In the climate of economic liberalism specific to the United States, judgement on all artistic expression is passed, in the final analysis, in the marketplace. Cultural big business (the recording industry, the motion picture industry, the theatre and publishing) accounts for the bulk of turnover, but it is true that art also benefits from subsidies. These come mainly from private patronage (nearly 55 per cent of subsidies are grants from non-profit foundations or gifts from big firms), the shortfall being made up by the federal administration (30 per cent) and the States (15 per cent).[4] But even activities that are subsidized or have managed to get sponsorship have to try, at least, not to lose money.

This sort of approach takes the accent off things like content and quality and places it on freedom of choice expressed in market shares (for example, mass-markets versus small but identifiable niches). Classifying works by aesthetic standards is less important than satisfying segments of the arts market, whether the consumers are after kitsch or the most sophisticated experimental performances. So that in a sense all forms of expression, of whatever origin, are judged on an equal footing. America is ready to reward with a smash-hit triumph – or bury with indifference – a foreign work (which by the same token becomes, or does not become, American). And the inverse is also true; products made in the US have become increasingly dependent on their popularity worldwide: in 1990 the Hollywood majors, the big production companies, earned 47 per cent of their income abroad.[5]

This global diffusion of artistic products has been supported on the one hand by the very mobile and cosmopolitan baby-boom generation, and on the other by the revolution in telecommunications and computer technology and the ubiquity of audio-visual media. The possibility of virtually instantaneous transmission of, and access to, the news and data banks of the entire planet constitutes a sort of cultural big bang. It smashes through the defensive barriers of specific cultures, no matter how entrenched they are. Television penetrates every household in every corner of the globe, multiplying cross-fertilizations, juxtapositions and the rapid circulation of fads and fashions, forcing eclecticism on everyone.

It is less a matter of an American culture being imposed on the world, however, than of a universalist approach originating in America being imposed on everyone. Moreover, cultural expressions that are highly specific, or that appeal to a small minority, are not rejected on principle if they can find a viable market or sponsors/patrons: examples include the music of John Cage, the minimalism of Philip Glass, Indian flute-players from the Upper Amazon, French experimental cinema.

Grooming the Elites

The accession to world leadership of a prosperous and powerful America placed it, from 1945 onward, at the centre of international cultural life. Its universities (a substantial proportion of whose research funding comes from the Department of Defense) are the planet's leading sources of scientific production. In the 1960s, New York leapt into the front rank of the world market for the plastic arts; in 1964, pop art exploded onto the scene at the Venice Biennale. But what has been imposed is not so much a new style as a very dynamic experimental approach, seeking innovation at all costs. In fact all American fine arts culture is marked with this voluntarist avant-gardism.

This systematic quest for the new at the expense of tradition thus enables every creative artist, American or foreign, to try his or her luck in the United States. The very notion of civilization is undergoing a mutation in artistic as well as academic and political circles. Before the Second World War it was implicitly understood that the truly civilized person was white, Anglo-Saxon and Protestant, or at least educated as such. After the 1960s, any person of culture or education could qualify for the title: Filipino doctor, Iranian engineer, black lawyer, German painter or French scientist. The barbarian became anyone hostile to progress, democracy, market forces, intellectual and social innovation: anyone rejecting the values of America, which had now become those of the whole "free world".

Foreigners and members of ethnic minorities – provided they were qualified and creative – were now welcome, and had some chance of gaining access to the establishment. In 1965, as we have seen, Congress approved the civil rights acts and a much more liberal set of immigration laws based specifically on the criterion of educational qualification. But the Americans went further: to give dynamism to this innovative and syncretic cultural approach, the White House established the National Endowment for the Arts (NEA) in the same year. For the first time, the state was going to take an interest in culture; the managers of the gestating World-America had become aware of a new attribute of power, which eventually acquired the name "soft-power": power stemming from the volume of cultural production.

This openness to the outside world was decisive in aiding the ascent of a new federal elite, more internationalist in outlook and without strong community attachments. The exercise of world leadership, the increasingly frequent contacts with older and more sophisticated civilizations, obliged American political, economic and intellectual leaders to groom themselves. John F. Kennedy had brought to the White House a taste for luxury, culture and good manners that was still not widespread in Washington. His assassination (and replacement by a boots-and-stetson Texas politician) and the Vietnam War brought that to a premature end.

But when the boys returned home after the Vietnam tragedy, the elite corps of the democratic empire and its wealthy offspring financed a commercial boom for quality products made in Europe. Porsche and Mercedes, Gucci, Dior and Savile Row became the distinctive insignia of social power. Expensive French restaurants became the places to dine; brie and Chablis replaced cheese and wine at private views in New York art galleries. Even "respectable" women started wearing sexy stockings and high heels. People bought switched-on magazines like *Gourmet* and *Architectural Digest* and began to take pride in Californian vintages. Fashionable creative people had finally gained access to the citadel. To attract increasingly sophisticated management cadres, big companies plunged into art patronage. Jimmy Carter was mocked as a "hick", but nobody was keen to admit liking the meretricious tinsel of Ron and Nancy's White House.

THE SOFT POWER OF WORLD CULTURE

The Reagan years were both the pinnacle and the swansong of this first great lesson in *savoir-vivre*. Meanwhile, owing to the energy of its eclectic approach, governmental America had absorbed and digested the refinement of the old cultures. Then, in its role as a producer of the universal, it started to prise these cultures from their national settings.

The Triumph of Eclecticism

The new American market was a temptation to many, including the French women's magazine *Elle*. Its American edition quickly became a success; but it required a less French, more international attitude on the part of the publication's staff. This globalization of the image of the modern woman is clearer still in the case of *Cosmopolitan*, an all-American magazine which has enjoyed worldwide success. *Elle*, with its packaged and homogenized but still sophisticated Frenchness, undoubtedly helped change the American woman's image of herself. *Cosmo* on the other hand, with its twenty-five foreign editions and its three million copies sold each month, has the mission of promoting this same image throughout the world, France included. The "Cosmo girl" works for a living, makes no secret of her ambition and knows what she wants in love as well as in her career. What she represents, finally, is the very model of an international woman freed from the constraints of local custom.[6]

These comings and goings across the Atlantic have become intense enough to persuade several great American publications and publishing houses to entrust their fate to foreigners (like the Briton Harold Evans at Random House or the Indian Sonny Mehta at Knopf). In 1992 a symbolic bastion of American "national" culture fell with the appointment of a British woman, Tina Brown, as editor of the *New Yorker*, that monument of the East-Coast intellectual press. To add insult to injury the magazine's prestigious "Talk of the Town" column was assigned to another Briton,

Alexander Chancellor.[7] Thus the United States, having mastered the processes of production of international culture, became a magnet for ambitious creators from every part of the planet. And they in turn helped fuel the great mechanism of American-made world culture.

Of course, mass culture took part in this development. By the late 1950s Elvis Presley, labelled "the first white to sing like a black", was popularizing the most important musical phenomenon of the second half of the twentieth century: rock music. For the baby-boom generation, rock had the same significance as jazz for the youth of the 1920s and 1940s. Except that this time, advances in record production and audio-visual technology meant that the whole world could join in. Rock became the means of communication between the younger generation of the whole planet, superimposing itself on all the national music traditions. This cultural vehicle is all the more powerful for being open to all foreign contributions, to folk music from India, China, Latin America and the Arab world, and even to classical music from Europe.

Rock has not killed national music traditions, but its planetary dynamic has exposed them to outside influence and scrutiny. The upheaval has been so rapid and radical that the current World Music, more than any other artistic expression, probably indicates how artistic creation will occur in the twenty-first century: increasing cultural crossbreeding will be combined with technological innovation (new instruments, sampling, digital sound and so on). There is however a corollary to this new high-tech syncretism: it becomes vital to safeguard or even strengthen national and local traditions, as they alone constitute the musical data banks essential for the great world synthesis. America, where the management of diversity in terms of a universal logic is the very basis of social life, obviously has a head start.

The Thousand Faces of the Democratic Empire

Audio-visual technology, the other great vehicle of mass culture, has evolved in a similar way. In the United States the cinema is not an art, as it is claimed to be in Europe, but an entertainment. The costly nature of the industrial processes by which images are produced means that film-makers are faced with the problem of their products' commercial viability. The American cinema has been compelled to think in terms of market share from its very beginnings, and even more so since the advent of television. This has proved to be a sound guiding principle. By the beginning of the 1990s America controlled nearly three-quarters of the world market for images (television and cinema combined). It is also the only national industry – in parallel with two large Latin American networks, Brazil's Globo and Mexico's Televisa – to have conceived universal products, of which the famous soap *Dallas* is the archetype.

Imprisoned by its economic constraints and obliged to be accessible to the largest possible audience, whose origins and identity are immaterial, audio-visual culture has freed itself of specific cultural references. It therefore has to make do with material common to everybody: the emotions, love and hate, friendship, jealousy, sacrifice, courage and cowardice. Blend this with the miniature of the American Dream we all carry within us: individual enterprise and success, social mobility for those who want it, the ordeals that must be endured on the way to the happy ending. It is pointless to look for content or any sort of propaganda for an American culture that, in any case, does not exist. Images produced in the United States reflect nothing but a concept of the individual, detached from a specific culture, grappling with the same challenges faced by all the other individuals on the planet. This is a realistic reflection of the condition of the citizens of World-America.

When the world news network CNN juxtaposes images from the four corners of the earth, it is not manipulating the information to deliver a pro-American message. All it is doing is demonstrating in programme after programme that the world is now interdependent and being internationalized, just like America itself. Anyway, CNN's news programmes in Spanish, German or Mandarin and MTV Latino show how this "local world culture" is developing. The message is personified by the reporters and presenters themselves – black, blond, Asian, Hispanic: everyone can become American, because America *is already everyone*! The viewer in Singapore or Moscow, Tokyo or Lima has ample time not only to identify with the production, but to dream of recreating America in his own home by consuming what he sees on the screen. Apart from Japanese mass-market electronic goods, are not most universal consumer products American (McDonald's, Kelloggs, Gillette, Zippo, Sebago, Uncle Ben's, Apple, IBM, *Reader's Digest*)?

This levelling of all cultural references in favour of televised emotion and market shares has been the most marked characteristic of the era of globalization of images. It has coincided with the accelerated internationalization of the United States itself and the emergence of an American democratic empire centred on a presidential government with a universalist vocation – a world power, ushered onto the planetary stage by television. This process was also put into play by federal elites who blurred the distinction between business and politics, between their own personal advancement and that of a deterritorialized central government, abandoning all particularisms.

It is by no means certain that this sort of process will continue, in any case in such a blatant manner. World Music aims to create a universal sound, but cannot continue to develop without a variety of musical traditions to supply it with raw material. Similarly, by the beginning of the 1990s, big-budget action films were no longer guaranteed box-office successes for Hollywood producers. People were starting to look elsewhere for stories that could be remade as commercial superproductions. Black cinema, in which community culture is allied with a universal language (the films of Spike Lee are a good example), or "remakes" of French and Chinese screenplays, seem to indicate one possible new direction for the American film industry. "World Image" thus seems doomed to follow the same path as World Music.

A world culture without references of its own, based on the perpetual reiteration of universal sentiments adapted to different market sectors — senior citizens, kids, housewives, ABC1 or C2DE consumers — seems certain to blunt the emotions and quickly run out of steam. So it must repeatedly put down roots in more concrete bodies — with content, the Europeans would say — mix them together and move frequently from one to another, like the wandering souls of the Pythagoreans.

So the promotion and maintenance of cultures rooted in their own traditions may be a *sine qua non* of continuing development for the mechanism of globalization. But this task of managing specific territories in the context of a universalist logic is only possible as long as there are living communities with enough autonomy to keep their art alive. The free market has become only one element in the equation. And the problem that now arises is how to administer this cultural internationalization. The American democratic empire has to reorganize its instruments of power to make it appear both the defender of specific identities and the site of their inevitable amalgamation. Identities, though, that are no longer in a position to decline the offer of access to the universal, because refusal to contribute to the world culture would consign them, through force of circumstances, to oblivion.

Finding a new configuration for the cultural power of World-America is the task of the-baby boom generation. An adolescence marked by cosmopolitan experience, and by the counterculture with its dreams of separation from conventional society, have prepared it rather well to respect particularisms while feeling at ease with the universal. Another useful development has been the widespread re-examination, since the early 1990s, of the very idea of the melting pot. In less than fifty years' time whites will no longer be the majority in the United States. The different communities still known as minorities – blacks, Hispanics, Asians, Native Americans – now routinely expect their cultural and historical roots to be taken into account. Multiculturalism has become an article of faith. And the old concept of the melting pot is giving place to new ones like "mosaic" or better still "salad bowl" (in which the savour of the American salad stems from the combination of ingredients all of which retain their own identities).

This new definition of American life shows especially clearly in the way history is taught. In secondary schools and many universities, Eurocentric history is being reconsidered; textbooks are being produced which treat all the world's civilizations on an equal footing. So that new generations of Americans will become familiar from early childhood with all cultures and heritages. History – even American history – used to play a limited part in school curriculums in the United States. As the twenty-first century dawns, Americans are suddenly in the unprecedented position of being able to weave the history of all humanity into their own national history.

A cultural revolution on such a scale could never be orderly. There is no shortage of worrying lurches and stumbles, and downright intellectual terrorism is not unknown. For example, some Afrocentric ideologies are not content to mirror white cultural centralism, and advocate full-scale apartheid. The risk of viewpoints quickly becoming irreconcilable is ever present. In Europe, for example, despite much well-meaning effort, nobody has yet managed to work out a version of European history acceptable to everyone. Perhaps the whole thing is electrically dead, perhaps there is no oil left to dress the salad in the American bowl. But in the meantime World-America is making itself a new personality, or at least acquiring the means to make one and redefine it continuously.

The so-called politically correct movement at the end of the twentieth century is nothing more than a radical expression of the need to respect all identities scrupulously, even in the choice of the words used to describe them. But America's particularisms correspond with those of the great cultural divisions of the outside world. The democratic empire thus already has the conceptual instruments to deal with the planet as it deals with its own citizens. The frontiers between foreign and national are dissolving bit by bit.

The end of the Cold War has confronted the American presidency with the problem of exchanging an international leadership role tolerated because of the Communist danger for a legitimate and accepted universal authority. When Bill Clinton formed his first cabinet "in the image of America", carefully representing both sexes and many ethnic groups, he also gave it the image of the whole planet. In the eyes of his fellow citizens and the entire outside world, he had to consolidate and legitimize the "triumphal presidency" he had inherited. That is the subtext of his early attempts to impose ethical relations on his colleagues and compel them to make a clear distinction between their private business and the service of the state.

Like modern Stoics, the senior staff of the democratic empire, drawn from the moral generation of the baby boom, must display at least some willingness to renounce personal ambition and devote themselves to the wellbeing of all. In his first speech to Congress, on 17 February 1993, Clinton did not forget to attack the paralyzing influence of "special interest groups" and "partisan bickering". Expounding his plan for budgetary rigour, he said that there would be "no sacred cows except the fundamental abiding interest of the American people".[8]

Of course, there is always a gap between a declaration of intent and the way things work out. There is not much chance that the new generation will embrace *en masse* the neo-Stoicism that is just becoming discernible on the political skyline. But a break with the somewhat elastic morality of the Reagan years seems likely. Corinne Brown, a Democrat newly elected to the House of Representatives from Florida, declared a few days after the November 1992 election, "I'm a tugboat, not a showboat, and I'm here to work and get things moving."[9] *E pluribus unum*, as it says on the ribbon in the American eagle's beak.

PART II

THE METAMORPHOSIS
OF GOVERNMENT IN
THE UNITED STATES

6

THE IRRESISTIBLE ASCENT OF THE
WHITE HOUSE

The splitting of the atom changed everything for the American nation. Is there a child of the baby-boom generation who cannot remember crouching under a school desk during nuclear alert drills, hands over eyes, giggling a bit but awaiting in imagination, with a frisson of real horror, the ultimate big bang? The widespread fashion for building backyard fallout shelters made the theoretical possibility of annihilation seem more immediate and frightening. In most countries, the launch of Sputnik by the USSR in 1957 was perceived as a convincing demonstration of Soviet scientific prowess. But in the United States everyone was aghast: the Reds had shown that they now had the ballistic means to inflict damage on American territory. The country felt vulnerable to attack from abroad, as never before.

The dynamics of deterrence and the resulting arms race called for the swift establishment of a caste of servants of the atom: strategists, engineers, senior officers, diplomats, researchers, scientists, spies, specialized industries. It did not take long for space to become the latest dimension of military strategy. In 1958, the White House had no trouble getting approval for the creation of NASA, whose budget grew fatter by the year. Science itself became a strategic issue, with research laboratories and specialized technical departments proliferating under Pentagon control. Federal public funds poured into military-oriented research in the universities. The defence industry swallowed an increasing proportion of the national budget.

In 1975, after the big demobilization that followed the end of the Vietnam War, there were still 1.8 million persons under arms, 517,000 of them overseas (314,000 in Europe, 156,000 in Asia-Pacific).[1] The president of the United States thus found himself at the centre of what Eisenhower, somewhat disapprovingly, called a "military-industrial complex". Never before had the presidency seemed so fundamental to the nation's security: the presidency wielded supreme nuclear power ("the Button"); and the relentless war of attrition against the Communist bloc was organized around the presidency. Never before had the well-being of the entire country seemed so dependent on *salus unius*, the well-being of a single individual.

THE POWER OF A STANDING ARMY

Partisans of the old Republic were seriously out of luck. Their time-honoured opposition to this sort of centralized power was an anachronism in the context of the Bomb. Although the massive demobilization of American troops in 1946, when the intervention could at last be scaled down, seemed to tip the balance comfortably in an isolationist direction, the cycle was soon upset by the Berlin blockade in 1948, the explosion of the first Soviet nuclear device in 1949, and the invasion of South Korea by the Communist North on 25 June 1950.

The first American troops to land on the Korean peninsula were so ill-prepared and vulnerable that they were badly mauled. It was not difficult to persuade Congress that only a large, well-trained army could prevent similar catastrophes in future. Henceforth, presidential power would rest on control of nuclear force – the ultimate attribute of power – combined with command of the most formidable conventional military apparatus on the planet. And this authority would prevail not just on American territory but throughout the "free world".

The Presidency versus the Republican Tradition

Nobody should be in any doubt that the Founding Fathers of the American Republic would have been deeply shocked by this concentration of power in the hands of the White House. Such was their mistrust of state power, in fact, that they suspected it of being naturally liable to abuses of all sorts. The 1787 Constitution therefore established a government divided and hobbled by strong internal contradictions. Decisions were meant to be difficult to finalize and only possible after a long process of negotiation between competing centres of power ("checks and balances"). The framers of the Constitution had not fought a war of independence only to bend the knee to a new king, albeit one who had been born in America and elected.

This time they meant, in the words of the preamble, to "secure the blessings of liberty to ourselves and our posterity".

The Constitution expresses this distrust of central government – and the executive in particular – in unambiguous fashion. Its authors start by rejecting a unitary state in favour of a federal structure in which the states enjoy extraordinary autonomy. They multiply the possibilities for institutional tensions by encouraging rivalries and overt antagonisms between the executive, the legislature and the judiciary. The president is certainly commander-in-chief of the armed forces, and may sign treaties, appoint senior officials and veto legislation. But he may not declare war or decree a mobilization by himself; and his decisions must be ratified by Congress, which has the means to overrule a presidential veto. Moreover, the president is not even elected directly by the people, but by an electoral college whose delegates were appointed by the legislatures of each state until the late 1820s.

This explicit curbing of presidential power corresponded to a model of the Republic in which the central state was conceived as a mechanism of mediation and coordination between the different local oligarchies, who actually controlled public life. There was no question of granting much independence to the presidency or even to Congress. The power base of these powerful regional elites lay elsewhere, in institutions they were certain they controlled: the state legislatures. These bodies appointed the members of the electoral college and, until the Seventeenth Amendment was passed in 1913, the senators themselves. They thus controlled the election of both the president and the Senate. Representatives were, it is true, elected by direct suffrage. But just in case they showed any autonomist tendencies, the states delineated the electoral constituencies; and representatives had to face the polls every two years.[2]

Needless to say, this oligarchic structure came under immediate pressure. Regional and other interest groups found the temptation to take advantage of federal power overwhelming. The East Coast merchants and bankers grouped under Alexander Hamilton's Federalist banner were soon in a position to do so. The big planters and farmers who dominated Thomas Jefferson's "Republicans' party" demanded a strict interpretation of the Constitution to defend states' rights against the federal administration. This polemic became swiftly inverted when Jefferson's election to the presidency in 1800 consigned the Federalists to the opposition.

These early skirmishes were already out of date when they occurred; for the state legislatures had lost a good deal of power as the federal Congress settled into the role of mediator. Of course, the states continued to defend their prerogatives, still essential to maintaining the positions of local oligarchies. But it had gradually become apparent that they were instruments of intervention, unsuited to the struggle between national coalitions. And there was constant pressure from the pioneer frontiers of the West, where growing numbers of new rich were clamouring for a role in politics. So the privilege of choosing the presidential electors was soon snatched back from the state legislatures and given to the state electorates instead. It therefore became crucial to articulate the power of the local legislatures with that of the national Congress. The House and the Senate became the central arenas of politics within the lifetime of the Founding Fathers.

In practice, Congress turned out to be an extremely adaptable institution. It became the main site for negotiations between the traditional interest groups, but also showed a capacity to make room for newcomers: western ranchers and entrepreneurs before the Civil War, industrialists and financiers during the Gilded Age, then the knights of the middle class and the tribunes of the urban and rural "plebs". It admirably fulfilled the role of defender of oligarchic freedoms against attempted encroachment by the federal executive. So the vision of the Founding Fathers, who considered the legislature the most important branch of government, survived against all odds until the 1929 crisis and Roosevelt's New Deal. "Government by Congress", denounced by the young "progressive" intellectual Woodrow Wilson in 1885, thirty years before his own accession to the presidency, became the distinguishing mark of the American Republic.

The Cold War and the Unmaking of Congress

Franklin Roosevelt's election in 1932 led (as we have seen) to a de facto revolution in the country's constitutional order. The White House took advantage of the climate of national emergency to acquire, for the first time, the means to intervene massively in economic life. The New Deal launched a spectacular increase in the power of the executive and the federal bureaucracy. The pre-eminence of Congress was called into question by the activism of a president who simply appropriated new privileges: the power to conceive and promulgate a legislative programme and the power to create and administer new state entities. Congress was also threatened by Roosevelt's populism, amplified by radio which enabled him to speak directly to the whole nation.

The Great Depression of the 1930s, and the invention of a true mass medium, undermined forever the prerogatives of the oligarchies and the traditional tribunes of the people. Both groups lost their former role as political mediators to a charismatic national leader. Their power had rested on three pillars: control of the political parties; control of the political institutions of the states; and control of legislative work in Congress. Now that power declined sharply. Henceforth, the president could go over the politicians' heads and draw directly on a new expression of citizenship: a national "public opinion" which could be called up at a moment's notice, and was recalcitrant to the usual political instruments.

The Roosevelt revolution might have come to nothing. After all, there had been other attempts to rearrange the institutions in the White House's favour: by Andrew Jackson (1829–37), by Abraham Lincoln (1861–65) during the Civil War, by Theodore Roosevelt (1901–09) and even by Woodrow Wilson (1913–21) during the First World War. On each occasion, Congress had quickly recovered its primacy by taking the lead in the ensuing republican reaction. But Roosevelt's achievement was saved by a historical development that compelled the United States to undertake permanent military commitments abroad: the Cold War.

This new international responsibility was spelt out in the Truman doctrine, announced by the president to Congress in March 1947:

> At the present moment in history nearly every nation must choose between alternative ways of life. One way of life is based upon the will of the majority. . . . The second way of life is based upon the will of the minority forcibly imposed upon the majority. . . . I believe that it must be the policy of the United States to support free peoples who are resisting attempted subjugation by armed minorities or by outside pressures. . . .[3]

American military history is an endlessly repeated cycle: intense periods of belated mobilization for wars which are often very bloody, followed by general demobilization immediately after the end of hostilities. The Founding Fathers had in fact written their own repugnance for a standing army of veterans into the nation's psychology, fearing the army as a solid foundation for a strong executive, open to possible abuse. To discourage temptations of this sort they imposed strict limits on the size of the regular national forces and on the responsibilities of the president/ commander-in-chief. Better still, the Second Amendment to the Constitution, adopted in 1791, stated without beating about the bush: "A well regulated militia being necessary to the security of a free State, the right of the people to keep and bear arms shall not be infringed." America was showing that it preferred an armed population to a standing army.

This disapproval of career soldiers had nothing to do with any pacifist tendencies. Starting with those who fought in the Revolutionary

War, virtually every generation of young Americans had some military experience: Indian wars, conflicts with Mexico, the Civil War, the Spanish-American War, the First World War, interventions in Latin America, the Second World War, the Korean War, the Vietnam War, the Gulf War. But until 1945, war only temporarily strengthened the power of the White House.

During the Civil War, Abraham Lincoln was able to decree the naval blockade of the South and shatter the legal ceiling on the number of conscripts without consulting Congress. Theodore Roosevelt's preference for strong government and American imperial expansion had the support of a great wave of public opinion. Backed by popular press campaigns orchestrated by the likes of William Randolph Hearst and Joseph Pulitzer, he managed to give the country a solidly based intervention force, starting with a modern navy. Even the devout Presbyterian Woodrow Wilson was willing, by 1917–18, to soil his hands with virulent propaganda for entry to the First World War and state intervention on all fronts: rationing, regulation of social conflicts and foreign trade, financing war industries.

But in spite of this direct association between war and executive power, the American Republic could always take comfort in a powerful antidote: once the war was over, the civilians who had fought it would see no reason for staying in uniform. In America, the people can only be called to arms in response to a direct and clearly identifiable threat. War has always been seen both as a crusade of Good against Evil, and a necessary job: you went to war, you won, you came home again. The atom bomb and the growing power of the USSR were going to change all that. The Bomb gave the American president power over life and death that was genuinely apocalyptic, something previously unknown in the history of humanity. As for the Soviet Union, its role was that of the absolute enemy, partner in a rivalry that could only end with the disappearance of one great power or the other. Meanwhile, Stalin had to be stopped from pressing his advantage in Europe or Asia.

The American military tradition favoured, as always, getting the job done as quickly as possible. There were even those who argued for prompt use of nuclear weapons to roll back the menacing Red Army. But in the late 1940s this option seemed too risky; given the superiority of the conventional Soviet forces in Europe, the atomic bomb seemed more effective as a deterrent. In 1947, George Kennan, in a famous article – signed "X" – in the magazine *Foreign Affairs*, defined the strategy of containment to which the United States clung through thick and thin until the implosion of the USSR in 1991 as "the adroit and vigilant application of counter-force at a series of constantly shifting geographical and political points, corresponding to the shifts and manoeuvres of Soviet policy".[4]

For the first time, America was choosing to embroil itself in a long war of attrition, with the corollary of having to maintain a huge standing army and develop a powerful, specialized arms industry. The White House had already consolidated its right to intervene in social and economic affairs; now it had at last acquired the military power that the republic had always denied it. Armed force, plus the economy, plus international political hegemony: nothing could resist such a concentration of power. The way was clear for a further increase in executive autonomy and the emergence of the "democratic empire".

THE POWER OF THE FEDERAL BUDGET

The Capitol's loss of authority to the White House was immediately apparent in the budgetary domain. Franklin Roosevelt had already dispensed with tradition by presenting his draft budget and legislative programme directly to Congress. The power over public finances exercised by the House and the Senate had already been eroded in 1939, with the creation of the budget office (renamed, in 1969, the Office of Management and Budget – OMB) attached to the presidency. Responsible for collating proposals from all the different government departments and agencies, the future OMB also made all the necessary compromises and coordinated the whole of the draft budget presented to Congress. The office thus became the only institution with an overall view of all the state's functions. The decision-making process in this fundamental domain was still constitutionally the responsibility of Congress, but the White House now had dominant influence over its timetable and content.

Control of Public Funds

Members of Congress did their best to respond. The Budget and Impoundment Control Act of 1974 set up a budget committee for both the House and the Senate and a congressional equivalent of the OMB, the Congress Budget Office (CBO). But the fragmentary character of legislative activity, combined with the strength of different lobbies and competing interests, did not favour the emergence of a common non-partisan position. So that although the Capitol's vote remained the decisive one, it had lost its essential advantage: absolute control of the purse strings.

This imbalance in the executive's favour was accentuated by the growing importance of the federal budget. Until the early 1930s, setting aside the period of American involvement in the First World War, the federal budget had never exceeded 4 per cent of gross national product (GNP). By the time of the attack on Pearl Harbor, after eight years of Roosevelt administration, it had climbed to 10 per cent. General mobilization boosted the figure for 1942 to almost 47 per cent of GNP; after stabilizing at the end of the War, the budget increased steadily from 11 per cent of GNP in 1948 to 22 per cent by the end of the 1980s. In cash terms, the increase is even more phenomenal: in 1982 dollars, the budget increased from $83.2 billion in 1940 to around $900 billion for 1993 (equivalent to $1,300 billion at current values).[5]

This vast mass of funds, distributed throughout the country to the most varied recipients, has produced what can only be called dependence on the federal government. This is not restricted to particular individuals and groups but extends to the states and local municipalities, whose expenses are partly covered by Washington. The executive has a determining role in allocating the federal manna. As a consequence of the application of social laws originally adopted under Roosevelt (and later extended under Johnson), an increasing segment of the budget has become more or less untouchable and its growth uncontrollable. The ferocious budget battle in the winter of 1995–96 showed how difficult it is to cut unemployment assistance or other social security programmes (for example, Medicare and Medicaid, health aid for the elderly and the poor respectively, or the various categories of retirement and military disablement pensions). Nor is it at all desirable for the state to default on interest payments on its borrowings. In total, counting commitments undertaken in previous years, the proportion of state spending over which Congress has only the most minimal influence is something like 75 per cent.[6] So that the budget debate nowadays, despite all its sound and fury, really only concerns the remaining 25 per cent (and even that includes a number of military credits which are also difficult to reduce).

Contrary to widespread belief, the levels of American military expenditure during the Reagan-Bush period were among the lowest since the Second World War. Only the great demobilizations that took place between 1948 and 1950, and after the Vietnam War – from 1975 to 1980 – entailed larger decreases. During the Second World War American defence spending had obviously reached high levels: over 39 per cent of GNP, nearly 90 per cent of federal government expenditure. The ceiling stayed very high throughout the 1950s and 1960s; under Eisenhower,

Kennedy and Johnson the proportions varied between 14.4 per cent and 7.5 per cent of GNP and between 69.5 per cent and 42.8 per cent of federal spending. During the Nixon and Carter administrations the figures fell to 4.8 per cent and 22.7 per cent respectively; but after the Soviet invasion of Afghanistan in 1979 Jimmy Carter decided to revive the military machine and got Congress to vote a noticeably higher defence budget. The build-up was continued by Ronald Reagan for the first three years of his presidency, until the White House itself started pressing the legislature to curb military spending (the famous "Rose Garden" agreement of 1984). But even during this period of strong growth the military budget never exceeded 6.5 per cent of GNP and 28.1 per cent of federal expenditure.[7]

Clients of the State

We have seen that the central government has greater budgetary power over social programmes than over funds allocated to the armed forces. Nevertheless the military have played a central role in strengthening the preogatives of the executive. The policy of arms development and production piloted by the Pentagon has established an immense network of specialized laboratories and companies working hand in hand with officials of the Department of Defense. It is well known that senior officers responsible for weapons procurement can retire to much better-paid jobs with the firms that supply them: this is the "revolving door" system attacked periodically in the press and in Congress.

The defence industries have taken good care to scatter their research and manufacturing establishments across the country, ensuring a presence in key states and electoral constituencies. This coverage of American territory is duplicated and reinforced by the network of army, navy and air force bases. The result is that whole regions are economically dependent on military installations or arms contracts. The military-industrial complex is thus the most powerful pressure group in the country. It has support from the Pentagon machine, the somewhat murky partnership between civil servants and arms manufacturers, the hundreds of military and civilian research establishments and their highly effective network of lobbyists in Washington. As if this were not enough, the local economic weight of bases and factories turns the senators and representatives concerned into passionate advocates of bigger defence budgets. During the legislative elections of 1987–88, the National Security Political Action Committee spent more than $10 million in support of its candidates, far more than any of the other PACs.[8]

Of course the armed forces budget is not quite untouchable, especially in the absence of the permanent threat posed by the Cold War. But given the size of the interests now involved, it is probably unwise to cross a certain political threshold. A number of voices on both sides of Congress have already opposed cuts deemed too radical on the grounds that they would be bad for employment and would risk damaging an enormous reservoir of weapons know-how that might be difficult to restore quickly in the event of new emergencies. The defence industry is not wasting energy mourning the fat years; it is getting itself into shape for the new strategic and budgetary environment. At the end of 1992, a wave of mergers and takeovers signalled the start of a clean-up of the sector. The process will leave the surviving firms with bigger shares of what may well be a smaller cake.[9]

Military credits are not the White House's only instruments of budgetary power. The client/patron relationship between the executive and the states is even more obvious in the area of infrastructural and social spending. Since the 1940s, the budget for local municipalities has remained more or less steady at around 5 per cent of GNP. And while the budget for the states has shown fairly steep growth, rising from 4 per cent to 7 per cent of GNP, it has not kept pace with the explosive growth of the federal budget. All the local bodies have nevertheless had to cope with the increasing costs of education, public services and social security, which account for nearly half of their expenditure. The result is a considerable increase in their fiscal dependence on the federal administration.

Thus, half the expenditure of the state of New Mexico has to be covered by Washington. Federal subsidies and gifts account for more than 40 per cent of the budget in eight states – including the biggest, California, and President Clinton's home state of Arkansas – and more than a third of the budget in around twenty others.[10] Richard Nixon, and later Ronald Reagan, decentralized part of these responsibilities under the pretext of a "new federalism" that would give increased power to the states. But in reality the revenues were not all decentralized in the same proportion, and this led to an even more extreme subordination for local bodies forced to borrow to fill gaping budgetary holes. Needless to say, this is not an ideal way to reduce mounting debts, or for that matter dependence on the federal government, which, like it or not, is the ultimate guarantor of all municipal debts within its territory. Making the states responsible for administering and funding social policy – an idea advocated by the Republican-dominated Congress elected in 1994 – is, paradoxically, another step in the same direction: a way of increasing the fixed expenditure of the states and thus their dependence on federal funding. It would relieve the central administration of many of the responsibilities and constraints of the welfare system, without reducing the power that goes with control of the money.

DECLINE OF THE POLITICAL PARTIES

While all the local government institutions were gradually becoming clients of the federal government, Congress was experiencing a parallel decline in relation to the White House. This weakening of the legislature stems directly from a revolution in American political life whose origins can be found in two historic phenomena, one technological (the new mass medium of television), the other sociological (the contentious outlook of the baby-boom generation).

TV Democracy

Just as radio played a key role in the growth of Roosevelt's power, television is essential to the development of a "democratic empire". The first presidential election decided by television was the contest between John F. Kennedy and Richard M. Nixon in 1960. The telegenic presence of the young senator from Massachusetts – seen at the time as the outsider – contributed in no small measure to his narrow victory. At that time 87 per cent of households had television sets. By the early 1990s the figure was 98 per cent, and more than 60 per cent of households were cable subscribers. American viewers spend an average of seven hours a day in front of their screens, and surveys indicate that two-thirds of them regard it as their main source of news. Indeed, half the American population considers TV a far more credible medium than either the written press or radio.[11]

The personalization of elections at the expense of the political parties and the use of advertising techniques in electoral campaigns (attitude surveys, marketing, public relations) were the first apparent consequences of the persuasiveness of televised information. The crucial role of images in all elections since the end of the 1960s has forced politicians to adapt to the medium. Television favours emotion and style, the spot and sound-bite suited to the endless reiteration of simple ideas. The screen is merciless and does not forgive the smallest mistake or momentary lapse. Hence, politicians are obsessed with a single question: how best to sell themselves to camera. The popular solution is to surround themselves with image specialists, professional "spin-doctors" who are not necessarily of the candidate's political persuasion. As a result, militants have become rarer in electoral teams, and their functions are gradually being taken over by mercenary practitioners of political advertising.

Nowadays, a campaign starts with a survey of the electoral constituency. When the main concerns of the voters have been identified, a range of appropriate themes is extracted for the candidate to adopt. These will figure prominently in the image created for him. And this image, in its turn, will be vetted, using marketing techniques, to ensure maximum impact on the TV-viewing electors. At the same time, "negative campaigns" may be mounted to undermine the image of an adversary. This method is particularly well suited to representatives, who have to face re-election every two years. But it tends to imprison the successful candidate in his role as a simple lobbyist for the particular interests of his constituency, and inhibit any wish he may have to lead the party or represent the general interest. This increased and personal dependence on the electoral base does have one advantage, however: it makes it more difficult for the representative to betray his electorate's trust.

The whole process is horrendously expensive, especially if the cost of air time is counted; and as the costs are increasingly unlikely to be borne by the parties, politicians have to find the necessary funding for themselves. Heavy financial support is needed from the very first moments of the campaign, when incumbents and challengers start scheming to get onto the party ticket. Incumbents can count on the experience of their personal teams, and also on the de facto support of the party bureaucracy. Challengers, under these circumstances, have only one choice: to set up their own organizations, something that in the long run reinforces the autonomy of politicians. The party machines suffer, especially as a large proportion of the funding obtained by candidates is swallowed up by personal promotion on television and thus does nothing to fill the party coffers.

The cost of electoral campaigns in the United States is increasing exponentially. In 1976, the average budget of a candidate for the House of Representatives was $73,000; by 1990 it had almost quadrupled to $284,000. The increase for prospective senators was even steeper, from $595,000 to $2,574,000. In 1976, no candidate for the House spent more than half a million dollars; in 1990, 168 of them did. And during the 1987–88 congressional elections, candidates spent a total of $458 million on the attempt to sell their images, the incumbents alone accounting for $294 million.[12]

The Decline of Political Parties during the 1970s

The 1970s had a decisive impact on the structure of American political life. In 1974, Congress passed the Federal Election Campaign Act in an attempt to clean up political morals after Richard Nixon's "dirty tricks". But the establishment of a Federal Electoral Commission, supposed to supervise the amount of money spent on political campaigns and manage the public funding component in presidential elections, had some unexpected results. For a start, it weakened the party directorates, which could no longer deploy funds as they chose. It also encouraged the untrammelled personalization of presidential elections, the federal contribution being paid not to the relevant party office, but to the candidate. And since the public subsidy, in effect, is proportional to the amounts raised privately by the contestants themselves, the candidate has every reason to hire a team of professional fund-raising specialists.

In 1975, the Supreme Court had the honour of severing the financial links between candidates and political party machines. By approving the formation of political action committees (PACs) authorized to make financial contributions to electoral campaigns, the judges created an immense new source of independent finance for any candidate at a stroke. In 1987–88, funds from the PACs represented 26 per cent of the budgets of successful candidates for the Senate and 45 per cent of the budgets of those elected to the House.[13] When the Court made its ruling there were already some seven hundred PACs in the United States. By 1990, the number had increased to 4,590 (of which 1,939 represented businesses, 783 professional associations and 370 trade unions).[14]

The decline of the parties is not simply a result of severing the financial links between the party machines and representatives or of the extreme personalization of politics caused by television; the baby boomers' irreverent attitude to the party bureaucracies has had something to do with it too. The manipulation of all aspects of party life by a mafia of elderly fixers in conclave – the notorious "smoke-filled rooms" – seemed distasteful to the "moral" new generation. The Democratic party's 1968 National Convention, held in Chicago, symbolized the new era. The delegates worked doggedly through their agenda, besieged by their own supporters, while rioting and police violence raged in the surrounding streets. The young activists, mainly from the Democrats' liberal wing and from radical-left groups, were calling for the democratization of the political parties. The wide mobilization of support for Eugene McCarthy's presidential candidature, and then George McGovern's, gave valuable practical experience: a host of amateur volunteers rose against the party directorate, lobbied energetically among the grass roots and ended by storming the machine itself.

The bosses were helpless in the face of this explosion of militancy among their hitherto sheep-like cohorts. At local conventions the balance shifted away from the docile mass of timid petty apparatchiks, and towards the much more demanding and assertive youth and minority activists. Encouraged by this grass-roots sympathy, the new wave insisted that national offices force local sections to agree to radical internal democratization.

The old regional bureaucracies had already been severely shaken by two Supreme Court cases – *Wesberry* v. *Sanders* and *Reynolds* v. *Sims* – in 1964. The decisions effectively established a new principle determining the delineation of electoral constituencies within the states: henceforward each of the constituencies had to contain approximately the same number of voters. This was to reduce a common form of gerrymandering: the submersion of demanding urban electorates in more tractable, immense, rural constituencies. Abandoned by the law, squeezed between the militant grass roots and the national leadership, the local bosses gave up and surrendered. This nationwide capitulation took the old regional oligarchies with it, notably the Dixiecrats, the powerful group of southern representatives and senators that dominated Congress until the late 1960s.

The revolution inside the Democratic party was bound to spread. Despite their very limited taste for that sort of thing, the Republicans were obliged to follow suit. In 1968, only seventeen states had held primary elections to choose the presidential candidate; in 1988 there were thirty-eight Republican primaries. The democratic agitation reached Congress itself in the early 1970s, causing an electoral massacre of the incumbents. By 1976, 55 per cent of sitting representatives had been elected less than six years earlier; between 1972 and 1976, 41 per cent of the Senate was replaced. Nothing of this sort had happened for decades, so solid had been the control exercised by the party machines.[15] Now these "Watergate babies" were simply rewriting the operating rules of Congress.

The Legislative Reorganization Act of 1970 launched what amounted to a major democratization of Congress.[16] The introduction of electronic public voting enabled electors, for the first time, to follow the day-to-day performance of their chosen representatives. The mode of operation of congressional committees and the internal working rules were also questioned. An early victim was the system of distributing responsibilities by seniority: the young representatives did not want to wait a decade or two before being given a place on one of the important House or Senate committees. By attacking the principle of promotion by seniority the newcomers were challenging the authority of the chairmen of the legislative committees. In the process they pressed hard for the adoption of the Sub-Committee Bill of Rights, which compels each committee to maintain at least four sub-committees. This new decentralized structure gave the young rebels who had stormed the old legislative fortress *en masse* real influence on deliberations and decisions. The subsequent proliferation of sub-committees – by 1990 there were more than two hundred in both Houses – is not at all surprising. Moreover, as their meetings were more private than those of the main committees, the sub-committees very quickly became the favoured venues for legislative horse-trading. Congress was thus being atomized while the members were emancipating themselves from party control. And the executive, the only federal body to retain its unity of thought and action, emerged from the turmoil as the main victor.

7

THE END OF THE AMERICAN
REPUBLIC

The wave of democratization started by the baby boomers in the 1970s ended by fragmenting the legislative branch. The party leaderships, already weakened internally, lost much of their authority in Congress. Votes cast by representatives in the House or the Senate were now instantly known to their electors and political adversaries, and to the local lobbies, without any mediation. This made it increasingly difficult to enforce party discipline; the interests of the constituency had to be seen to come first.

For members of Congress, therefore, any wish or pretension to represent the general interest had to take second place to the immediate demands of their constituents. Members were more independent, but also more solitary and therefore more vulnerable to pressures of every sort. Stripped of the identity and support provided by a party, they had to fall back on their own resources to interpret issues, spot political pitfalls, keep the lobbies at arm's length and maintain contact with their electors. In addition to these concerns, the elected representative is responsible for a numerous personal staff whose future employment depends entirely on his or her political fortunes.

THE TRIUMPH OF CLIENTELISM

The authority of the political parties had not disappeared completely, but their role had changed: instead of defining a programme or projecting an ideology, they now had to act as efficient machines for selecting and preparing presidential candidates for election. The obstacle race for the party's nomination is an excellent probationary exercise, eliminating lightweight contenders and helping people fine-tune their personal organizations for the subsequent single combat before the electorate. Moreover, the fact that the two main parties are well-established provides a useful cultural framework that simplifies the democratic choice: elections crystallize around a contest which is nearly always binary, in which each candidate is easily identifiable with a familiar set of political attitudes and landmarks. Of course, circumstances often force Republicans and Democrats to behave similarly once in office.

In exceptional situations the political leaderships in Congress may still appeal to party discipline (although a clear party division between Democrats and Republicans has featured in less than a tenth of congressional votes in every year since 1946).[1] The parties still possess some financial clout and a residual capacity to mobilize their supporters. But most of the time representatives and senators are left to their own devices and the direct pressure of interest groups.

The Budgetary "Law of the Market"

The Founding Fathers envisaged a conflictual cohabitation between the different power centres (Congress, judiciary, presidency, states and local governments), articulated around a single fixed point: the prerogatives of the federated states. This model survived more or less intact until the New Deal. As the power of the administration increased during the 1930s and 1940s, a new system of collaboration between the different levels of government took shape. The scale of the economic crisis, followed by the war effort, encouraged the formation of a sort of "sacred union" around a federal government that distributed aid, subsidies and sacrifices.[2]

This cooperation did not survive the relaunch of the social state and the announcement of Lyndon B. Johnson's Great Society programme. By the 1970s the role of the federal budget had become so decisive in the states and local municipalities that cooperation gave place to widespread and ferocious competition. The fragmentation of Congress and the proliferation of subsidies, programmes and regulations on the national level had created a situation in which every organization – from Congress itself to small-town councils – had to compete with all the others to secure its own share of federal funds.

The relations between the federal, state and local branches of government are now defined less by constitutional rules than by a sort of budgetary law of the market. Federal resources have become, in effect, a vast financial market that has to be conquered like any other. Each government echelon, each lobby, has to turn itself into an enterprise for securing funds. To this end, they develop a network of pressure groups and their own policies of communication, public relations and advertising. Thus the model is not that of a hierarchized state in which each level of government passively receives the share of resources decided on the level above. In the United States it is more a matter of equality for all in the scrum around the federal gold mine.

What has evolved, therefore, can be described as a star-shaped client system with the federal administration in the central "godfather" role. The system is not hierarchical in the strict sense, as the clients retain a broad measure of autonomy in managing the funds they obtain. The power of the boss is based not on control of the use of the subsidies he provides, but on his ability to generate and distribute funds. Moves by the Republican-dominated Congress elected in 1994 to distribute federal funds to the states in the form of block grants, without specifying their end use, further accentuate this mode of organization.

At the base of the client system are the different associations of individual beneficiaries and the private and semi-public local businesses employed as sub-contractors on infrastructural projects. Obviously these clients of the central state are spread across the whole American territory, and constitute a powerful lobby influencing the local governments – more than 83,000 of them[3] – responsible for the management and final distribution of the money. As the number of subsidies increases, there is a need to hire more civil servants to administer them.[4] It is thus no surprise that the number of people employed by local municipalities has increased dramatically, rising from 3.461 million in 1952 to 9.846 million in 1987 (more than 58 per cent of the entire United States civil service, federal and state administrations included).[5]

Among these ground-level institutions of the American administrative system, the big towns occupy the front rank. The 1964 Supreme Court decisions on the delineation of constituencies had already greatly increased the influence of the urban electorate, which now has enough weight to alter the political balance within the states, forcing governors and state assemblies to consider its demands. The ghettoization of inner cities, inhabited by poor, marginalized populations living in appalling conditions, makes the large municipalities natural candidates for social aid from the federal government. The main metropolitan centres thus constitute some of the more formidable lobbies: their influence extends far beyond their own local clienteles and looms large in the career of many national politicians.

Local governments are vulnerable to incessant pressure from their "client-constituents", although they themselves are a very powerful interest group. Not content with lobbying the administration, Congress and state governments on their own behalf, they also seek support from their colleagues and opposite numbers throughout the country. Neither White House nor Capitol is at all eager to tangle with bodies like the National League of Cities or the US Conference of Mayors. The weight of this political pressure is multiplied by the convoluted arrangement of local governmental units: counties, municipalities, school districts, townships, towns, special districts. Each category is also a client for federal and state aid, and each has its own lobby (the National Association of Counties, for example).

The ten million-odd civil servants who run these tens of thousands of local administrative machines also maintain direct contact with their patrons: the federal and state departments responsible for their various functions. This practice leads to cooperation between the two bureaucracies – national and local – which both have an interest in multiplying programmes and struggling to obtain ever-larger shares of public resources.

This complicity between civil servants naturally extends to the structures of the states, the main victims of the growing power of central government. Although they depend on the federal budget for a third of their finance, the states are still the main suppliers of funds to local municipalities, providing more than half their revenue. The "new federalism" launched by Ronald Reagan on the pretext of decentralization further aggravated the situation: the states had a range of responsibilities restored to them – mainly in the area of social policy – without being given the means to discharge them. The "Contract with America" proclaimed by the Republicans elected in 1994, with its strong decentralizing drive, threatens to make the bill even larger. Nor has the revolt by taxpayers, who refused to countenance any increase in taxes throughout the 1980s, given much help in sorting out state finances. The governors and their individual and collective lobbies (including the important National Governors' Conference) have found themselves knocking on the federal administration's door along with everyone else. Along with the state legislature pressure groups and the four million state civil servants[6] they have become assiduous frequenters of Washington's corridors.

The Managers of Politics

As clients of the federal government, the mayors, governors and other local officials are – like their various legislative bodies – virtually on an equal footing. Their skill in securing and managing funds has become the essential criterion for discriminating between them. This metamorphosis of political activity into economic activity favours the professionalization of staffs. More and more counties and municipalities are openly delegating their executive functions to a professional manager, while governors and their offices are slowly acquiring a business mentality.

We have seen that members of Congress, too, have been compelled to visualize political activity like managers. The legislative reforms of the 1970s further accentuated this transformation of representatives, who are now little more than budgetary lobbyists (working essentially, of course, for their electoral constituencies and thus for their own re-election). Members of both House and Senate have granted themselves very generous travel allowances so that they can make frequent visits to their regions. The right to virtually unlimited free postage enables them to mount massive promotional mailing campaigns and opinion polls among their elector-clients. Each representative also has the right to employ eighteen full-time and four part-time assistants (senators employ thirty-eight people on average). Legislative committees and sub-committees have been allowed to increase their permanent staffs as well (from a total of 546 employees in 1950 to 2,999 in 1989). Counting all the ancillary services – Library of Congress, Congressional Research Service, General Accounting Office, Congressional Budget Office, Office of Technology Assessment – there were no fewer than 30,000 persons working for Congress in 1989, including some 11,500 personal staff attached to the representatives and senators.[7]

So barely two decades after the landslide victory of the "Watergate babies", a caste of professional specialists in federal affairs has blossomed in the legislature. It joins the already swollen ranks of civil servants working for the executive: counting everyone, from the cabinet to the cleaning staff, the federal government employs some three million people. Washington is thus becoming the base for a symbiotic relationship between different pressure groups, which obviously have an interest in doing each other favours and multiplying budgetary programmes and lines of credit: the staffs of members of Congress and congressional sub-committees, the personnel of numerous departments and agencies of the executive and the various public and private lobbies based in the capital.

The individual legislator is submerged in a multitude of competing subjects for discussion and a mass of draft laws under debate, any of which may have direct implications for his constituency (and therefore his political future). His personal staff thus has to act as a board of directors, responsible for steering negotiations in the sub-committees so as to eliminate threats to the boss's career. But the member's image also has to be maintained in the constituency itself: in 1990, over 40 per cent of representatives' personal staffs, and over 35 per cent of senators', were based "at home".[8]

Thus a good deal of the general activity of Congress boils down to the exchange of individual favours between representatives, a practice known as "log-rolling". In the process, paying scant attention to national financial constraints, the members multiply new lines of credit to satisfy the categorical demands of their electorates (the "pork barrel"). Under these conditions, it is hardly surprising that the federal budgetary deficit should have doubled (in constant terms) since 1960. Despite ringing declarations, despite the Gramm-Rudman-Hollings Act of 1986, which instituted automatic cuts in state finances, the leaks in the federal coffers have continued to get bigger. Compared to other industrial powers, however, America has a modest annual public finance deficit (around 3 per cent of GNP in 1995). The Clinton administration has managed to stabilize and even reduce the federal budget deficit; the Republican-dominated Congress says it wants to balance revenue with expenditure in seven years' time. So Capitol Hill would still like to attack the problem, but only if essential things – the core of social spending and the bulk of the military budget – are left alone, and no member of Congress is ever asked to vote for cuts liable to be resented in his constituency. In the heat of the budget battle in January 1996, Speaker of the House Newt Gingrich, self-proclaimed leader of the "Republican revolution", even accused President Clinton of misinforming the people by claiming that Republicans wanted to cut social programmes: it was unfair, he said, to call a reduction in the rate of growth a cut in spending.

LIBERTY, EQUALITY, COMPETITION

The White House sits enthroned at the centre of this immense spider's web of decreasingly public, increasingly private interests. Ever since the Second World War it has fought to widen its margin of manoeuvre for dealing with this magma of clients and bureaucrats. The presidential staff has almost doubled since 1945, reaching a total of 1,500 people at the beginning of the 1990s. Appointed directly by the president and totally dependent on his personal destiny, this staff acts as his shield against the avidity of the lobbies. The spoils system gives the president patronage over another 3,000 high-ranking posts in the administration, without counting a further 20,000 appointments over which he has indirect influence. These people, the Praetorian guard of the executive office, manage the American "democratic empire".

Happiness through Money

The truth is that the president of the United States is a classic patron. Although he is certainly the prisoner of his clients, he is not answerable to any one of them in particular. He defines the general interest, within an immense system of patronage that extends abroad through military cooperation and development aid, through the right to give or withhold access to the American market, or through the de facto right of veto in bodies like the International Monetary Fund or the World Bank. With politics in the United States reduced to an economic competition for shares of the public finance "market", the many lobbies in contention inevitably represent only local interests.

This fragmentation of clientele is very useful to the White House in consolidating its independence and shoring up its role as the unifying symbol of American society and hub of a World-America. It enables the White House to oppose one pressure group or another by organizing coalitions of interests around large-scale national projects. A notable example is the North American Free Trade Area agreement with Mexico and Canada (NAFTA), signed by the Bush administration in the autumn of 1992 and ratified in 1994 under pressure from the Clinton administration: certain American regions and industries have been deliberately sacrificed to the larger objective of extending the domestic market to the whole of North America. Conversely, though, a collection of competing lobbies has little serious hope of being able to define a coherent foreign policy, or indeed of offering real opposition to the broad policy options defined by the president. Thus since the 1950s the presidency has acquired an effective monopoly of strategic information while retaining control of the armed forces and national security, a power it has extended over a large part of the planet in the name of defending the "free world".

The resulting political organization is formidably flexible and pefectly adapted to the expansion of the American model. The basic principle of the democratic empire is also the most universal: make money. In "the pursuit of happiness" – a right proclaimed in the Declaration of Independence –

it is thought legitimate, even admirable, for the individual to seek to improve the material conditions of his existence. The private entrepreneur, the civil servant, the elected representative of a small town, region or state, senator and citizen, American and foreign-born, are equal in facing the same challenge: how to obtain the largest possible slice of cake.

To the old Calvinist bedrock of American society, however, the combination of individual responsibility and competition does not mean the law of the jungle. Competitive egalitarianism must observe some rules if it is not to collapse into savagery pure and simple. These rules are those of American law (and Anglo-Saxon law in general), combining a certain level of business morality – paying taxes, keeping honest accounts, observing standards of weight and quality, respecting signed contracts and the laws of fair competition – with the greatest freedom in formulating contracts and undertakings.

All is permitted but the explicitly forbidden; hence the central role of the law. As political practice metamorphoses into lobbying and making deals, the arbitrating function devolves increasingly on the courts. The over-use of the US legal apparatus and the multiplication of cases brought before the Supreme Court (just over 1,000 a year in 1950, 4,500 in 1990),[9] are symptomatic of this growing social function. So that, de facto, it is the Supreme Court and not the legislature that decides the great debates of American society. Its role is that of an Areopagus of high priests, augurs of social law, who share with the charismatic president-*imperator* the honour of "uttering the sacred".

This democratic ideology – money-making, kept within bounds by the cult of the law – can be applied to any human endeavour: business of course, but also the civil service, culture, science, charity and trade unions. Slowly but surely, economic success is becoming the only gauge of social relevance for a whole range of initiatives and institutions. This permanent competition certainly has a pitiless side. But it is also extremely dynamic because it is totally neutral between particularisms. Whether you are white, black, yellow or mulatto, Christian, Jewish, Muslim, Buddhist or flying saucer enthusiast, whether you want to corner a whole economic sector or just carve out a comfortable niche, in America or elsewhere, the same question always applies: how to go about getting your share.

The Dream of the Have-nots

What could be more universal than the wish to survive from day to day and ensure material happiness? The American model is extraordinarily attractive: it asserts without any beating about the bush that everyone should have the chance to climb to the top of the social ladder. The fact that only a tiny minority of individuals actually achieve this is of small importance; it only takes a handful of successes to keep the dream alive. This aspiration is deeply destabilizing for all hierarchical or closed societies in which social mobility is hampered by tradition or culture. As the democratic empire permeates the planet, it promotes the most ambitious, the most cunning, the toughest and the best organized: those who in the final analysis will do anything to succeed. The strength of the democratic empire is irresistible precisely because it mobilizes the most dynamic actors and activities at all times. Few traditional cultures will be able to resist this all-conquering individualism. An old civilization like Europe, which has learned painfully to value social balances and rejects what it perceives to be the rule of the strongest, may try to put off the evil day. It may try to mobilize its collective resources, it may even make room for some of the new conquistadors who appear in its midst, while compelling others to leave. After all, how many of the most strong-willed and gifted Europeans have chosen to emigrate after failing to break down the barriers of rigid social stratification? But sooner or later Europe has to face the terrible competition with something more enterprising than itself.

Japan, somewhat differently, has been trying to play the role of collective predator. But it too is beginning to suffer for its failure to observe the Anglo-Saxon law of the market, having discovered the political limits of its strategy for economic conquest. In the face of growing hostility from its economic partners Japan is being compelled, slowly and painfully, to accommodate more individualist attitudes. Once outside these few favoured territories, however, there is not much point in extolling the benefits of traditional cultures and loyalties which are meaningless to the young Africans, Arabs, Asians and Latin Americans struggling to escape from misery at any price. For them, despite the violently mixed feelings of fascination and hatred it inevitably arouses, Washington's democratic empire is still a hope, not a threat. A hope continuously nourished by the images that flow through the satellite dish.

In this egalitarianism of personal ambition focused on money, the other side of the coin is the exclusion of the losers. There is not much flexibility round the edges of the money-making ideology. People survive in an incessant struggle to keep the other competitors from encroaching, or they "drop out". America itself, with its millions of homeless, its squalid urban ghettoes, its marginalized communities and its ever-increasing senseless violence, is the prime example of this absence of social solidarity.

But the endemic revolt of the drop-outs has little chance of turning into widespread opposition or upsetting major social balances, as it might in better structured societies. Incapable of formulating a credible alternative ideology – at least in the closing years of the twentieth century – opposition movements and simple expressions of violent despair end, like everything else, by succumbing to the law of the market. The only option on the political horizon for those who have been excluded is re-entering society and rejoining the race. Devoid of clear objectives, most outbursts of collective fever among the excluded end by turning back on them (and their own communities), driving them to look anew for individual solutions, legal or otherwise.

This fragmentation of objectives also lends itself perfectly to effective management by the central government through a delicate mixture of social subsidies and precisely targeted repression. When the Watts district of Los Angeles goes up in flames, order is restored – using as much violence as necessary, but remembering to read the arrested rioters and looters their Constitutional rights – and then an emergency federal aid package is decreed. In the final analysis, recurrent social explosions look very like another method of lobbying: revolts seem to be aimed primarily at obtaining a bigger share of public funds. For the federal administration, therefore, solving the problem is not the first priority. If a solution is found so much the better; but this is something that depends mainly, almost by definition, on the people concerned. For the government, the essential thing is to prevent an "inevitable" fringe of losers from jamming the social dynamic, especially during periods of economic slowdown.[10]

THE NEW IMPERIAL NOBILITY

In the final years of the twentieth century the American domestic model is being universalized, as we shall see, through the transformation of the planet into a sort of World-America. The democratic empire is going to be built on the will and ambition of each of its "citizens": a status for which – let us not forget it – everyone in the world is a candidate. A measure of misery and exclusion will be tolerated, on condition that the general prosperity is constantly fed by a permanent, creative competition in which everyone can dream of winning the jackpot. This is what the White House is saying when its representatives in the World Bank insist that priority in the granting of development aid should be given not to governments, but to small and medium enterprises in poor countries.

The power of the American market, something no one can afford to ignore, will enforce respect for the laws of open economic competition. The imperial armed forces will intervene, alone or with allies, whenever a local disorder threatens to interrupt major strategic exchange flows – Iraq endangering the free movement of Gulf petroleum, for example – or to pollute the mediatized projection of sacrosanct values, like the armed looters who sinned against human rights and private property by appropriating food aid intended for starving Somali populations.

Victory of the New Generation

This global administration will need civil servants devoted to the empire, not just a mass of lobbyists. The president of the United States, both commander-in-chief and symbol of unity in the triumphal cult of World-America – *imperator* and *pontifex maximus* rolled into one – has to have an extensive network of collaborators imbued with some sense of the general interest. The Supreme Court is already taking on the role of a "religious" college responsible for the "sacred" character of the law. But priests alone are insufficient for the task. Nor is it possible to administer a highly complex global reality through state servants who place their own specific interests – "American" interests – above those of the world power. The big boss of a universal client system cannot allow himself to be sucked into his clients' local rivalries. Paradoxically, the extension to the rest of the world of an order based on the individual ambition to make money requires a barrier to exist between business and the service of the White House. The democratic empire is condemned to promote a state nobility or risk breaking up.

The sacralization of the president's person, starting in Ronald Reagan's first term, coincided with the arrival of a new elite of businessmen at the controls of the state. These big operators, whose horizons encompassed the world market – bankers and currency traders, defence industrialists, oilmen, corporation lawyers, directors of multinational companies – held most of the key posts in the executive, managing the triumph of the White House until George Bush's defeat in November 1992.

But this politico-economic elite had difficulty distinguishing between public service and private interests. Many a juicy contract bypassed the correct channels, through cosy personal networks of businessmen, lobbyists, congressmen and departmental secretaries. The revolving-door system already established by the Pentagon and its arms suppliers spread to other domains. People gave up complaining when a member of the administration was recycled by the private sector to lobby his former federal department. But the Defense Department's purchasing policy – the famous $3,000 screwdrivers and bomb-proof coffee machines – created scandals and began to alarm the public. So did the rumours implicating senior government figures in deals involving outrageous corruption or illegal influence-peddling. It is easy to understand why every president since 1981, Bill Clinton included, should have pressed for the line item veto: an extension of the presidential veto to cover not just the federal budget as a whole, but each specific line of credit. It is a way of trying to limit the uncontrolled expansion of the client game.

Abuse of congressional privileges, and the dubious personal conduct of certain politicians in relation to the bottle or their female staff, became the pretexts for a tidal wave of national indignation. The congressional elections of November 1992 took place amid cries of "Out with the incumbents!" In fourteen states (and without even knowing whether it was allowed under the Constitution) the electors approved amendments setting limits on the number of times a member of Congress could stand for re-election. Many representatives accused of misconduct – often over mere peccadilloes – chose not to stand, while others had already been weeded out in the primaries. A few of the old guard did manage to get re-elected, but with such reduced majorities that they were going to have to toe the line to survive. The resulting renewal of Congress was as sweeping as the great clearout of the early 1970s that brought the Watergate babies to power. In another sign of the times, the 1994 congressional elections saw the triumph of a new generation of particularly active young Republicans led by another baby boomer, Newt Gingrich.

The Return of Virtue

The new generation's success owed an enormous amount to this desire to clean up Washington. The newly elected Clinton (and Newt) "babies" in any case repeatedly professed their faith in a renewal of civic virtues. The new tenant of the White House chose to start his term in office with a programme to moralize the upper reaches of the civil service. Soon after his election Clinton introduced a code of ethics – the strictest ever decreed in the United States – that would apply to the 1,700 persons who were to form the top rank of his administration. The most important clause requires them to refrain from lobbying their former federal departments or agencies for five years after leaving the government, and forbids them to represent any foreign interest for life.[11]

The new president relied heavily on the newly elected members of

Congress to push through his legislative proposals on the reform of campaign financing and restraining the lobbies. These proposals accompanied plans for substantial cuts in the size of the federal bureaucracy. They amounted to a direct attack on clientelism, not in the social body (where it is the main driving force of the American model) but at the top levels of government. The plan to give student grants that would be repaid by several years of public service was another indication of Bill Clinton's declared intention to relaunch the civic spirit and restore respect for the state. The Republican party's "Contract with America" carried a similar strong moralizing charge, especially the measures which aim to subject members of Congress to the same rules and laws as other citizens.

In a country where politics had been reduced to a quest for funds this caused considerable surprise. Reforms of this nature, carried to their logical conclusions, would mark a clear distinction between an elite consisting of big fixers and an imperial nobility motivated by honours and a taste for power. Of course, the change was not going to be completed overnight. The White House could expect, at best, some sort of improvement in the ethical conduct of its senior officials. The challenge facing the members of the Clinton team and Newt Gingrich's young Republicans was to persuade people to set aside their money-making instinct – still regarded as necessary and positive – in the interests of the state, at least while on the state payroll.

This new element was not going to amount to a revolution unless the president could also secure the famous line item veto, putting Congress at his mercy.[12] But it represented, at least in intention, a real break with the past and the political attitudes of the previous generation. Ever since the establishment of the spoils system by President Andrew Jackson in 1829, the upper levels of the American civil service have been unavoidably politicized. They have kept pace with changing realities as politics gradually metamorphosed into a vast client network. At the end of the twentieth century, as the American model is extended to the rest of the planet, they are under pressure to move towards a new form of neutrality based on technocratic competence and an understanding of the general interest of World-America.

The American federal elite, both Democrat and Republican, is perfectly aware of this new challenge. Proclamations in the "Contract with America" on reducing the size of the administration and making it more efficient echo, in a different form, the campaign to "reinvent government" mounted by the Clinton-Gore duo. And it is significant that the Republican leaders in Congress, Bob Dole and Newt Gingrich, share at least one objective with Bill Clinton: to secure the line item veto for the presidency.

In fact the new Republican majority goes further in the imperial logic preached by the Democrat White House. On one hand, it would like the federal administration to pass on as many of its domestic policy responsibilities as possible (except in the key areas of keeping order and economic regulation) to the states and other "provincial" authorities. On the other hand, it supports the retention of a strong military apparatus and wants Washington to be able to intervene, unilaterally if necessary, in all areas of international life – economic, political, military, cultural.

This gradual increase in the central government's autonomy from its provincial roots implies a governing group of senior officials devoted primarily to the grandeur of the empire rather than to their own private business. It thus assumes the adoption of a new, more "moral" attitude by the new federal elite. In its early stages, imperial Rome saw itself as an attempt to rebuild the old values of republican Rome on a new foundation. The "American renaissance" being trumpeted by Newt Gingrich is not so far removed from Bill Clinton's calls for the restoration of middle class and family values. "We need new solutions founded on old values," the American president told an audience of academics in 1995. He went on to quote Vaclav Havel: "Politics after all is a matter of serving the community, which means putting morality into practice."[13]

The democratic empire has urgent need of a meritocratic *nobilitas*. It is an irony of history that the task of creating it should have devolved on the baby boomers. A generation that has fought for civil rights and the democratization of institutions in the name of moral values is now responsible – in the name of those same values – for establishing a new aristocracy. An imperial nobility cannot win legitimacy, however, without being seen as a group open to talented recruits and dedicated to the public good. Frequent ceremonies and big events with blanket media coverage, in which the president and his retinue are shown to be accessible to the ordinary citizen and concerned for the people's happiness, project this image: a sort of modern, televisual populism, previewed on the occasion of Clinton's televised economic seminar in December 1992 and officially launched as a style of government with the celebrations and "open day" that marked the new president's arrival in the White House.

Things have come full circle. At the country's inception, in the small "holy experiments" of New England, the magistrates – democratically elected and responsible to their constituents – served a community governed by religious law. As the twenty-first century dawns they may well be reverting to this role as "nursing fathers", but this time their allegiance will be to the triumphal presidency alone, the community having fragmented and enlarged to cover the entire world. The first president of the baby-boom generation saw fit to drape himself in an ancient symbol of contractual obligation that was dear to the first Puritan colonies – the *covenant* – in an attempt to return to the country's roots, to re-establish the legitimacy of a government becoming increasingly emancipated from its territorial limits. "We need", Clinton wrote, "a New *Covenant* for American Security after the Cold War, a set of rights and responsibilities that will challenge America's people, leaders *and allies* to work together to build a safer, more prosperous and more democratic world."[14]

8

THE BIRTH OF WORLD-AMERICA

Although its power was manifest by the beginning of the twentieth century, America was still very provincial. It refused to get involved in the customs or quarrels of the old European states, which it saw as decadent, and contented itself with its rude pioneer culture. Piously, voraciously, it went on constructing its utopia without reference to other events on the planet. There were so many spaces left to conquer, so many new needs to satisfy, that the rest of the world was seen merely as a source of emigrants and supplementary markets for agricultural surpluses.

The Americans thus chose to live as if the United States were a remote, untouchable island. Its policy on national security was isolationist; its economic policy consisted essentially of defending nascent industries with robust customs tariffs. The First World War opened the door to the outside world; and a few years later, Roosevelt's wish to promote free trade compelled industrialists to pay attention to external reality. But the atavistic mistrust of a planet populated by savages, always ready to ensnare America in the toils of their destructive passions, was still very much alive.

War and victory in Europe and the Pacific finally overcame this prudent reticence. Henceforth America was to be irremediably implicated in global events; for it had become, *nolens volens*, the leader of the "free world", eyeball to eyeball with the Soviet empire.

THE JOB OF WORLD LEADER

In 1946, President Harry S. Truman was wondering whether he would be able to resist the pressure for immediate demobilization of the troops. His worries were well-founded: so deafening was the clamour to "send the boys home" that by 1950 only 600,000 men remained in the American army out of the 7.2 million under arms at the end of the war. The secretary of state, General George Marshall, described it gloomily as "a rout".[1] But the Berlin blockade by the Red Army in 1948 and the start of the Korean war in 1950 cut short this renewal of isolationist sentiment.

The Shortage of Qualified Personnel

The White House now found itself responsible for defining and organizing the West's defence plans. The policy of containment, adopted at the beginning of the Cold War, envisaged maintaining a prolonged siege until the USSR collapsed of its own accord. Washington thus undertook to manage a vast network of political and economic alliances, along with the formidable troop deployments needed for the task.

After 1947, the American presidency had two new specialized instruments to help with the management of its worldwide interests: the Central Intelligence Agency (CIA), in charge of espionage, counter-espionage and analysis of international affairs; and the National Security Council (NSC), attached directly to the Oval Office and responsible for following events from day to day. In 1949, Congress gave its permission for the creation of the first integrated Department of Defense in United States history. This rapidly expanded into a many-tentacled organization, with its own intelligence services and bases scattered all over the planet.

In 1946, the president acquired a Council of Economic Advisers to help him keep up with international economic affairs. This body was required to monitor the state of the national economy, and also to evaluate problems raised by the network of multilateral arrangements established by the United States: the International Monetary Fund and the World Bank (1945), the Marshall Plan and the General Agreement on Tariffs and Trade (GATT, 1947) and the Organization for European Economic Cooperation (OEEC, 1948). The administration also had heavy responsi-bilities within the United Nations Organization (UNO), established in New York in 1945; and in regional political and military alliances like the Organization of American States (OAS, 1948), the North Atlantic Treaty Organization (NATO, 1949), the Pacific Pact (1951) and the Southeast Asia Treaty Organization (SEATO, 1954).

The resulting demands were brutal for a country that still had relatively few people with experience in international affairs. There were a lot of new jobs to fill both in the United States and abroad: 110 new diplomatic missions were opened between 1950 and 1990.[2] The international departments of universities expanded to train the specialists required. Independent think-tanks researching security and foreign policy problems proliferated in Washington. The executive was not alone in calling for a new generation of civil servants whose horizons would not be limited to America: Congress also had to adapt to the new world leadership role. Senators and representatives – especially those with seats on foreign affairs, armed forces or trade committees – found themselves obliged to hire ever-increasing numbers of advisers specializing in international affairs.

On-the-Job Training

The press soon found that it too needed to take account of America's extended influence in the world. Although most of the media in the United States still pay virtually no attention to events occurring outside the national frontiers, since the 1950s a handful of leading newspapers and quality news weeklies have greatly increased their foreign coverage. At the beginning of the 1980s the creation of the CNN television network, specializing in live worldwide news, placed planetary actuality at America's immediate disposal.

One of the main conduits of international experience available to American leaders is the Pentagon. The rotation of officers between posts at home and abroad calls for a great deal of preparatory work; although they often live in closed American enclaves, the military are expected to familiarize themselves with the culture and customs of the region in which they are stationed. Army "field manuals" are well known for their precision, their passion for sociological detail and – occasionally – their talent for getting things wrong. Members of the armed forces do not necessarily become dedicated cosmopolitans in the course of their careers, but they do have contact with people from different cultures. This field apprenticeship in international affairs was extended to civilians in 1961 with President Kennedy's creation of the Peace Corps. Former volunteers in this development aid organization began to be appointed to senior posts during the early 1970s.

This movement towards a more internationalist conception of American interests could not stay restricted to the political and military elites for long. The world markets opening up under White House pressure were a new frontier that was far too promising to be ignored by businessmen. In 1960, exports of goods, services and revenues represented 5.9 per cent of America's GNP. The liberalization of trade accelerated the integration of the American economy with the rest of the world, and vice versa. By 1991, exports had reached 12.4 per cent of GNP and looked like becoming the most dynamic sector in the country. Over the same period the value of imports increased from 4.6 per cent to 12.4 per cent of GNP.[3]

This explosion of international trade inevitably had a profound impact on American businesses. It was no longer simply a matter of knowing how to administer sales and purchases abroad. As the economy became more integrated with the outside world, enterprises had to master policy on investment outside the national territory and learn how to manage currency exchange rates, overseas stock markets, international instruments for raising capital and so on.

A DOLLAR WITHOUT FRONTIERS

The development of economic interdependence between America and the rest of the world soon rendered a purely national outlook obsolete. At the beginning of the Carter administration in 1977, total United States assets abroad were worth $519 billion. In 1991, after ten years of Republican government, their value had reached $1,960 billion. Over the same period, foreign assets in the United States increased from $328 billion to $2,321 billion,[4] almost half of GNP, estimated at $5,671 billion at 1991 values.[5]

Making a Career Overseas

America is thus at the centre of world capital exchanges. On the one hand, it is the main direct investor in foreign markets, with $655 billion in accumulated shares in 1991.[6] On the other hand, since the early 1980s, it has also been the main beneficiary of a growing tide of direct offshore investments, absorbing almost half the planetary total; British, German, French and Japanese investors, for example, all seem content to bet on the future of the American economy. The value of direct foreign investments in the United States increased from $56 billion in 1977 to $487 billion in 1991.[7]

So despite the gigantic size of the American domestic market, the more dynamic businesses could not ignore the phenomenon of inter-nationalization. A whole new area of expertise was urgently needed by the industrial and financial groups. There was a need for expatriate managers to help run foreign subsidiaries, negotiate cooperation agreements with outside partners and administer company accounts in several currencies using increasingly exotic financial products. By the end of the 1980s, for the first time in the history of American business, it was becoming possible to base a career on a period of service outside the national borders. One spectacular example was that of Jack Smith, who became Executive Director of General Motors at the beginning of 1993: his appointment followed a stint in Europe where he was credited with putting GM operations back in order (and profit). Smith brought with him his European right-hand man, the Spanish Basque J. Ignacio Lopez de Arriortua. The Spaniard – already known to the Detroit giant's parts suppliers as "The Grand Inquisitor" – made it clear to suppliers, many of whom had worked with GM for decades, that their costs would have to come down by 20 per cent if they wanted to keep their contracts. And he added insult to injury by suggesting a method of his own for achieving the desired economies.[8]

Another significant example was the transfer to Brussels of one of the largest chemical products divisions of the American group Monsanto, whose base is in St Louis, Illinois. The emigration of one of the company's power centres would have been unthinkable a decade earlier. The point was underlined by the reclassification of North America as a regional market with the same status as Europe or Asia. The architect of this globalist great leap forward, Bill Slowikowski, even insisted that half of the management posts in Brussels should go to non-Americans, in an attempt to create an entirely new business culture. Difficulties included most of Monsanto R&D remaining in the United States; and an attempt to transfer computer files to St Louis that resulted in "data all over the place". But the real challenge had been changing people's attitudes and ways of working from "vertical to horizontal". This had made the operation something of a "trial by fire". Although R&D people were "coming over one at a time and starting to think completely differently", Slowikowski said, his staff were "going through a lot of things which we need to co-ordinate on a world-wide basis".[9]

The end of the Reagan decade thus marked the beginning of the internationalization of the American economic elite. The middle class was not excluded from the phenomenon. A growing number of jobs in the United States depend indirectly on relations with the outside world; more importantly, those Americans who are able to save are looking to the world economy. Hence the proliferation of investment funds in shares and bonds. In 1980, there were 564 such funds in the United States. By 1992, there were more than 3,000; their share value passed from $134 billion to more than $1,000 billion in the same period.[10] Shares, bonds and monetary instruments are acquiring greater importance to individual households, as shown by the proportion of Americans' total personal income provided by dividends and interest payments: 11 per cent in 1970, 14.6 per cent in 1980 and 17.5 per cent in 1991.[11]

The Planetary Stock Exchange

The majority of investments in the United States are restricted to the domestic market. Given the very high yields often obtainable from foreign stock markets, however, increasing numbers of financial managers have taken to globalizing their investments. Between 1989 and 1992 the amounts invested in international bonds and shares were multiplied by six and three respectively, while the amount invested in all funds only doubled.[12]

The fact that a large proportion of these financial shares is in personal savings – pensions and life insurance funds – further accentuates the importance of investment funds in American saving. These very large investors abandoned their proverbial provincial caution at the end of the 1980s, and began investing for the first time outside the national territory. The arrival on the scene of these financial mammoths transfigured the international investment market, whose net flow reached a total of $102.2 billion in 1991. The proportion of foreign shares in American pension funds rose from 2.2 per cent in 1988 to 4.4 per cent in 1991, with 7.2 per cent forecast for 1994. The race for globalization by the world's stock markets was such that, by late 1992, foreign investors held nearly 9 per cent of shares in all the world's stock markets.[13]

The American middle class has been caught up in the great game of the planetary stock exchange. It has become one of the players, either directly through the agency of a currency trader or fund manager, or indirectly through a pension fund. The telecommunications revolution and the deregulation of financial markets have given the small saver in Missouri or Colorado easy access to the world market and day-to-day information on the trials and tribulations of his or her portfolio. A mass of financial newsletters has sprung up to help him or her make decisions. Little by little, the investor is being forced to keep an eye on everything that might affect the prices of shares or bonds – economic events, political upheavals, natural catastrophes. The globalization of their savings is giving middle-class Americans a new vision of the world: the territory of the United States is only one element – still decisive perhaps, but no longer overwhelmingly predominant – in an expanded universe.

If America is starting to take an interest in the outside world, the inverse is equally true. Liberalization of trade and financial flows works, of course, in both directions. We have already mentioned the attractiveness of the United States for direct foreign investments, whose cumulative value was $487 billion in 1991. They were still outweighed by the financial holdings – shares and bonds combined – of non-American individuals. These reached a cumulative value of $559 billion in 1991, with a further $154 billion in Treasury bonds and $396 billion in shares held by foreign governments.[14] And just as the Americans have staked their savings on the smooth running of the world economy, the world for its part depends increasingly on the sound economic health of the United States. By 1991 the foreign stake in America amounted to some $2,500 billion in accumulated assets, equivalent to more than 40 per cent of GNP for the whole European Union – quite an advance on the 1980 figure of $543 billion.[15]

INTERNATIONALIZATION OF THE UNITED STATES

The rapid globalization of the political and military elites, middle-class savings and American financial instruments has inevitably affected regional governments as well. The growing interest of foreign investors has tempted every American state to do all it can to capture some of the capital pouring into the country. During the 1992 presidential campaign, Bill Clinton drew attention to the regular trips he had made to Europe and Asia to support the economic interests of his home state, Arkansas, which can boast that it has opened trade promotion offices in Brussels, Tokyo and Taipei. This line of argument was also meant to short-circuit Republican claims that the Democratic candidate knew nothing of world affairs.

The former governor of Arkansas is hardly a special case. These days, very few state governors hesitate to don the pilgrim's cloak and wander abroad trumpeting the investment opportunities available back home. As we have seen, Western and Japanese businessmen do not take much persuading. In every American region, the presence of foreign capital virtually doubled during the decade from 1980 to 1990. The bulk of the investments was concentrated on the eastern seaboard (New York, New Jersey and Pennsylvania), in the northern Midwest (Illinois and Ohio in particular), in the South-East (especially the two Carolinas, Georgia and Florida) and in Louisiana, Alaska, Texas and California (the last two absorbing nearly a quarter of the total between them).[16] The economic health of many states thus increasingly depends on their international connections. By 1990, foreign companies provided 14 per cent of jobs in Delaware, 11.2 per cent in Hawaii, 8 per cent in South Carolina and between 5 and 7 per cent in nineteen other states.[17]

Dissolution of the National Territory

The signature of the North American Free Trade Area (NAFTA) treaty in 1992 underlines the existing economic relationship between the individual states and Mexico and Canada. The Mexican market already absorbs nearly 30 per cent of exports from Texas, 19 per cent from Arizona and 8 per cent from California, as well as 14 per cent from North Dakota, 11 per cent from both Missouri and Kansas and 10 per cent from Arkansas.[18]

NAFTA seems certain to accentuate this cross-frontier interdependence. There is every expectation of the development of a relationship between the United States and Mexico analogous to the process of integration between the United States and Canada inaugurated by the bilateral agreement of January 1988. Thus the state of Washington lives in virtual symbiosis with the neighbouring Canadian province of British Columbia, and the towns of Seattle and Vancouver are not far from comprising a single economic entity. Around the Great Lakes, the province of Ontario and the states of Michigan, Wisconsin, Illinois, Indiana, Ohio, Pennsylvania and New York form an economic area that grows more homogeneous by the day. On the East Coast, trade and investments between Quebec and the American North-East are increasing.

This brings to the North the gradual erosion of frontiers already experienced in the Southwest as a result of Mexican and Hispanic immigration. The prosperity of all the Canadian provinces is becoming extremely dependent on the United States. The constitutional crisis that has been threatening to split the country since 1991 is a further encouragement to the Canadian provinces to strengthen links with their nearest American counterparts. The NAFTA agreement therefore seems likely to have a decisive impact on North American geography. On one level, it promotes the extension and integration of the North American market "from the Yukon to Yucatan". On another level, it will bring about the reorganization of North America into five great transnational regions: (1) the California/Texas/Mexico triangle; (2) the North Pacific axis comprising British Columbia and Washington State, centred on

Seattle and Vancouver; (3) the Great Lakes region; (4) the Saint Lawrence, comprising Quebec and New England; (5) the South, opening onto the Caribbean islands and Latin America, focused on the decision-making centres of Atlanta and Miami (the latter already de facto financial capital of the huge Caribbean and Central American region).

Washington, D.C.: Capital of the Planet

The internationalization of the United States is thus proceeding at dizzy speed. The main architects of this historic upheaval were members of the Reagan administration. A fair proportion of Reagan's senior appointees were business people from enterprises with transnational interests, like Wall Street brokers Merrill Lynch or international engineers Bechtel.

It cannot be denied that this economic revolution was bought on credit. At the beginning of the Reagan administration, in 1981, America was the world's leading creditor. By the time "Ronnie" left the White House in 1989 it had become the world's biggest debtor. For eight years Reagan had treated his fellow citizens to an economic boom financed largely by the rest of the world: the value of American internal and external debts increased from 26.3 per cent to 42.9 per cent of GNP, reaching a total of some $2,200 billion in 1989.[19] However, we should note that this percentage, which began to diminish after 1990, was lower than those registered during the Roosevelt, Truman, Eisenhower and Kennedy administrations.

Vociferous lip-service apart, the White House and Congress show a curious lack of interest in any holes in the federal coffers. This is not just simple political irresponsibility, even though Congressional allergies to budget cuts and tax increases are well known. Until the early 1990s, the United States was fully aware that the rest of the world was far too dependent on its economic power not to continue financing its growth. Where was it safer to place capital, given the uncertainties that still enveloped Europe and Asia-Pacific?

America thus benefited from an uninterrupted flow of foreign private loans and investments. It is also blessed with a unique privilege: that of being indebted in its own currency. Since the dollar is the world's main reserve currency, the United States can hope to live on credit for some time to come. The Americans are not about to be declared bankrupt by anyone. Under these conditions debt appears more a badge of strength than of weakness; note, for example, that the big loans taken out during the Reagan era, contracted in strong dollars, are being repaid during the 1990s in currency whose value has halved. Numerous Japanese savers are still wondering how American government bonds came to seem such a good investment.

With the United States at the centre of the international financial system, the entire world becomes de facto American national territory, at least where the management of financial loans is concerned. There are, however, limits to investors' confidence. A deficit that was completely out of control would arouse anxieties about the American state's ability to honour its commitments. The main thing is that the imperial drain must never become so large that it threatens to ruin the provinces. The problem has some parallels with another manifestation of power, nuclear deterrence, which works only if the players can prove at all times that they can keep control of the inevitable atomic arms race. Just as the Bomb cannot be "disinvented", the American debt cannot be made to vanish. With a federal deficit that reached $332 billion – 5 per cent of GNP – in 1992, the White House and Congress had to demonstrate their ability to master the processes of budgetary decision making.

After two years as president, Bill Clinton had reduced the government deficit to a relatively modest 3 per cent of GNP. In 1995, the "real" budget – setting aside a $200 billion deficit in federal finances due almost entirely to debt interest payments – was practically balanced. The debt itself had nevertheless reached the astronomical level of $3,300 billion. Although this sum, expressed as a percentage of American national wealth, is on the low side of average for an industrialized country, its very size makes it a heavy drain on national and world savings. Since the 1994 congressional elections, the Republican Congress and the Democrat White House have consequently been vying with each other to come up with plans to eliminate the budget deficit totally within seven years. But whether these radical intentions can be realized remains to be seen.

Meanwhile, the globalization of America is already being reflected in domestic policy. Deliberations in Congress, decisions from the White House or the Supreme Court and new laws, all have a direct and increasingly profound impact on the rest of the planet. Monetary and financial decisions by the Federal Reserve or new trade regulations can limit the margins of manoeuvre even of states as powerful as Germany or Japan. For a large number of foreign industries, these decisions can make the difference between success and bankruptcy. So it is not difficult to understand why a wide range of external interests are starting to get involved in the American political process.

There are two privileged channels leading to some measure of influence in Washington: the famous "lobbies" – established and officially registered interest groups – and the political action committees (PACs), which are legally entitled to finance electoral campaigns. Of course the great majority of these groups represent interests that are American and strictly sectoral. But in recent years more and more foreign countries have been appearing in the system. By 1991, no fewer than 112 countries were paying for the services of a recognized lobbyist (two in some cases, one hired by the government and the other by its embassy), not counting those acting for foreign businesses or associations of producers. In 1992 there were some 850 non-American interest groups, including governments, embassies and ministries, with a political foothold in the capital of the United States. Among the most active are Japan (145 groups), Canada (62), Britain (60), Germany (45), South Korea (37), France (32), Brazil (26), Taiwan (22), Mexico and Italy (19 each) and Israel (16).[20]

Foreign financial contributions to American electoral campaigns are difficult to estimate exactly. But although they are small compared with the gigantic sums provided by the national PACs, they are important enough to have generated a polemic during the 1992 presidential campaign. During the 1985–86 congressional elections, foreign enterprises established in the United States officially gave some $2.2 million to a variety of Republican and Democratic candidates (a sum representing just under 4.7 per cent of the total contribution from American businesses). The equivalent figures for 1987–88 and 1989–90 are $2.37 million and $1.33 million (4.5 per cent and 3.8 per cent of the total, respectively).[21] As we know, Bill Clinton has instituted an ethical code of conduct for his senior colleagues: when they leave their government jobs they must refrain from representing foreign interests for life, not just for a year as previously.

The United States thus enters the last decade of the century in the aftermath of an extraordinary metamorphosis. In the space of just forty years, its economic and political life has become so entangled with that of the rest of the planet that we now need to think in terms of a single large entity, a World-America. A good example of this new reality was seen on 3 November 1992, the day the Americans elected their forty-second president. Hour after hour, all over the world, the television networks covered the vote count live, with blanket commentary and news stories. It was as if everyone knew they were watching a "domestic" election, an event crucial to the future of their own nations, their own families: a sort of restricted world suffrage, the vote available only to those with

American citizenship, influenced by foreign pressure-groups rich enough to use the established indirect channels.

With the destinies of the whole planet bound up with the fate of the United States, America cannot afford to neglect the rest of the globe. US interests – political, economic and cultural – are so extensive that the difference between national and international politics is becoming quite tenuous. Washington's power elites must arbitrate increasingly between strictly national options and the need to take wider commitments into account. A typical example is the NAFTA agreement: some of the mid-western states will be forced to sacrifice jobs and lose investment for the sake of the new economic dynamism that should result from the creation of an enlarged North American market.

The territory and population of the United States remain, of course, the foundations of American power. But they are no longer the sole references and have become one of the spaces – albeit the most crucial – of the vast entity of World-America. Little by little, the internationalization of American political and economic leaders is transforming the White House, and even Congress, into a sort of world political centre: a decision-making nexus centred on an ability to mediate between a multitude of disparate interests involving all nationalities.

PART III

CONSTRUCTING THE
UNIVERSAL
DEMOCRATIC EMPIRE

9

ECONOMIC LEADERSHIP

With its Soviet enemy vanquished, the American presidency now finds itself the sole heir to a turbulent planet. Nothing can be done from now on without the leadership of the last surviving superpower: the Gulf War, the "philanthropic" intervention in Somalia, the Arab-Israeli peace negotiations, GATT, the relaunch of the world economy, the peace agreement in Bosnia. "The buck stops here", read the famous sign on President Harry S. Truman's desk. It is even truer today.

In this radically new universe the American elites have a head start: they were the first to become aware that the globalization of economies and decision-making processes was inevitable. American political and economic leaders – apart from those who still yearn for insulation from a "barbaric" planet – know that there is no going back. The future of the country and its prosperity are irremediably linked to its ability to fulfil its role as leader of the world.

STEERING WORLD GROWTH

"The fact is that for now and for the foreseeable future, the world looks to us to be the engine of global growth and to be the leader," Bill Clinton proclaimed in 1993.[1] A model based on classical hegemony no longer applies, however. Worldwide economic integration has blunted the tools of power available to national governments, even that of the United States. Washington has neither the means nor the ambition to impose a pyramidal world structure with America enthroned at the summit and its vassals arranged below in order of relative power. The new metaphor for the democratic empire is rather that of the hub of the world: a centre, separate from the rim of the planet, but rigidly connected to it by innumerable spokes of interdependence that form a single assembly.

Integrating the World with America

In the middle of the Iraq–Kuwait crisis George Bush, who had presided over the collapse of the bipolar world, proclaimed "a new order of peace" which would last "a hundred years". Bush, a cold warrior whose outlook was primarily political and strategic, believed that his task was to construct a new, stable planetary balance, centred on American military power which was now without rival. The precarious transition from the dangerous but predictable universe of East–West confrontation to a new world order whose permanence would be guaranteed by American supremacy over all other potential decision centres, whether friendly or unfriendly, had to be managed as well as possible. The White House would act through a sort of Meccano of power, the network of institutions set up by the United States over nearly half a century (the World Bank, IMF, GATT, UNO, NATO, OAS and so on), to establish a new permanent configuration for the balance of forces between states.

"What we need to elect in 1992 is not the last president of the twentieth century, but the first president of the twenty-first century," Bill Clinton stated several months before the 1992 presidential election.[2] The first baby boomer to be elected to the supreme magistracy is known to prefer the idea of a "new covenant" to that of a "new world order." The vocabulary is significant. Where the veterans of the Cold War saw a vast chess game of coercive political and military pressures, the new generation sees a chance of establishing a legitimate leadership. Only the United States, the new president proclaimed, could play the role of leader in reducing human suffering, continuing the march towards democracy and human rights, and maintaining growth in the market economies.[3]

The distance separating George Bush from Bill Clinton was nevertheless infinitesimal. Both came out clearly in favour of maintaining and extending America's managerial role. Both saw the planet as a space in the process of unification, which it was their responsibility to administer. The difference was that the outgoing president was still entangled, via the logic of the old politico-military alliances, in a game that consisted essentially of controlling a delicate arrangement of balancing blocs. The new occupant of the White House slipped more naturally into the role of central formulator of the values – economic, political, juridical, cultural, ecological – that ought to rule the lives of all human beings.

The difference between the two generations is nowhere more evident than in the economic domain. Bush and his secretary of state, James Baker, gave priority to opening up the world market simply as a way of promoting the growth of the United States. The pre-eminence of the American economy was supposed to be unassailable, provided competitors played the free-trade game fairly. For Bill Clinton, on the other hand, the task was to strengthen America's economic power in order to "help lead the world into a new era of global growth".[4] In an overt reference to the weight of the United States in the world economy, the new president proclaimed: "I say that if we set a new direction at home, we can set a new direction for the world as well."[5]

Instead of integrating America into the outside world for the good of America, the world was going to have to be integrated into a strong America for the good of humanity. "We must tear down the wall in our thinking between domestic and foreign policy," Clinton explained.[6] The Cold War was history. Security problems could no longer be defined "in narrow military terms".[7] The economy was becoming the central political issue, and the president would henceforth be able to call on a National Economic Council responsible for international economic affairs, which works in a similar way to the National Security Council. Integration of the whole planet around a dynamic American nucleus: that was to be the great challenge of the new covenant.

Managing "Common Threats"

The White House is situated at the centre of a vast process of globalization. Its task is to sketch the broad outline of the process and encourage the private sector in the United States to assume its historic leadership role. The state has been thoroughly rehabilitated after a decade of Reaganite *laissez faire*. But there is no question of reviving a narrowly protectionist and national industrial or social policy, as people in Europe might imagine. On the contrary, public power will be used to speed the globalization of markets and underwrite rules of operation permitting the ordered expansion of World-America under Washington's direction: "success in the global economy must be at the core of national security in the nineteen-nineties. Without growth abroad, our own economy cannot thrive. . . . Without global growth, healthy international competition turns all too readily into economic warfare, and there can be no true economic justice among or within nations."[8] And it falls to the Americans, of course, to take responsibility for a vigorous and balanced development of the world market.

The head of the democratic empire must also be ready to assume an essential role in reconciling the dynamism of the market economies with the containment of "common threats to all people":[9] environmental damage, the proliferation of weapons of mass destruction, drugs, and so on. With the assistance of a militant environmentalist, Vice-President Albert Gore, the White House is now in a position to work out a body of minimum guidelines and obtain the acquiescence of its foreign allies and clients. These guidelines are meant to regulate environmental protection worldwide, set conditions for the trade in advanced technologies and co-ordinate the struggle against narcotics. "On the environment and other global issues", the new president wrote, "our very survival depends upon the United States taking the lead."[10] George Bush was to go down in history as the last commander-in-chief of a long Cold War that divided the planet. Bill Clinton introduced himself as the first *imperator* who intended to lay the institutional foundations of a civilization that, for the first time in human history, might incorporate the entire world.

The conviction that America is the only entity with the power to set the world in order is not just an indication of conceit in a country that can claim to be the great victor of the terrible, clanging twentieth century. The Washington elite can command genuine advantages: not just unrivalled military strength but, more importantly, the extraordinary power of the American market, whose weight effectively dominates the world economy. The United States does not have the dominant position that it had in the late 1940s: it can no longer profit from being the only industrial nation left unscathed by the Second World War, and it has lost the exorbitant privilege of producing more than half of the world's wealth. But its gross domestic product, equivalent to $7,000 billion, still exceeds that of the whole European Community and represents a quarter of the GDP of the entire planet.[11] The size of the American economy doubled between 1980 and 1992, an expansion over just twelve years equivalent to the creation of two markets the size of the German economy.

It is often forgotten that the United States made room for its European and Asian partner-competitors on its own initiative. The Marshall Plan, launched in 1947 to save the economies of non-Communist Europe, was explicitly intended to revive the world economy through the rapid reconstruction of allied and enemy economies alike. As Secretary of State George C. Marshall explained, referring to the utter collapse of the Old World:

> The modern system of the division of labor upon which the exchange of products is based is in danger of breaking down. . . . The consequences to the

economy of the United States should be apparent to all. It is logical that the United States should do whatever it is able to do to assist in the return of normal economic health in the world, without which there can be no political stability and no assured peace.[12]

Since the end of the Second World War, America has avoided mercantilist temptations and bound its own prosperity firmly to that of the entire planet.

TECHNOLOGICAL DOMINATION AND PRODUCTIVITY

Throughout the Bush administration, despite one of the most marked recessions since the 1940s, the United States had one of the lowest unemployment levels in the OECD – 7.2 per cent in October 1992. Although much higher than the rates normally claimed in Japan (always a special case), this is still a marked improvement on the peaks measured between 1980 and 1985 – 9.5 per cent – before the Reaganite revival took effect.[13] Better still, the figure had dropped to 5.6 per cent by the end of Clinton's first year in office. The same superiority is apparent in figures for per capita GNP calculated in terms of effective purchasing power. With $22,000 each, Americans have a substantial lead in standard of living: 35 per cent more than the Germans and 25 per cent more than the Japanese.[14] In 1991, the United States was the country exporting the most goods – $422 billion, equivalent to 12.3 per cent of world exports – and also the biggest importer – $487 billion or 14 per cent of world imports.[15] Despite the strong performances of competitors, American exports after 1986 increased, not just faster than world trade, but 40 per cent faster than German exports and 75 per cent faster than Japanese.[16] Moreover the American share of total industrial production by the twenty-four OECD countries was larger in 1990 than in 1970.[17]

Leaner and Meaner

Falling productivity in the American economy was one of the main arguments of those who started claiming, in the middle of the 1980s, that America was in terminal decline. History seemed to endorse this view. From 1889 to 1937, the United States showed an average annual labour productivity growth rate of 1.9 per cent. Between 1937 and 1973, this figure was an extraordinary 3 per cent. Since then, however, it has dropped to 0.9 per cent, the lowest rate for more than a century, inferior to those of its major competitors.[18] These mathematical averages do not tell the whole story, however. Since the 1982 recession, American industry has been engaged, as it has been several times before during the last hundred years, in a vast process of modernization and ruthless restructuring: brutal internal reorganizations, massive lay-offs, radical changes of profile, spectacular takeovers, gigantic mergers. This trend towards accelerated rationalization began in manufacturing industry and then spread to the services, which by the end of 1991 provided 78 per cent of non-agricultural employment.[19]

Concerning the "de-industrialization" of the United States, it is worth noting that, despite the grim conjuncture, the industrial sector has been leading the American economy since the second half of the 1980s. Between 1980 and 1991, the productivity of manufacturing industry increased by 55 per cent, far more than in Germany and Japan, which achieved gains of under 40 per cent.[20] In the last quarter of 1992, American industrial productivity showed an annual growth rate of 3.8 per cent,[21] and the share of American-made manufactured goods in the world market has been growing by 0.6 per cent a year since 1987.[22]

As for the service industries, they became hugely inflated during the Reaganite "miracle on credit", which was nevertheless the longest period of consecutive growth since the Second World War. Transport, retailing, banking and catering all recruited vigorously for a decade; and even with workforces swollen by 30 per cent,[23] they managed to delay the inevitable onset of rationalization. This arrived, brutally, at the beginning of the Bush administration and largely explains the curious cycle of recession and "soft recovery" that characterized 1990 and 1991. During the Reaganite growth period the dynamism of the services sector helped compensate for the effects of industrial modernization, and it was still there when industry restarted. But under George Bush the restored vitality of the manufacturing sector was unable to cope with the enormous wave of modernization in the services.

Ronald Reagan's successor was simply unlucky. Shortly after his electoral defeat in November 1992, economic indicators suggested that the vast movement to adapt the American economy to the environment of the twenty-first century was approaching completion. After the summer of 1991, the productivity of the whole American economy started growing at the rate of 2.5 per cent a year, reaching 4 per cent in the third quarter of 1992.[24] Bill Clinton thus inherited a much healthier situation, with American business becoming a good deal leaner and meaner in all sectors.

A study of productivity throughout the world, published in 1992 by the McKinsey Global Institute, with input from the winner of the Nobel prize for economics Robert Solow, caused surprise by showing that the United States was well ahead of the other industrial countries. In 1990 an American worker produced the equivalent of $49,600 in goods or services, compared with $47,000 from a French worker, $44,200 from a German and a mere $38,200 from a Japanese. In industry, the hourly production of German and Japanese workers is only 80 per cent of that of their American colleagues.

Although Japan, for example, can claim superior productivity in electronics and some heavy industries (car and machine manufacture), it is quite far behind the United States in nearly half of its industrial installations. Since the end of the 1980s, moreover, America's competitors have been finding it much more difficult to make up the difference. And the gulf between the US and Germany has actually widened. The United States is absolutely dominant in the services sector (with the exception of luxury restaurants, in which the French still lead). In the retail trade, Americans are 56 per cent more productive than the Japanese, 31 per cent more than the French and 4 per cent more productive than the Germans. In banking, they are 32 per cent better than the Germans and 36 per cent better than the British. In telecommunications, France and Japan are abreast of the United States, but Germany is trailing 20 per cent behind. In air transport, American personnel are 20 per cent more productive than Europeans.[25]

Priority to Innovation

Productivity is not the only important measure of modern economic power. Research and development (R&D) activity is equally determining. And here, too, the United States is far ahead of all its competitors, even though the lead has been somewhat eroded since the mid 1970s. In 1991, the American government and private enterprise devoted 2.8 per cent of GNP to research, the same percentage as the Japanese and the Germans.[26] It is not always remembered, however, that given the difference between American and other GNPs, the $160 billion invested in R&D annually by the Americans outweighs the combined efforts of Japan, Germany and France. As a result, the Americans still make 37 per cent of the world output of high-technology products[27] and have a market share equivalent to 20 per cent of world exports in this sector.[28] In the area of patents, licences and royalties, America's "technological balance of payments" was

$1.3 billion in surplus in 1989, with the United States pocketing four times as much as it paid out.[29]

It is true that R&D in America is heavily dependent on the defence industry, which gets more than 60 per cent of the federal funds allotted to research. Until the early 1980s Americans expected usable amounts of technological fallout from the military laboratories. But in most of today's vanguard sectors the innovation process is much more rapid in civilian industries. Thus, since 1984, the federal government and local municipalities have given priority to scientific research on all fronts. They have encouraged businesses to set up joint research centres with universities, stimulated the exchange of information between federal, university and private laboratories and striven to improve and coordinate transfers of technology.[30]

As a result, hundreds of research centres have been set up over the last decade, attracting scientists and engineers from all over the world. The United States – whose policy on brain imports has always been more liberal than those of Europe and Japan – has thus restored its traditional dynamism in technological innovation. At the dawn of the Clinton era it still appeared a formidable competitor, even in areas where it had declined between 1970 and 1990.

So the new president inherited a widely improved national economy fit for its role as world "locomotive". There remained, of course, the task of cleaning up the inequities left by years of uncontrolled Reaganite growth. Clinton accordingly announced programmes for renovating neglected roads, railways and bridges, new housing and the revitalization of depressed inner-city economies. The federal budget deficit – the heaviest burden left by the two Republican presidents – occupied a central place in the Clinton reforms (and in the Republican leadership's priorities).

The executive and the legislature therefore expressed determination to regain control of the reputedly "untouchable" budgetary headings whose growth had become exponential. Clinton and Gingrich both proclaimed their intention of attacking the most sacred cow of all, responsible for the biggest hole in public finances: health costs. To demonstrate that he was staking his personal prestige on this issue, the president even entrusted the task to his wife Hillary. Budgetary measures were, however, only one aspect of the White House's political programme. It made no secret of its wish to concentrate on matters seen as having much greater strategic importance: the consolidation of American scientific and technological leadership and the integration of foreign markets into the economy of World-America.[31]

INFORMATION SUPERHIGHWAYS

Everyone – Republican or Democrat, businessman, politician or expert – is convinced that advanced technology, with mastery of the flows of information and intellectual capital, have become the motors of economic growth. The future belongs to enterprises whose arsenals include a high proportion of grey matter. But little is known about how to exploit the new gold mine. The problem has become acute since the end of the 1980s with the appearance and proliferation of "borderless labs".

Borderless Laboratories

The American computer firm Hewlett Packard is a case in point. Its PCs, designed and marketed in Palo Alto, California, are assembled in Grenoble, France, from components made in Malaysia and part-assembled in Singapore. Fifty per cent of sales are on the American market.[32] However, Hewlett Packard has moved part of its product development division to Singapore, where one of its local engineers recently developed a component leading to the launch of a new line of printers.[33]

This example of a "borderless lab" is far from unique. Between 1985 and 1989 there were nine hundred transnational alliances affiliating American high-tech enterprises with partners abroad, or involving direct investment by non-American firms in companies in the United States.[34] Some of the cooperation agreements announed in 1992 – IBM-Siemens, Intel-Sharp, Apple-Motorola-Sony – confirmed this tendency to globalize research and development activities. Although American enterprises spend only a tenth of their R&D budgets abroad, the phenomenon causes disquiet among those who believe the "pirating" of American technological treasures to be a threat. Would not a more protectionist policy be a good idea?

The response of political leaders, and even of most firms working in the advanced technology sector, has been a definite no. It is felt that the internationalization process is not only inevitable but positive, as it brings greatly enlarged financial and human resources to bear on the process of innovation. By contrast, any attempt to withdraw into a protected national territory would mean falling behind technically and losing competitive edge. So the priority is not to shut out the rest of the world, but to try to ensure that America not only pilots the globalization but profits from it; to "harness the global economy for the benefit of all of our people", as Bill Clinton put it.[35] In this context, the main American objective is to develop a material and human infrastructure that is clearly superior to that of its competitors. This is a *sine qua non* for attracting investment and talented researchers from all over the world; for acquiring – as Hewlett Packard did – the means to profit from the potential of foreign partners, abroad as well as in the United States.

The debate between protectionists and internationalists was decided in favour of the latter not only by the notoriously "free-tradist" Bush administration but by Bill Clinton as well. Clinton's determination is clearly expressed at the top of his electoral programme, "Putting People First":

> In the emerging global economy, everything is mobile: capital, factories, even entire industries. The only resource that's really rooted in a nation – and the ultimate source of all its wealth – is its people. The only way America can compete and win in the twenty-first century is to have the best educated, best trained workforce in the world, linked together by transportation and communication networks second to none.[36]

In other words, industrial policy now consists of investment in know-how, brains (talented and qualified staff) and information. Or, as the new occupant of the White House urged, "putting the American people first without withdrawing from the world and people beyond our borders".[37]

The High-Tech Challenge

Although reform of vocational training and the education system figured high on the new administration's list of objectives, technological development was regarded as utterly crucial. Clinton embraced the idea of a federal agency to encourage and coordinate civilian R & D, along the lines of a particularly efficient military body, the Defence Advanced Research Projects Agency (DARPA). The new civilian agency would be expected to bring enterprises and universities together to conduct advanced research in "biotechnology, robotics, supercomputers and environmental technology". Where the last of these is concerned, the ambition is to "create the world's most advanced systems to recycle, treat toxic waste and clean our air and water".[38] Budgetary deficit notwithstanding, fiscal concessions were going to be available to firms taking the plunge into high tech. And public funds would support programmes like "intelligent" freeways and supersonic commercial aircraft.

Nor were the military programmes neglected, despite their exposure to budgetary cuts following the end of the Cold War. The American president reaffirmed his support for maintaining the defence industry's research and development capability, so that US arms superiority would not be eroded. There was no threat to the laboratories, the teams of researchers and engineers and the production facilities devoted to national defence. Clinton even went so far as to agree to the project, defended by George Bush, of an anti-missile shield, a less grandiose version of the Reaganite fantasy SDI or "Star Wars".

But the president set most store by the ambitious project of information superhighways, for which Vice-President Albert Gore was made responsible. The term refers to a high-speed information network linking universities, enterprises, hospitals, public administrations, libraries, government laboratories, schools and even individuals. Based on the High Performance Computing and Communications (HPCC) programme developed by Gore and approved in its day by the Bush administration, this network was supposed to set up a national system of computer links drawing on a mosaic of interconnected supercomputers. The White House issued an eloquent list of possible uses: helping firms to collaborate in research activity, making technical and legal information instantly available, alerting small and medium enterprises to commercial opportunities abroad, making cooperation in medical research and diagnostics more rapid and efficient, giving scientists instant access to the latest discoveries (and enormous computing power), making libraries and laboratories more widely available to teachers and students, stimulating individual creativity and the creation of new enterprises.

In a report entitled "Technology: The Motor of Economic Growth", published in September 1992, Bill Clinton declared that the network could do for the productivity of individuals, at work or in school, what the "interstate highways of the nineteen-fifties" had done for the system of passenger and goods transport.[39] The new president clearly saw this project – which by its nature is also open to foreigners – as having a role in maintaining American technological leadership in the twenty-first century, rather like the space race launched by John F. Kennedy in the 1960s.[40]

An effort on this scale has no meaning unless it is aimed at the entire world market. Nicholas Brady, former treasury secretary in the Bush administration, summed up the constraints of World-America perfectly. Pointing out that most of the industries that make America the leader of the new world economy – pharmaceuticals, software, telecommunications, aerospace and computers – prosper through trade, Brady said that if competition is the lever that will enable a country to increase its productivity in the twenty-first century, then "trade is the pivot".[41]

Although the new administration fully shared this view, it was not content simply to defend a more muscular form of free trade than its Republican predecessors. The baby-boom generation saw America, along with all the other countries in the world, as being inextricably integrated into the global economy. A simple commitment to freedom of trade would perpetuate the old vision of state entities negotiating access to their respective markets in accordance with rules supposed to ensure a measure of equality amid the flow of exchanges; while today, the fact is that capital, products, services, companies, even manufacturing and research processes have become globalized. So that although free trade is more necessary than ever if this globalized ecomomy is to work, it is no longer sufficient, by itself, to ensure profit. The important thing now is to attract the activities with the highest added value onto one's own territory.[42]

The national origins of managers, companies, technologies and investors have become unimportant. Bill Clinton himself applauded – on condition of some measure of reciprocity – the wider opening of the American market to foreign investment: "with it come new ideas as well as capital, new technologies, new management techniques, and new opportunities for us to learn from one another and grow."[43] The president of the new democratic empire clearly defined the economic challenge of the twenty-first century as "how to maintain a high-wage economy in the United States without ourselves adding to the protectionist direction that so many of the developed nations have taken in the last few years".[44] But the success of this strategy cannot be guaranteed by the quality of America's labour force and infrastructures. The United States must also master the key economic element of the new millennium: information and its circuits.

10

MASTERING THE INFORMATION CIRCUITS

Silicon Valley is the great industrial myth of the generation born during the 1940s and 1950s. What young entrepreneur in the United States has not had dreams based on the modern version of the rags to riches story: teenage computer nerd cobbling microchips in a garage to billionaire head of (say) Apple or Microsoft? The reputation of this high-tech Mecca in northern California is well established now. Only a few years ago, in the late 1980s, it was fashionable to predict its demise. But in the last decade of the century Silicon Valley has re-emerged as the world's most formidable concentration of talent, innovatory spirit and entrepreneurial will.

It contains a unique cocktail of electronics engineers, academic researchers, specialized ancillary enterprises, venture capitalists, specialist computer lawyers and public relations experts. It is a place where companies are set up in a few hours, and liquidated just as quickly. Silicon Valley is the advanced industrial complex best adapted to an economic environment that calls for permanent innovation and abrupt changes of strategy. It is easy to understand why Bill Clinton, himself in his forties when first elected, used it to symbolize American power, and chose a firm from Silicon Valley to start his great modernization programme.

In a world where production is increasingly fragmented, where capital can whip round the globe several times in just a few minutes, mastery of information has become crucial. "Most important of all", the new president affirmed, "information has become global and has become king of the global economy." He went on to define the central place that computer technology and telecommunications would occupy in the future: "In earlier history, wealth was measured in land, in gold, in oil, in machines.

Today, the principal measure of our wealth is information: its quality, its quantity, and the speed with which we acquire it and adapt to it."[1]

THE BRAIN OF THE WORLD ECONOMY

Obviously, this wish to integrate and relaunch the world economy with information technologies in the central role is based on the extraordinary strength of the United States in this area. But how real is this advance over the rest of the world? The prophets of American decline harp on the irresistible growth of Japanese strength in the information technologies. Japanese firms, they point out, control 80 per cent of the world market for memory chips. And they are omnipresent in the market for portable computers and electronic organizers.

Computer Technology: America's Crushing Dominance

The truth is that with the exception of dynamic random access memory (D-RAM) chips and liquid crystal (LCD) screens, the Japanese trail a considerable distance behind the Americans. The world computer market from top to bottom, from the PC via the commercial work station and big mainframe system to the supercomputer, is not far from being an American monopoly. IBM, Apple, Compaq, Del and Hewlett Packard have already occupied all the terrain. A handful of European survivors like Olivetti, Bull and Siemens-Nixdorf are a long way behind, with a global market share of about 10 per cent.[2] In the PC domain the most important Japanese manufacturer, NEC, is only the fourteenth biggest in the world, with 1.5 per cent of the American market. In 1992, the entire Japanese industry only accounted for 7 per cent of office computer sales in the United States. Moreover, the Japanese firms NEC and Toshiba, which began with a head start in the portable sector, saw their share of the United States market plummet from 43 per cent in 1989 to under 25 per cent in 1992.[3] Meanwhile, American firms had finally made up their minds to attack the Japanese market. From 1990 onwards, IBM and Compaq were steadily increasing their sales in the Japanese archipelago by waging a ruthless price war. Apple's performance in Japan was doubling every quarter.[4]

In addition to this crushing dominance of the computer market, the United States holds a near monopoly on systems architecture. Between them, Apple and the partnership of Intel and Microsoft (the world's biggest producers of microprocessors and software, respectively) effectively dictate the design of the architecture of most of the planet's computers including, of course, the various Asian clones. American manufacturers may use a lot of Japanese components, but they still manage to maintain a constant six- to nine-month technological advance over their Japanese competitors.[5]

The United States is also unrivalled in the area of innovation and mastery of the technological sectors of the future: MPP (massively parallel processing) for supercomputers, RISC (reduced instruction set computing) architectures, flash memories (reprogrammable chips that retain data when the current is switched off), software, new architectures, multimedia products, digitalization and even "à la carte" computer services. To give one example, Intel controls four-fifths of the output of flash memories, which are simpler than earlier chips and, since 1994, cheaper to make. The market for this recent product, worth $130 million in 1991, should be around $10 billion by the year 2000.[6]

The Japanese assault on the memory-chip market during the 1980s thus ended in a Pyrrhic victory. D-RAM chips are the basic components of the entire computer industry. The intention had been to use Japan's undeniable superiority in production engineering to gain control of this "industrial rice" of the modern age. The problem was that these chips went the same way as rice and became a generic product; the Japanese near monopoly has been undermined by new arrivals from Korea and Taiwan, whose products are even cheaper than those of Japan's mature industry. In just a few years, the Korean firm Samsung has emerged as the biggest world producer of D-RAM chips, and seems likely to beat its Japanese competitors in bringing the next two generations of chips (16 and 64 megabyte) to the market. By 1992 Samsung and the other two big Korean manufacturers, Hyundai and Lucky-Goldstar, already controlled a quarter of world sales between them.[7]

The Japanese memory-chip industry is thus squeezed between Asian competitors who outperform it at the lower end of the market – and soon, perhaps, at the top end as well – and the Americans, who are unrivalled in developing new chips. Even the immense research effort deployed by Fujitsu to develop a 256-megabyte chip was hit by the slowing down of the D-RAM market in the early 1990s.[8] Memories have become a simple raw material produced by a number of makers of different nationalities: very useful to the United States, which does not have to depend on Japan as sole supplier. To add insult to injury, the American semiconductor industry, which had practically closed down as a result of Japanese competition, edged back into leadership of the world market in 1992.[9]

THE TWENTY-FIRST CENTURY WILL BE AMERICAN

The Software Monopoly

So that at the dawn of the twenty-first century, there is not much chance of America's hold on the computer industry being challenged in any serious way. Lord of both domains – hardware and software alike – the United States can depend on the power of the world's biggest internal market and a government eager to encourage technological advance and investment in new equipment.[10] American firms are also actively preparing for the globalization of markets by weaving a planetary network of alliances centred on themselves. To survive, IBM president Jack Kuehler explained bluntly in September 1992 at a joint conference with Toshiba and Siemens executives, computer firms have to be able to meet global competition. "Survival is our first priority. Nationalist concerns come second," he added.[11]

Kuehler knew what he was talking about. IBM, a true dinosaur of the computer industry, confronted with the dinosaur's fate of extinction, decided at the end of 1991 to undertake a radical restructuring of its activities. The giant ended by smashing its corporate culture and centralized, inward-looking structure, and transforming itself into a federation of smaller, more autonomous units, able to react quickly to developments in the market.[12] This quest for a new flexibility, which involved tens of thousands of redundancies and a broad diversification into services, flowered in a mass of new cooperation agreements with competing American and foreign businesses.

IBM is just one of many examples. The underlying tendency is for American firms to establish a sort of star-shaped world network, not unlike the model of client relations that links Congress and the White House with the states and local communities. They are certainly rendered more dependent by the immense industrial net they have thrown over the planet. But by virtue of their powerful internal market and near monopoly of software production, the Americans are in a position to reserve the activities with most added value, and thus the biggest profit margins, for themselves: a way of promoting the overall growth of the industry, while abandoning the less attractive sectors to partner-competitors abroad. Thus, since the end of 1991, IBM has established all sorts of agreements with Hitachi, Siemens, Toshiba, Tata Industries (of India), Bull, Toyota, and so on. Apple has done the same thing with Sharp, Sony and Toshiba. And within the United States, the American industry has been consolidating its position with mutual agreements between the big players: IBM, Intel, Apple, AT&T, Microsoft, Motorola.

The alliance between the two computer giants IBM and Apple, sealed in October 1991, shook the entire industry. It is no small thing, after all, to witness the betrothal of the planet's two main computing systems, and to realize that they have decided to define the technological standards of the future (especially in the strategic multimedia sector) in private, between themselves. Multimedia seems the most promising area for developing not just the computer market, but the consumer electronics market as well.

Multimedia systems – "telecomputers" combining the technologies of computing, audio-visual equipment and telecommunications – are the great hope of the (mainly Japanese) electronics firms whose market started crumbling at the beginning of the 1990s.[13] However, the development of multimedia products depends first and foremost on advanced software, which Japan is still incapable of producing. Japanese firms have consequently tried to forge alliances with American partners: Sharp signed up with Apple, NEC and Toshiba with AT&T, Sony with Motorola and Apple, Matsushita and Toshiba (again) with AT&T (again). But cooperation with the United States has a price. For example, Apple and IBM did form a joint association, Kaleida, to develop multimedia products. It was open to European and Japanese members, but only if they agreed to the technological norms defined by the Americans becoming the international standard.[14]

THE WORLD'S NERVOUS SYSTEM

The decisive question of who is to set international standards also lies at the heart of the battle for control of telecommunications. If computing is the brain of an integrated world economy, telecommunications constitutes its nervous system. The world market (services and equipment combined) is growing by 10 to 15 per cent annually, stimulated by rapid and widespread deregulation and uncontrolled technological innovation.[15]

The Planet's Central Switchboard

By 1990 a thousand million telephones, linked by cable or satellite, covered the planet. The traffic volume sextupled during the 1980s and was expected to reach sixty or seventy billion minutes a year by 1995. Services valued at $175 billion in 1986 were forecast to rise to $576 billion by 1995. The corresponding figures for the value of equipment are $88 billion and $169 billion.[16] The market is by no means saturated, however. The "emergent" economies of Asia and Latin America – not to mention the East European countries – are certainly going to have to modernize their ancient, ramshackle systems. The chances are that the world will invest more money in telecommunications between 1993 and 2000 than it did over the whole century following the invention of the telephone.[17] Services are about to see an explosion due to the development of digital technologies; the future belongs to "intelligent" or "personal communication" networks, able to transmit not just voice messages, but data and even images.

Since the production and transmission of information lie at the heart of all added value in the computer-age economy, mastery of the world communications network has emerged as a major political imperative. It was not by accident that the United States appointed Alfred Sykes president of the Federal Communications Commission (FCC) in 1989. Sykes made no secret of his objective: to maintain American leadership in this field by pushing for internal and external competition, innovation, deregulation and the opening of foreign markets.[18] Before Sykes's appointment to the FCC the Americans had been suspicious of free trade in this very sensitive sector: America was the only market that, lacking a state monopoly, was open to competition. American representatives at the GATT negotiations had therefore always refused to extend most favoured nation status to cover intercity and international telecommunications services. But in December 1991 Washington took the offensive: the GATT ruling was accepted on condition that the other countries concerned would agree to radical liberalization measures.

There are good reasons for the United States to feel confident. First, because America is the world's biggest telecommunications market. Next, because the process of deregulation and privatization has been so rapid, with Canada, Britain and Japan following the American example along with twenty or so other countries in Europe, Asia, Africa and Latin America. The national cartels are henceforth subject to competition from efficient global companies, forcing the state monopolies to become more open and international to avoid falling behind technologically.[19] Winning markets abroad has become a matter of life and death: it is the only way to meet the exorbitant cost of research, keep up with the speed of innovation and retain a strategic vantage point in the networks of transnational enterprises. In 1985, only five telecommunications companies were bought by foreign firms, for a total of $399 million. In 1990, there were sixty-seven such takeovers, involving a total of $16.5 billion;[20] in a market that, less than ten years earlier, had been divided into virtually hermetic compartments.

The front runners in this globalization race are three American companies – the giant AT&T, MCI and US Sprint – and two British ones – BT (British Telecom) and Cable & Wireless. AT&T – American Telegraph and Telephone – leads the pack. The second biggest group in the world (below the Japanese firm NTT and above BT), it has the stated objective of earning half its revenues abroad by the year 2000. Before its monopoly of the American telephone market was dismantled in 1984, it had no more than a hundred or so employees based outside the United States. Less than a decade later, after acquiring the computer maker NCR in 1991, it had over fifty thousand.[21] AT&T also possesses one of the most prestigious reseach centres on the planet, Bell Laboratories, and can boast the biggest R & D budget of the sector: $2.6 billion a year, far more than NTT, France Télécom or BT spend, and more than the entire research expenditure of a medium-sized industrial country like Belgium.

This enormous power pursues a strategy aiming to ensure a massive presence in three areas that will determine the course of the world telecommunications industry in the twenty-first century: expansion abroad; the marriage of computing with telecommunications in equipment and services; and mobile communications. In this battle of the titans AT&T is only the leader of a battalion of American companies, all of them determined to transform the United States into the central switchboard of a great planetary network.

Networks in Space

Taking part in international competititon may have become indispensable, but it is nonetheless an extremely costly adventure. Different technologies develop so quickly that it is often difficult to know which one to back. Big firms are therefore obliged to chase several hares at the same time, without any guarantees of success. To be sure of missing nothing they have to be present everywhere, especially in the markets with real growth potential. Hence the watchword: "Think globally, act locally." In 1992, American firms accordingly launched an all-out offensive on the former Communist countries, whose networks stand in urgent need of comprehensive renewal. When it bought the Telfa equipment factory in November 1992, AT&T was taking an option on 50 per cent of the Polish market; and it was already well placed to seize a good slice of the Russian market (through an agreement with Dalnya Sviaz-DALS), as well as those of Armenia and the Ukraine. Hughes Aircraft (a General Motors subsidiary) had secured a contract with Tatarstan to install the first large-scale telephone satellite link system.[22]

In fact the Americans, while maintaining a strong presence in fibre-optic "cable" technology, seem to be concentrating on the development of wireless satellite communications. Their lead in this sector is crushing; not only is its space industry the world's first and biggest, but the United States leads Japan, and everyone else, in VSAT (very small aperture terminal) technology to supply private companies with secure communication through orbiting satellites. The satellite/radio-telephone combination also represents the most dynamic market in the sector. The most practical solution for states with obsolete communications systems may well be to leapfrog more developed recent versions and jump directly into the twenty-first century. This is the case, for example, with the fast-growing economies of the Asia-Pacific region; South Korea, Thailand, Malaysia and Indonesia are racing to acquire communications satellites (all of which will be made by American firms, Hughes Aircraft in particular).[23] In Eastern Europe, Estonia and Hungary have already inaugurated mobile wireless telephone systems; Russia, the Czech Republic and Poland are working on theirs.

The American firms Motorola and AT&T have a solid technological lead in cellular telephone component manufacture. The market looks very promising, having grown from 5.3 million subscribers in 1989 to 13 million in 1991 (7 million in the US alone), with strong growth in Southeast Asia and Latin America.[24] The jackpot in this area is the "personal communicator", combining the functions of mobile telephone, fax, electronic mailbox and computer. These "third generation" systems are unlikely to be introduced before the end of the century. But intermediate systems using a network of low-altitude, non-geostationary LEO (low earth orbit) satellites have already been planned by Motorola and Loral Qualcomm as well as TRW, Ellipsat and AMS (belonging to McCaw, Hughes and MTEL). From a technical point of view, this projected system requires a very large number of LEOs in orbit, something that would favour countries like the United States with experience in making space hardware.

The American emphasis on mobile satellite communications is not at all to the taste of the European telecom companies, which have put their money on ground-based cellular systems. The battles over radio frequency allocations and the imposition of an international digital standard will therefore be decisive. Negotiations on these matters between the Americans, the Europeans and the Japanese were launched in 1991 and had not made progress by the end of 1992. It looked as if the United States was in no hurry to adopt rigid standards that might obstruct the development of new technologies by American firms. But at the world administrative conference on radio, which took place in Torremolinos in February and March 1992, Washington secured a sizeable victory. With massive support from Third World countries and from Russia, the conference approved the allocation of new frequencies for LEOs and for satellite communications in general. This decision was of the utmost importance: it represented the guarantee American firms demanded as a precondition for the large investments needed to perfect these technologies.[25]

The Americans have also sought to extend their advantage in the field of space telecommunications by exploiting the advance of deregulation. Hitherto, private companies wishing to offer a satellite communications service were dependent on the benevolence of the big multinational bodies Intelsat and Eutelsat, controlled by state-owned telephone companies. But Washington did not stop at deregulating the American internal market (a move promptly followed by the British): in November 1991, Alpha Lyracom – the first company in the world to run a private international satellite – was given permission to attack the high ground of international telephone communications. The target was to reach complete deregulation in five years, enabling private firms to launch and run their own satellites and to invest in private telephone networks for the use of big multi-national companies.[26] There is no need to point out that the size of the United States's internal market puts the Americans in a good position to impose any technical standards that they develop, or decide to adopt, on the rest of the world.

For the time being, the watchword is a simple one: flexibility. Europe in particular has been forced to count the cost of rigid attitudes. For example, the successful adoption of a European digital standard (GSM) for cellular radio-telephones, intended as a protectionist measure, has rebounded on its promoters to some extent. It is difficult, in practice, to keep communications segmented by region. So the European standard ended by favouring big companies with an eye on the world market, like Motorola and the Swedish firm Ericson, firms with the means and the flexibility to adapt to any and every standard.

Computing and telecommunications will be to World-America what paved roads once were to the Roman empire. American leaders, in any case, draw an explicit analogy between communication circuits and road networks. Just as all roads led to Rome, all the planet's information flows will one day pass through Washington. The United States nurtures the ambition to become the main switchboard of the entire world. And the field of operations stretches far beyond the terrestrial surface: space, too, is seen as a territory open to colonization, in which the computing superhighways of tomorrow are already under construction.

The main concern is not, however, to monitor the content of the messages that crackle across the earth's surface. That task would be pointless as well as titanic. Only strategists and the military have any interest in keeping secret certain information – very little of it at that – which is "sensitive" because it touches on American security or technological leadership. The real objective is the simpler one of maintaining a presence in places where information flows intersect, and thus having priority access to the information – for whatever it is worth – as well as some influence over its onward transmission.

Dominating the planet's brain and nervous system, while obviously necessary, is not sufficient in itself to ensure harmonious administration of the democratic empire. Road maintenance is one thing; guaranteeing the free flow of traffic is another. The day-to-day functioning of a rapidly integrating world depends increasingly on a handful of major strategic flows: energy, capital, images. Interruption of these exchanges, even on a local scale, could very quickly paralyse the whole activity of World-America.

11

CONTROLLING THE STRATEGIC
FLOWS

The United States was never quite like the other world powers. It is true that, being an essentially maritime state based primarily on control of main trade routes rather than on territorial conquest, it shares certain characteristics with Britain. But the Americans, unlike the British, have always had a profound aversion to the idea of personally running the institutions or social life of other peoples. The "empire of freedom" asks only for allegiance to its principles – respect for political, economic and personal freedoms – and to its role as ultimate decision-maker. Apart from that, everyone can organize as they choose in order to cut their own slice of the big cake of world economic development. Liberty, equality, competition!

The prosperity of World-America is largely unaffected by the variety of specific institutional forms it contains. Local disorders – even tragic and bloody ones – are of small importance as long as they pose no threat to the real foundation of this transnational system: the free circulation of people, money, goods and ideas. Maintaining the security of the main strategic flows has therefore always been central to White House foreign policy. At the dawn of the twenty-first century, three great currents of exchange constitute, so to speak, the veins and arteries of the democratic empire: the petroleum trade, cross-frontier capital movements, and circuits for the transmission of televised images.

PETROLEUM

American domination of the world oil market goes back to the very beginnings of the industry, in the latter half of the nineteenth century.

The United States at that time produced about 90 per cent of world output. Throughout the first half of the twentieth century, the "Seven Sisters" – the famous oil majors, Exxon, Shell, BP, Mobil, Chevron, Texaco and Gulf, five of them American – kept tight control over production and prices of the black gold, dictating the law of the market in their own interests. The picture altered in the 1960s with the appearance of the "independents" – European state firms and new American companies – and the increasing power of the OPEC oil-producing countries. At the beginning of the 1990s, however, fourteen of the world's twenty leading petroleum companies were still based in America.[1]

Neutralizing OPEC

The two great oil shocks of the 1970s caused deep turmoil in the market. They also exposed the utter dependence of industrialized countries on what had become their main source of energy. Since the beginning of the 1980s, therefore, control of oil prices and security of supply arrangements have emerged as central strategic issues. Despite efforts to conserve energy and proliferating new sources of crude petroleum, Europe and Japan – and to a lesser extent the United States – remain seriously dependent on Middle Eastern supplies, a situation likely to worsen until at least the turn of the century. Part of the problem is that exporting countries like Mexico, Indonesia and China are themselves undergoing very rapid economic growth, thus consuming a larger proportion of their own oil output. This reduces the quantities of non-OPEC crude available to the world market.

Since the end of the Cold War, American companies and the American government have had one declared objective: to regain control of crude oil prices and production flows. The administration led by George Bush, a naturalized Texan and former oilman, was very receptive indeed to the arguments of petroleum lobbies. At the dawn of the twenty-first century, they aim to re-establish American authority over oil movements in the Middle East, and to buy up prospecting rights and unexploited reserves in the rest of the world, especially on petroleum's "last frontier", the former Soviet Union. Once again the traditional – and atypical – collaboration between the federal state and a particular industry is expected to work wonders.

Operation Desert Storm, mounted by the White House to rescue Kuwait, did not have the recovery of control over the region's oil resources as an explicit objective. The outcome was nevertheless spectacular: the American president's show of force enthroned him as honorary de facto president of OPEC. By intervening massively and in person, America made itself the sole guarantor of security for the Gulf monarchies: an essential role, since the preservation of Saddam Hussein's regime in Baghdad poses a continuing potential threat to the whole region. Saudi Arabia's immense reserves give it control over the volume – and thus the price – of OPEC oil reaching the market. But the very survival of the Saudi regime has become even more dependent on American protection; and it is therefore unlikely that Riyadh will take any initiative that would seriously displease the White House. Washington has another powerful means of persuasion: the power to decide whether or not to lift the embargo on Iraqi crude. Thus the whole delicate balance of quotas within OPEC is at the mercy of an American decision.

The Rush into Russia

American companies are also at the forefront of the search for new reserves all over the world. In 1989, their investments in oil exploration abroad overtook those made inside America for the first time. By 1992 the five biggest American groups were making nearly two-thirds of their investments abroad, from Colombia to Yemen.[2] This wish to ensure an American presence in the world's main production areas was exposed in 1991–92 during the NAFTA negotiations. Using pressures that sometimes strayed outside normal diplomatic practice, Washington persuaded Mexico to accept a significant loosening of the regulations governing oil exploration, and refinery and distribution operations, on Mexican territory.

The biggest prize remains, however, the right to develop oilfields in the former Soviet Union, which contains the world's biggest reserves after those of the Middle East. The White House listed this as one of its primary objectives on the eve of the July 1991 London summit of G7 (the seven most industrialized countries); the aim of integrating the Soviet and Eastern European energy sectors into the world market was to be "actively pursued".[3] Chevron's acquisition of exploration rights over the immense deposits at Tengiz and Korolev in Kazakhstan, in May 1992, epitomizes the American stampede for the former Soviet Union's black gold. The contract – which allocates a swingeing 80 per cent of future profits to the San Francisco-based company[4] – also constitutes a perfect example of collaboration between a business and the White House: James Baker, who was secretary of state at the time, made no attempt to dissimulate his lobbying intentions when dealing with the authorities in Alma-Ata. What with Amoco in Azerbaijan, the Stan Cornelius Consortium in

Uzbekistan, Marathon Oil and McDermott in Sakhalin, Pennzoil in Tyumen, Conoco, Texaco and Occidental Petroleum in the Komi Republic and Phibro Energy and Anglo-Suisse in Siberia, the presence of American companies in the former "Evil Empire" overshadows the handful of French, British and Italian successes.[5]

So at the close of the twentieth century, the American petroleum industry seems to be recovering its former splendour. And it is difficult to identify anyone – private company or government – capable of challenging its dominant position. Especially now that American oilmen are already preparing for the future, encouraged by new American environmental legislation, with heavy investment in natural gas and the clean energy sources of tomorrow. One sign of the times was the public complaint made by France in July 1991 that the New York Mercantile Exchange had a near monopoly of futures contracts for crude petroleum: 80 per cent of all transactions.[6] The United States may still only aspire to control the key points of the world economy's brain and nervous system, but it is already master of the arteries and veins that carry its sticky black lifeblood.

MOVEMENTS OF CAPITAL

America is also pre-eminent in the domain of financial flows, although here the competition is more vigorous than in the petroleum industry. The American capital market nevertheless remains the biggest and most sophisticated on the planet. At least half the transactions on the world currency market are made in dollars, and three-quarters of international credits are payable in American currency. But the New York and Chicago stock exchanges and brokers, as well as the large US regional banks, are condemned to perpetual innovatory effort to keep ahead of the pack which, led by the dynamic City of London, bays at their heels. In January 1992 William Donaldson, president of the New York Stock Exchange, chose the Manhattan pit's bicentenary celebrations to make a clear statement of its ambition "to become the central floor of the world stock market".[7]

Financial Syndicates

Mastering the accelerated globalization of capital movements will be one of the most important economic and political issues of the early twenty-first century. Whoever secures a dominant position in this area will have a hold on the very sinews of the world economy. The sums involved are so gigantic that they are outside the control of even the most powerful states.

In June 1992, when the foreign exchange reserves of the planet's seven main industrial countries totalled $350 billion, the ten biggest British banks alone were trading $20 billion *each day*, and the world foreign exchange market was handling something like $1,000 billion a day.[8]

The internationalization of production processes and the extremely rapid progress of computing and telecommunications, added to the wave of deregulation that took place during the 1980s, lie behind the new world financial market and the irresistible advance towards round-the-clock, 365-day stock transactions. Increasingly powerful companies need a financial infrastructure that enables them to raise funds throughout the world. They see this as an essential tool for mergers or cooperation with foreign competitors, for acquiring firms based outside the national frontiers, for supervision and protection of their multinational investments. They also need markets with extensive liquidity, served by efficient, fast-moving establishments with imposing financial capacity.

The money war is now raging. It is giving rise to technological innovation in the big stock market information networks, to new and increasingly sophisticated financial products. In this struggle there are two sectors that play strategic roles: global issues of shares or bonds, and the financial instruments known as derivatives (options, "swap" contracts and futures). In the first of these, investment or merchant banks compete for the fabulously profitable privilege of representing big firms who wish to raise loans or issue shares on the international market. The second is linked to the competition between the world's bigger stock markets to attract the largest possible volume of transactions.

The explosion in global issues of securities was caused by international firms' need for capital, and by the wave of state company privatizations in Britain and the Third World. Such issues totalled $15 billion during the first half of 1992, compared to $8 billion for the whole of 1990. General Motors supplies a convenient example of this financial globalization: in May 1992, the Detroit vehicle giant raised $2.1 billion by selling 40 million shares in the United States, 6 million in Britain, 4.5 million in the rest of Europe and the same number in the Far East.[9] This type of international financing seems likely to increase throughout the 1990s, for the privatization of major public enterprises is expected to continue in Latin America, Southeast Asia and even Europe.

Operations of this kind are usually administered by a syndicate of financial establishments, one of which performs the role of supervisor. Obtaining the mandate of "global coordinator" in juicy operations like the share issues of the 1980s has thus become a basic instrument of growth for the big merchant banks and, by the same token, a factor in their great power as the twenty-first century dawns. The Americans are getting the lion's share of this too, far more than the British. The Japanese have lurched from one setback to another in a field where great cultural flexibility is needed to capture clients from an enormous variety of investment traditions.

Apart from its adaptable, fast-moving operators, the United States benefits from the raw strength of its domestic financial market. Foreign companies, governments, even supranational organizations like the World Bank look to America first when it comes to long-term financing; for the amount of investment capital is far larger in the US than anywhere else, and the American saver is known to fancy foreign paper.[10] Besides, a very large number of American firms, having taken the gamble of internationalizing themselves, seem to be permanently in pursuit of global capital. Financial coordinators based in the United States thus usually have the considerable advantage of playing on home ground. Especially as the regulatory authorities have shown themselves to be pretty understanding. To give a leg-up to the national financial establishments, the Securities and Exchange Commission (SEC) even went so far as to depart from the sacrosanct rules of disclosure that apply to the internal market. Regulation 144A, for example, has the effect of allowing foreign firms, when selling shares to US institutional investors, to make only such disclosures as are required by law in their country of origin.

The Derivatives Boom

Derivative financial products helped initiate what amounts to a revolution in the world capital market. They are a sort of abstract futures contract on stock indices, currency or interest rates and so on, and attract larger funds than the concrete products on which they are based (shares, currencies). They have the added advantage that they are often much more liquid (that is, easily and rapidly negotiable). In 1992, when the stock-market capitalization of all the shares in the world was worth around $9,000 billion, derivative products were worth $10,000 billion. In 1987, the over-the-counter derivatives market – electronic quotations made outside the regulations of the traditional stock exchanges – was worth $866 billion. By 1992 it had reached $4,300 billion.[11]

These products also play a leading role in the process of permanent innovation in the markets. The sophisticated techniques devised in the course of their development – most notably, "swaps" on exchange rates

– are spreading rapidly into other segments of the financial market: shares, goods, even insurance. So much so that the classic stock exchanges are starting to adapt their contracts to suit the needs of derivatives operators. For example, the New York Mercantile Exchange (NYMEX) in 1992 invented a crude petroleum futures contract conceived specially to attract capital from over-the-counter traders.

By the beginning of the 1990s derivatives were the most profitable, dynamic and innovative sector of the entire world finance market. The internationalization of company strategies can only favour this pivotal role in the planetary circulation of capital. Confronted with the increasing volatility of a globalized market, big companies are more or less compelled to resort to derivatives to protect their foreign investments and reduce their exposure to currency fluctuations. For the main function of derivative products, surely, is to determine costs and revenue flows in advance, thus sheltering the companies from any nasty political or business surprises.

The United States still has a lead in this sector despite stiff competition from the European markets, London in particular. Indeed, the City can boast that it is the main marketplace in the currency sector, with a third of the world market. The Chicago Board of Trade (CBOT) and the Chicago Mercantile Exchange (CME) – the inventors of share options and currency futures in 1973 – still had 40 per cent of the total world market for futures contracts in 1992. Only two years earlier, however, their share had been nearly 70 per cent.[12] Although the volumes traded in the two American exchanges are growing at a substantial rate, the main beneficiaries of the explosion in this type of product have been the LIFFE in London, the MATIF in Paris and the Terminbörse (DTB) in Frankfurt.

The CBOT, the CME and their cousin the CBOE (Chicago Board Option Exchange, the world's main options market) have one permanent and insoluble handicap: they are physically situated in a time zone that is out of step with the rest of the world's stock market "day". So that to stay ahead of the competition, they have had to call on their talent for technological innovation. In June 1992, the two Chicago giants accordingly launched Globex, an electronic, round-the-clock, over-the-counter market operating on a world scale. It is still unclear how successful this system will be in attracting investors, but the stakes are so high that by the end of 1992 MATIF had already joined Globex, and the LIFFE and DTB were negotiating to do so. Despite CBOT's second thoughts about Globex, there is certainly a risk in being excluded from a market quotation system launched by institutions that handle nearly half of a $10,000 billion market.

The CBOT and CME know perfectly well that they will not be able to recover their former monopoly. But the limited creativity of their Japanese counterparts and the fragmentation of the Europeans (who would rather fight over leadership of the Old World than compete with the American giant) help compensate for their geographical disadvantage. The Chicago exchanges – like the big American investment banks – have a strategy based on promoting networks of cooperation with their foreign competitors. The resulting arrangements place them almost automatically in a leadership role.

This vision is shared by the whole American financial community, starting with the Wall Street traders who, after the October 1987 market crash, engaged in a much-trumpeted modernization and rationalization of their business. They were so successful that in 1992 they celebrated not only the recovery of their position as world leaders, but the best year's profits in their history. The American bankers, whose mega-mergers in 1991 gave them the means to restructure their sector in depth and return them to profit by the end of 1992, recovered their confidence too; they went on to attack the archaic banking laws dating from Jefferson's presidency in the nineteenth century and the Glass-Steagall Act of 1933. "It's a question of making American banks competitive again in the outside world," explained BankAmerica president Richard Rosenberg in August 1991 during the merger of his establishment with Security Pacific, at that time the most important in American banking history.[13] There is not much doubt that the Americans hold the biggest option on leadership of the financial markets of the twenty-first century.

WORLDWIDE IMAGES

The globalization of images is an essential component of the triumph of World-America. The spectacular performance of CNN during the Gulf War in 1991 underlined the importance of a medium supplying live news to all the planet's political and economic leaders. Through CNN, the authorities throughout the world, and the general public, simultaneously receive the same live news and thus the same emotional spin. But this instantaneous, ubiquitous image diffusion is not limited to the news. Along with straightforward information journalism, other images – cinema, soap operas, sports, game shows – are being universalized at record speed. Independently of cultural differences, everyone's dreams, aspirations, feelings and anxieties are being integrated in a vast transnational audio-visual network. Control of images – news and fiction – is indisputably one of the principal stakes of the early twenty-first century.

The Hollywood Monopoly

There is no point in trying to be subtle: in this domain, United States dominance is quite simply overwhelming. America's audio-visual industry is not just more financially solid, technologically advanced and better diversified than any other; it also dominates a domestic market that accounts for nearly half the world market, and from which foreign competitors have great difficulty extracting 1 per cent of the receipts.[14] Thanks to this extraordinary backyard, which enables production costs to be amortized before exports even begin, the Americans enjoy a position of de facto world oligopoly. Depending on the country concerned, they pocket between 50 and 85 per cent of local box-office takings and between 80 and 90 per cent of the video market. The spectacular result is that the film industry is the second most important American exporter (after civil aircraft manufacturing), and 40 per cent of its sales are made abroad.[15] Of all the cinema and television images viewed each day by the planet's inhabitants, three-quarters are "made in USA".

Since the late 1980s the image industry has been thrown into turmoil by the generalization of new technologies like cable, satellites, video, pay-TV and interactive television. Hitherto, cinema had been a highly specific economic activity carrying enormous financial risks and no advance guarantee of success. Although analogous constraints are still present, the multiplication of sources of finance and outlets for the product has made it possible to adopt more classical management procedures: revenue forecasts, cost control, diversification of investors, intensive marketing, spreading the risk. But the revolution that overturned the economy of this sector favoured the seven biggest American production companies – the majors – owing to their solid financial backing. They alone are in a position to supply the national and international markets with a steady flow of saleable products. The crisis of the 1960s (caused by competition from TV) and the deregulation of television under the Reagan adminis-tration both accentuated the phenomenon of industrial concentration: the majors were eventually absorbed by enormous American or foreign conglomerates with interests in other industries and services. In buying Columbia Pictures from Coca-Cola in 1989 the Japanese electronics firm Sony was following the same strategy as Gulf and Western with Paramount, Rupert Murdoch with Fox and Matsushita with MCA-Universal. By the early 1990s the globalization of the American image industry was well advanced.[16]

The anguished nationalistic cries that greeted the arrival of the

Japanese in Hollywood soon died down. To make products that earn money on the world market, the film industry continues to depend on specific forms of creativity and know-how, practices in which the Americans effectively reign supreme. If there was ever a software-dominated sector, this is it. So we may have to wait a while for the pleasure of watching a Japanese Rambo butcher stupid, brutish white troops with a bazooka. In practice, foreign capital simply gives the majors more clout and helps tighten their control over the production of images. And the gaps between the majors are filled by very active and dynamic American independent producers, competing for the specialized niche markets (horror films, minority films and so on). The picture is one of a near-invincible American armada controlling the seaways and inlets of the world audio-visual network.

It goes without saying that American producers are best placed to take advantage of the rapid internationalization of image diffusion. Although they compete ferociously for shares of the domestic market, they have little hesitation in forming alliances to conquer markets abroad. As the twenty-first century dawns, it is Europe that lies at the heart of their expansion strategy. The European Union in particular represents nearly half the majors' box-office takings outside the United States. But the market does not stop there: the modernization of television infrastructures in the Old World is creating an appetite for programmes that the European industry may have trouble satisfying. The import quotas and programming policies applied by the Europeans have merely aroused the commercial aggressiveness of American producers who, since the late 1980s, have been wriggling through holes in the protectionist fence using a series of astute expedients: minority co-productions, producing films in Europe (in Britain especially) and taking massive shareholdings in local production and broadcasting companies.[17] At the same time, since the collapse of the Soviet empire, American companies have plunged into co-productions and joint ventures with the new Eastern European producers. That is a market no one can ignore, with 3.64 billion cinema tickets sold each year in the former Soviet Union alone.[18]

The American image industry's dominance of production and diffusion has not lulled it into neglecting the hardware. A new technology, high definition television (HDTV), could upset the market once more at the end of the century. Japanese and European equipment makers rushed into development of two different HDTV standards (MUSE and Mac respectively), but America chose to await a breakthrough to something more advanced. The FCC president, Alfred Sykes, accordingly persuaded the commission to delay its decision on an HDTV standard for the internal United States market. The idea was to give American firms a chance to develop a standard that would be more modern than their foreign competitors' efforts.

The FCC knew that time was on its side: it was going to take until 2000 at least to develop wide flat screens and HDTV-compatible sets that could be sold at mass-market prices. By early 1993 it looked as if Alfred Sykes – about to retire after years of faithful and capable service – had won his bet: American companies had made giant strides towards perfecting an all-digital standard (which would also, incidentally, be vastly superior for the multimedia integration of computers and images). At a stroke, this made hybrid analogue-digital standards like MUSE and Mac seem terribly out of date. The Japanese withdrew voluntarily from the competition and decided to go along with whatever standard the FCC eventually approved; and the Europeans had to shelve their Mac system. Since the United States has the planet's biggest audio-visual market and is the biggest producer of programmes, it is hard to imagine the rest of the world holding out indefinitely against adoption of the American digital standard.[19]

The American fiction oligopoly has a good few fat decades ahead of it. Only a couple of big Latin American organizations, which in any case are more partners than competitors, are managing to keep up with the Americans in this race for a globalized image. The television mega-networks Globo (Brazil) and Televisa (Mexico) have both managed to conceive and sell universal programmes. Indeed, Televisa can even boast of having captured the lion's share of the internal US Hispanic market. The Mexican giant, which faces fierce competition in its own domestic market, makes no secret of its global ambitions. Thus, in early 1993, it snapped up 50 per cent of the capital of the American firm PanAmSat, one of the few operators of a private satellite for TV transmissions. The existing satellite, it is true, only covers the Atlantic region, but PanAmSat planned to launch three more satellites to cover the rest of the world by 1996.[20] In 1995 Televisa took the decisive step of starting production of programmes in English for the world market.

The CNN Empire

In the smaller, but strategic, domain of news and current affairs, the international breakthrough by CNN launched another race for globalization. Poor sport, however, owing to the runners' gross inequality: Japan and Europe lack the means to invade the American airwaves, while their own territories have become the principal battlefields of the world audio-visual industry. It looks as if the Asian and European markets, increasingly saturated with cables, satellites and dish aerials, are going to be the fastest growing in the last decade of the century. The Atlanta-based CNN, half of whose 50 million viewers lived in the Old World, made no secret of its plans to double its foreign audience before the end of 1993.

In October 1991, CNN beefed up its presence in Asia through an agreement with the Japanese network Asahi TV, which agreed to pay $40 million for the right to transmit the American firm's output. At the same time, to widen its audience (still thought to be too concentrated in Korea and Japan), the Atlanta firm was negotiating with the Jakarta government to hire channels on an Indonesian satellite. There was only one adversary able seriously to resist this offensive: another English-speaking network, the BBC. The grand old lady of Portland Place decided to hang on to her share – which she put at 5 per cent – of the 170 million anglophone Asians. The BBC hoped to ensure exposure for its World Service Television through an alliance with the Hong Kong firm HutchVision, which already owned a satellite network (STAR TV, music and sports) and a one-third interest in AsiaSat 1, a superb device covering a potential market of 2.7 billion television viewers, from China to Indonesia and from Japan to Turkey.[21]

The fact that this battle between the BBC and CNN for the news market in Asia is being fought over the ruins of a great Japanese project merely underlines the power of English-language news and current affairs. The Gulf War was a very serious shock to Japanese broadcasters. Lacking American resources and know-how, the archipelago's networks had to be content with rebroadcasting footage shot by CNN, ABC or CBS. "CNN is trying to impose American-style news on the rest of the world," complained the president of the biggest Japanese network, NHK. The response to the challenge would be made by GNN (Global News Network): a network producing non-stop news from an "Asian perspective", based in New York and broadcasting in English, with powerful but discreet Japanese participation. The dream started to collapse in December 1991. None of Japan's Asian neighbours had much enthusiasm for the idea of an Asian world-view promoted by the Japanese. And the Western partners indispensable to a project on this scale – $778 million a year in investments – had their own reservations about Japanese-style journalism, thought to be too influenced by the economic and political powers of the archipelago.[22]

The CNN monopoly of international live reporting is often seen as an intolerable attempt to impose the American world-view on everyone. As the Japanese GNN disaster shows, however, it is pretty well impossible to sell the whole planet any national or regional perspective on current affairs. The English-speaking media, with their individualist outlook and overtly independent posture vis-à-vis the powers that be, do not claim to express any specific culture, American or other. On the contrary, they regard themselves as a universal service based on values that can apply to all humanity: human rights, freedom of expression, political liberties, free enterprise and trade; Good as opposed to Evil. American culture, as we have seen, consists essentially of exalting the individual and the individual's participation in universal passions, regardless of his or her origins. CNN, even in its coverage of events in the US, insists on reporting purely individual stories and clings to its role as part of an independent fourth estate. George Bush discovered this to his cost. Would any Japanese, German or French presenter have dared ask his president or prime minister, during an electoral campaign and on live worldwide TV, to answer questions on his alleged extra-marital relationships?

This tension between American universalism and specific concepts of news coverage weighs heavily on the experimental European global news network. Euronews, which started broadcasting out of Lyons on 1 January 1992 in English, French, German, Italian and Spanish, purported to inform the European public from a European angle. The project seemed something of a gamble in an Old World notoriously crotchety about its particularisms. Moreover the bosses of Euronews were public service channels, cautious by definition on governmental issues.

At the beginning of 1993, a year after its launch, only the southern European countries, along with Belgium, Finland, Cyprus and Egypt, had put capital into the new venture. But how could it stand up to the BBC or CNN without the support of the British, the Germans and the bigger Scandinavian countries? Quite apart from the fact that Euronews, capitalized at under $5.5 million, lacked the means to provide comprehensive permanent live coverage of Europe, let alone the world.[23] It is an absolute law of television news that even analysis of the highest quality cannot compete with the emotional impact of live footage. In any case, CNN is busily exploiting this area of European weakness. In December 1992, the Atlanta firm took a 27.5 per cent shareholding in the new German news network N-TV, which was to relay CNN footage. Of course, anyone with a solid presence on German screens is well placed to gain market share throughout Europe.

Military leadership, promotion of democracy and the fight to open markets: these are the three elements essential to the expansion of World-America. The end of the Cold War has not cast any doubt on this conception of power; at best, it has placed more emphasis on the economic variable. "My international economic and trade strategy will guarantee our position as an export superpower, extending our global economic reach in tandem with our security presence," proclaimed George Bush in September 1992.[24] Bill Clinton went somewhat further: "Our economic strength must become a central defining element of our national security policy."[25]

The Cold War veteran and the baby boomer had at least one common objective: integration of the world's economies, centred around the American economy, to create a vast world market that would be a source of prosperity for everyone. American management alone has the capacity to lead humanity towards this single universal and democratic market. The struggle against protectionism, against the division of the world into competing economic blocs, is thus of primary importance; as is the definition of rules for international trade. An institutionalized, universally accepted juridical and political framework is essential to prevent distortions and unfair competition that might lead to new economic confrontations (direct military clashes having become less likely).

"If individual liberty, political pluralism and free enterprise take root in Latin America, Eastern and Central Europe, Africa, Asia and the former Soviet Union," predicted Bill Clinton, "we can look forward to a grand new era of reduced conflict, mutual understanding and economic growth."[26] For the president of the United States – and for his predecessor – what really mattered was the extension to the rest of the world of the American model: free trade in a market economy driven by entrepreneur-innovators seeking personal profit, the only model thought capable of ensuring happiness and prosperity for all humanity. In this battle to consolidate the democratic empire, free trade plays a determining role.

12

ORGANIZING PLANETARY TRADE

Computer networks, instantaneous communications, the growing de-centralization of enterprises, the speed with which capital and images are moved about: these things have turned the conditions of world trade upside down in a very short space of time. The development of new products and the internationalization of production processes have increased the pressure to dismantle customs tariffs and other national barriers to the great flows of goods and services.

Throughout the second half of the twentieth century, world industrial cycles have tended to follow the same logic: as more profitable activities with greater added value have arisen in the rich countries, the older, mature industries – textiles, steel, shipbuilding and so on – have been passed on, first to "intermediate" economies, then to poor countries.[1] The economic interdependence created by this world redistribution of production according to profitability has greatly stimulated international trade.

Since the 1980s the machine has been running at full speed. The manufacturing processes themselves have started being globalized within each industry, especially in the more advanced sectors. We have seen for example that in the case of computers, the advanced countries reserve for themselves the stages of production with the highest added value (like software and systems architecture), and subcontract the other phases (assembly and memory chips) to poorer countries able to provide cheap labour. The result is a planetary production network whose prosperity depends on the removal of all obstacles to free trade.

This globalization of trade also engenders a specific dynamic of its own: to be competitive, a product now has to be aimed at the entire world market. To be comfortably placed in a national market – even one as large as America's – or a single region – even a rich one like Europe – is no longer enough to guarantee survival, especially in the industries of the future (telecommunications, computing, television, environmental industries and so on).

MUSCULAR FREE TRADE

America's claim to the status of economic hub of the world depends on its capacity to manage this process of transition to an economically integrated planet equipped with clear working rules observed by all. As in a number of earlier periods of their history, the Americans are putting their faith in the openness and dynamism of the latest frontier awaiting conquest.

Breaking up the Economic Blocs

When the Cold War finally ended, there seemed every chance that the world economy might fragment into competing blocs. "Euro-optimism" reached its peak at about the same time as the fall of the Berlin wall. With the enlarged single market scheduled for 1993, Western Europe – delivered at last from the permanent threat of the Red Army – was already seeing itself as a new economic superpower. The economy, everyone thought, was going to be the main factor in establishing the hierarchy of power in the next century. European Union (EU) leaders started adopting a bossy tone towards the other two heavyweights, the United States and Japan. Warnings from Tokyo and Washington against the construction of a "fortress Europe" were even perceived as an inverted tribute to the Old World's revived dynamism.

This view of the world is, of course, diametrically opposed to the growing globalization of economic and political power; in fact, it tends to revive the old concept of an international society ruled by the balance of powers. It is easy to see why Japan also found it seductive. The major phase of Japanese economic expansion had peaked, more or less, by the late 1980s. The crisis deepened after 1991, but had still not been officially acknowledged. With a touch of verbal arrogance, Japanese industrialists and politicians dropped their usual reserve, and began predicting an American decline and the emergence of a new world power centre in the Asia-Pacific region. In Paris and Bonn, as well as in Tokyo, it was thought inevitable that three large blocs would appear, each doomed to gird its loins for a great economic confrontation with the other two.

These yearnings for independence – for which the allies can hardly be blamed after decades of enforced subservience to White House leadership – became apparent at a moment when the United States itself was undergoing a rare crisis of confidence. The American economy was entering a period of slowdown, soon to evolve into one of the sharpest recessions since the 1950s. The disappearance of the Soviet adversary had left Washington's foreign-policy makers in some disarray. Without the familiar point of reference that Moscow had become, what could America's primacy be based on now? The prophets of doom were already digging a grave for the "American century"; economic and political decline would lead to general loss of authority. What was coming was a terrifying new world of unending trade wars, all against all, like crabs in a barrel.

In the event, the Bush administration reacted to the danger with quite astounding vigour and opportunist skill. The Bush-Baker duo can claim, more or less, to have established the necessary instruments for modernizing and extending the international economic institutions set up under the aegis of the United States after the Second World War. The former president summarized his strategy clearly in a speech delivered to the Detroit Economic Club on 10 September 1992. His first objective was to increase the power of the American economy by setting up an enlarged North American free market centred on the United States. The next stage was to "develop a strategic network of free trade agreements"[2] with the whole of Latin America, the countries of Southeast Asia and the former Communist countries of Eastern Europe. This network would eventually be powerful enough to "reduce internal barriers to competition . . . in *North America*, Western Europe, Japan, and elsewhere".[3] The new rules governing the globalization of exchanges would have to be established while all this was going on. In addition, the White House wanted a swift conclusion to the multilateral GATT negotiations, and was lobbying for the adoption of new criteria for management of development aid.

NAFTA: An Enlarged North American Market

NAFTA – the free trade treaty between Canada, the United States and Mexico – remains the Bush administration's major achievement. NAFTA represents the first attempt at instituting freedom of trade between industrialized and developing countries. A large trade zone with 360 million potential consumers and a combined GNP of $8,000 billion, NAFTA forms the biggest solvent homogeneous market on the planet. The European area (the EU plus EFTA) may be comparable in total GNP, but it is far from homogeneous: the same product is sold differently in different countries. Asia's heterogeneity is even more marked.

The North American market will not be a sort of new EEC, a conglomerate of disparate economic zones two or three centuries old with different, often contradictory, regulations and traditions. The crushing weight of the United States – which generates 87 per cent of the total GNP – means that, in reality, the other two countries are being integrated into the American economy, to be subjected eventually to American standards and practices. In the long run, however, according to an independent survey published in February 1993 by a federal agency (the International Trade Commission), the Mexicans stand to gain most from NAFTA. In the long run, the Mexican GNP, for example, is expected to grow at a maximum annual rate of 11.4 per cent in constant value, against just 0.5 per cent for the US and Canada. The difference in the growth of wages is just as marked: a maximum rate of 16.2 per cent a year for Mexican workers, against 0.3 per cent for Americans and 0.5 per cent for Canadians.[4] Lawrence Eagleburger, George Bush's last secretary of state, saw all of this as a way to "consolidate our nation's continental base . . . as well as benefit the economies of all three nations".[5]

President Bush might have been predestined to carry out this new enlargement of the American economic zone: during his business career in the Texas oil industry he had had a great deal of contact with Mexican society, which he liked and had come to know well. He had even named his company Zapata Petroleum. NAFTA is a genuinely revolutionary development in relations between the North and South banks of the Rio Grande, and oil inevitably played an important part in the negotiations. Apart from opening up the service sector, Mexico had to agree to a partial opening of its petroleum industry to American capital. Thus, the price of free access to its northern neighbour's huge market was a partial sacrifice of Mexico's biggest sacred cow: national ownership of its petroleum, first decreed in 1938.

Washington, it is true, also had to make some concessions. It is not going to be easy for fruit, vegetable and sugar growers, or for some segments of American labour in the automobile, textile and electrical goods industries, to compete with their Mexican equivalents. So that, whatever is done to reduce the violence of this period of economic transition, some regions of the United States are certain to be sacrificed, at least in the short term, to ensure the overall prosperity of the new North American grouping. NAFTA therefore represents a crucial moment in the organization of World-America: it is unusual for an American president to make an overt frontal attack on powerful national interests on behalf of a larger project extending well outside the political and economic setting of the American nation alone. The treaty with Canada and Mexico is a clear indication of the presidency's increased autonomy in relation to the political institutions and national lobbies. George Bush's own statements confirmed this wish to internationalize the scope of the Washington government: he saw the enlarged North American market as a necessary stage in the creation of a greater world market. NAFTA, he explained, should "further strengthen our position" as "the largest fully integrated market in the world". He added: " . . . my intent is to use our attractive domestic market as the basis of a muscular free trade policy that will strengthen America's global economic reach and complement our world-wide security presence."[6]

A LEVER TO OPEN UP THE WORLD

Most of the trade agreements signed under the NAFTA umbrella conform to the GATT regulations stipulating that a regional free trade zone should not raise new barriers against external partners. The White House believed that the economic integration of North America should serve as a "lever" to force the rest of the world to open itself to freedom of trade, and should not in any case result in a "fortress America". Long before the treaty was signed on 17 December 1992, George Bush had stated clearly that NAFTA was only a first step towards the creation of a free trade system stretching from Alaska to Tierra del Fuego.

The Great Alliance from Alaska to Tierra del Fuego

In June 1990, a few weeks after the start of negotiations with Mexico and Canada, Bush launched his Enterprise for the Americas Initiative (EAI). Open to all democratic states south of the Rio Grande, the EAI aimed to promote economic and political reform and dismantle trade barriers throughout the American hemisphere. To this end, the project was supposed to mount a direct attack on three crucial problems: trade, investment and debt. To stimulate trade, it was thought useful to begin by signing framework agreements setting out the principles that ought to regulate commerce and investment and establishing a basis for regular consultations. Eventually, these were to result in bilateral free trade agreements with the United States; investment policies giving priority to privatization and reforms to strengthen the market economy; and – last but not least – reducing the debts of countries making a firm commitment to the new way of thinking.

Such was the sheer, ambitious scale of this White House initiative that a very unusual tide of approval and hope swept through Latin America. Virtually every state in the region had already signed a preliminary outline agreement by the beginning of 1993. Better still, the first agreement of this type with a regional grouping – Mercosur: Brazil, Argentina, Uruguay and Paraguay – was signed as early as 19 June 1991. Meanwhile several Latin American states were citing the provisions of the "Brady plan" to negotiate a reduction in their debt service requirement.

The EAI had the immediate effect of starting a race to liberalize markets and set up free trade zones in Central and South America. The prospect of eventually gaining free access to the great North American market induced a number of states in the region to launch themselves into radical economic reforms at a gallop: reduction of price controls, subsidies, regulation and public deficits; openness to foreign investment; downsizing the role of the state. Development strategies based on import substitution and protectionism, which in some countries had been in place since the 1950s, were dropped to make way for more open economies.

Mercosur and other regional economic organizations (like the Andean Pact and Caricom) have been encouraged to accelerate their own march towards free trade. Mexico has taken on the function of a sort of airlock between NAFTA and the southern continent. After signing a free trade agreement with Chile in 1991, in August 1992 the Mexicans reached agreement with their five Central American neighbours on the creation of a free trade zone by 1996. In 1994, they signed free trade agreements with Colombia and Venezuela (creating the "Group of Three"), and with Bolivia. But this sea change in Latin American economic policy, which amounts to a revolution, remains contingent on Washington's ability to keep its promises by opening up the vast American internal market. Bill Clinton's hard struggle to get the NAFTA treaty ratified by Congress in November 1994, and the opening of negotiations over Chile's membership, were reassuring to leaders south of the Rio Grande. The summit meeting of the Americas in Miami a month later brought together all the countries of the American hemisphere (except Cuba), and took the new step of deciding to create a continental free trade zone before 2005. There are many obstacles; but the common support for emergency aid to Mexico during the January 1995 peso crisis, from both the Democrat president and the Republican Speaker of the House, further strengthened this vast process of integration.

Meanwhile, the Bush and Clinton administrations have succeeded, in less than four years, in promoting the biggest inter-American rapprochement since Kennedy initiated his Alliance for Progress in the 1960s. Washington has acquired the means to consolidate a rear base for World-America extending well beyond North America: 600 million potential consumers and a combined GNP of $9,500 billion. The White House waxed lyrical over the potential benefits of the attempt to integrate the hemisphere: "The American republics stand poised as never before to create an unprecedented partnership of developed and developing nations to secure democracy, promote prosperity, and join together to confront the new challenges of the post-Cold War era."[7]

Anxieties in Asia-Pacific

From Washington's point of view, NAFTA, the EAI and the Miami process are just an instrument – a crowbar – for promoting free trade across the whole planet. Before it was even in place, this instrument had shown itself to be highly effective, especially where the East Asian countries were concerned. These states were already disturbed by the blockage of the GATT multilateral trade negotiations and the threatened appearance of a "fortress Europe"; now they were looking at an enlarged North American market that might succumb to runaway protectionism. But freedom of trade and, above all, access to the American market are absolutely indispensable to the economy of a region which depends heavily on its exports. Asian politicians and industrialists are aware that the United States alone absorbs somewhere between 13 and 32 per cent of their foreign sales.[8]

Fears in the Asia-Pacific states that the world might separate into mutually hostile commercial citadels also applied to investment flows: it was assumed that Mexico's privileged access to the American market would attract investors and multinational companies to set up shop on the south bank of the Rio Grande, at the expense of the Asian "dragons". Savings due to geographical proximity could, it was thought, easily cover the difference between Asian and Mexican wage levels. Not to mention the cultural advantages: American firms have more contacts and feel much more at home with their Hispanic neighbours. The Chinese expatriate communities, which are in fact the motor of the Southeast Asian economies, felt particularly threatened. Working essentially through the family and clan networks that give them such freedom and business agility anywhere from Malaysia to the West Coast of the United States, the expatriate Chinese felt rather lost (and certainly very under-represented) when faced with the vast space of Latin America.

The speed with which the Bush administration concluded its negotiations with Mexico gave rise to a certain confusion in Asia. Under the circumstances, the idea of setting up an economic zone to defend Asian interests seemed an attractive one. But the obstacles were considerable. So dependent are the region's economies on the world market that its governments are reluctant to take a step that cannot do much to solve the problem of trade outlets, but could easily provoke a protectionist backlash from foreign trade partners. Asia-Pacific, which had never before formed a large regional organization, was thus torn between two projects. One, proposed by Malaysia at the end of 1990, was for the creation of the East Asia Economic Group (EAEG), excluding the English-speaking powers (Australia, Canada, New Zealand and the US). The other, put forward by the Australian goverment a year earlier, envisaged creating a forum for Asia-Pacific Economic Cooperation (APEC). This body would embrace Japan, South Korea, the three Chinas (China, Taiwan and Hong Kong), the six members of the Association of South-East Asian Nations (ASEAN, comprising Indonesia, the Philippines, Malaysia, Singapore, Thailand and Brunei),[9] the two countries of Oceania (Australia and New Zealand), Canada and the United States.

APEC versus an Asian Bloc

The White House perceived instantly that the Malaysian proposal threatened its strategy for integrating the world economy: the EAEG would become a sort of Asian bloc, led by the main regional economic power, Japan. Obviously, there could be no question of allowing America's main competitor to acquire a sort of hinterland that would include the fastest-growing economic zone in the world. The State Department, while embracing the idea put forward by the Australians, quickly – and none too gently – set about neutralizing the Kuala Lumpur project. To deter the Seoul government from joining the EAEG, for example, the American secretary of state, James Baker, went so far as to remind his Korean opposite number that Malaysia – unlike the United States – had never "shed its blood for your country".[10]

In reality, however, Washington did not need to twist too many arms. The other members of ASEAN were reluctant, in any case, to join an organization that might place them under de facto Japanese economic supervision, and perhaps even lead them into confrontation with the

United States. And Japan itself, in the throes of an economic crisis and struggling to disentangle its trade problems with America, sought to distance itself from Malaysia. The EAEG was more or less buried by the end of 1991. Meanwhile, the Bush administration was piling on the pressure to institutionalize APEC, which so far had simply been a forum of discussion. APEC, James Baker explained in November 1991, was not a regional bloc that would cut Asia-Pacific off from the rest of the world. It aimed to become a catalyst for economic integration, trade liberalization, and growth.[11]

The strategy employed by the Bush administration to convince its Asian partners owed much of its success to its subtlety. To assuage worries about the agreements with Canada and Mexico, the United States highlighted the importance of the new, enlarged North American market as an outlet for Asian exports. It painted a rosy picture of the advantages of Mexico as a site for Asian industries seeking freer access to American consumers. The White House also indicated that it would favour a free trade agreement between the ASEAN countries (AFTA). Provided that this treaty, modelled on NAFTA, does not create new obstacles, it should in fact stimulate trade, not just within ASEAN, but with the rest of the world as well.

AFTA, whose basic principles were accepted at the beginning of 1992, thus became, paradoxically, an instrument that could be used to prevent the political crystallization of a powerful Asian bloc. Consisting of countries whose economies are competing rather than complementary, this new free trade zone is unlikely to start working properly for at least a decade or two; but in the meantime, it can only accentuate the tendency of its members to integrate with the world market. Especially with Washington assuming the mantle of regional leader, aided by a mass of bilateral trade and investment agreements with Singapore, the Philippines and ASEAN itself.

On 24 June 1992, this orgy of diplomatic activism was crowned with the institutionalization of APEC: the fifteen member countries decided to set up a permanent secretariat, based in Singapore, with its own working budget. The rotating one-year presidency went first to the representative of the United States, whose role would be to get the organization working: as Lawrence Eagleburger explained, to clear the terrain for arriving at an investment code, a code of administrative conduct, an agreement on intellectual property, a customs treaty, a mechanism for settling legal disputes, an agreement on civil aviation and a trade agreement covering specific goods and services.[12] They set up, under United States leadership, the nucleus of a politico-economic organization representing half the "gross world product", including all the most powerful Pacific economies, with the door invitingly open to Mexico and Chile. However history remembers George Bush's presidency, this is certainly one of the finest feathers in his cap. Bill Clinton has not dropped the baton. He held the first big APEC summit in Seattle in 1993; the following year, in Bogor, Indonesia, encouraged by the United States, the organization decided to create a free trade zone before 2020.

The White House's successes in Latin America and Asia-Pacific complete what amounts to an outflanking strategy, designed to contain the principal economic competitor-partners in Japan and Europe. The Asian and South American free trade zones, and the prospect of their integration with the enlarged North American market, present an extraordinary challenge to Japan and Western Europe, both of which understand that they cannot live cut off from the rest of the world.

Development of the single European market has stimulated trade inside the EU, certainly. But by privileging its "domestic" market the Community has lost ground elsewhere, especially in strategic, advanced areas. In technological innovation the Old World is dropping further and further behind its American and Japanese competitors. And a growing share of the Community's GNP goes on subsidies to prolong the lives of industries sliding into obsolescence.[13] Japan is in the disagreeable situation of the biter bit: its economy is increasingly dependent on the goodwill of its foreign customers, but it also has to face stiff American and Asian competition in its own domestic market. The Europeans and Japanese are thus squeezed between American domination of future technologies and a battalion of emergent countries who are more competitive in the traditional industries.

So by preaching the advantages of a network of trade agreements linking the enlarged North American market with South America, Southeast Asia and Eastern Europe, the White House has placed a sort of noose around the economic power of its main competitors. Brussels and Tokyo must both choose between opening up their markets, thus integrating with the main body of World-America, and slow strangulation through loss of export markets. A choice the *imperator*-president is also forcing on the United States and its internal protectionist lobbies.

13

SHARING THE PROSPERITY

APEC, NAFTA and the whole star-shaped web of free trade agreements promoted by the White House resemble so many levers for forcing the doors of markets that show protectionist tendencies. Sandra Kristoff, a senior official of the State Department under the Bush administration, explained early in 1993 that the policy was intended to enable the United States to reach the whole world, not to exclude anyone or cut itself off. For, as she said, "history and economics" both show that inward-looking "protectionist trade blocs" do not stimulate trade, "either in the bloc itself or in the rest of the world."[1]

The integration of the world economy into a vast network centred on Washington implies an attack on everything that obstructs the free circulation of goods, capital, enterprises and technologies. It is worth remembering that these obstacles are essentially political in nature; national and regional laws and regulations, business cultures, consumption patterns and different lobbies are local protectionist particularities, under-written in the final analysis by national states. It follows that promoting the values of the democratic empire – giving priority to market laws, freedom of enterprise and movement, and ruthless competition subject to rules accepted by all – must involve a frontal offensive on the prerogatives of these states.

THE WAR BETWEEN THE RICH

Towards the end of the 1980s, America began to adopt a stern attitude towards its biggest economic partners, Japan and the European Union, accusing them of dragging their feet on the liberalization of their domestic markets. Neither George Bush nor Bill Clinton has hesitated to threaten severe commercial reprisals. At the same time, the White House has made the success of the Uruguay Round one of the main objectives of its economic policy. Launched in 1986, these talks were generally aimed at promoting a new liberalization of trade in the areas of agriculture, services, intellectual property and foreign investment.

The White House versus the United States

The American offensive was not limited to trade problems alone, however. The United States was also pressing for a general redefinition of the role played by the big international economic organizations dating from the Bretton Woods agreements of 1944: the International Monetary Fund (IMF) and the World Bank. Henceforth, the economic organization of the whole planet, which had functioned under American leadership since the Second World War, was to concentrate on promoting policies of de-regulation and privatization, and the opening of frontiers to trade and capital movements. What this meant, in a nutshell, was that the nation states, including the United States of America, were to have their sovereign economic powers expropriated by World-America.

One major threat still hangs over this great project for an ever more integrated world: the protectionist temptation in Japan, the EU and America. It was not for nothing that George Bush conceived his "strategic network of free trade agreements" as a weapon against the partisans of frontier closure, not only in Tokyo and Brussels, but in Washington as well. Ever since the presidency of Franklin Roosevelt, the White House has fought a protracted guerilla campaign against the demands for state protection made by various American industrial lobbies. Although the battle has not invariably favoured the defenders of free trade, it has gone their way more often than not during the second half of the twentieth century.

The priority given to the Uruguay Round and the signature of the NAFTA treaty are a gauge of the central government's determination. It demonstrates the American presidency's continuing readiness to sacrifice individual American interests, if need be, on the altar of World-America's ambitions. International free trade treaties also represent a powerful internal anti-protectionist instrument, conferring a measure of strategic autonomy on the White House. This is periodically codified in the famous "fast track" resolutions adopted by Congress: during the ratification process, the legislature promises to refrain from exercising its right to amend agreements already negotiated by the executive. This is an effective way of neutralizing the weight of individual lobbies.

Opening up Japan

Despite its muscular protectionist legislation, America can still pride itself on being one of the planet's most open markets. Japan is obviously a very different matter. In 1989 the Bush administration proposed a dialogue with the Tokyo government, entitled "Structural Impediments Initiative" (SII). Its goal was to identify the cultural and institutional obstacles that make penetration of the Japanese market so difficult for foreigners. The talks – the first economico-cultural negotiation in history – produced an initial SII pact, signed in 1990. Tokyo undertook to look into the monopolistic practices of its big companies (the *keiretsu*) and also, more importantly, to improve the quality of life for the Japanese. Extraordinarily detailed in some ways – for example, on increasing the floor area of Japanese apartments – the agreement instituted a reform of the distribution sector, allowing big stores to be established alongside the traditional network of small retailers. In return, partly to save face for its interlocutors, the Washington government promised to reduce its budget deficit, revise its education system and encourage American businessmen to "think in the long term".

From the White House point of view, the SII talks only represented the starting point of an all-out offensive to open up the Japanese market. As its trade deficits continued to accumulate, Washington raised the stakes by threatening to close the American economy to the Japanese if they persisted in not importing American-made products. The Japanese industrialists were forced to retreat, but only with the greatest reluctance: a withdrawal is not necessarily a rout. Japan negotiated hard before agreeing to a "voluntary" ceiling on vehicle exports, and undertaking to buy 20 per cent of its semiconductor requirements from abroad. So that early in 1993, the Japanese trade surplus with America reached a record level. The Tokyo government had to resign itself to the fact that henceforth, economic relations with its main partner and customer would be very like political arm-wrestling.

The Japanese economic strategy had reached its political limits. It is simply not viable to concentrate permanently on winning market shares to the exclusion of every other consideration (even that of paying dividends to the shareholders). Before playing the predator, you have to be sure that you really have the necessary means. And Japan, despite its industrial prowess, is a long way from being able to browbeat a power like America.

The stagnation of the Japanese growth rate at the beginning of the 1990s exposed the country's heavy dependence on its foreign customers. With the collapse of its domestic market, Japan found itself in the position of an offshore production platform serving the American, European and Asian markets. Japanese industry could survive only in a world where free trade reigned. Tokyo therefore had every interest in a swift conclusion of the GATT negotiations. But how could it secure that result without yielding something in exchange? Especially with the United States using the GATT talks to extract concessions that would upset the internal machinery of the Japanese model: opening the rice market, liberalizing the finance and service sectors, opening consumer markets to foreign firms, strengthening the anti-trust regulations, and so on.

As America is the main trade outlet for Japanese industry, protectionist whims in Washington pose a permanent threat to the archipelago's economic health. The idea of a free trade agreement between NAFTA and the ASEAN countries, proposed by George Bush in 1992,[2] deepened the anxieties in Tokyo. Had the White House really decided to favour competing Southeast Asian countries? If so, the Land of the Rising Sun might find itself increasingly isolated in the middle of a fast-integrating world economy.

The Capture of "Fortress Europe"

These robust forms of pressure are also brought to bear on the Europeans. But American practice is more subtle in the Old World. In principle, the United States supports the integration of the European market into a larger, more homogeneous entity. It hopes that this enlarged free trade zone will stimulate business and provide new opportunities for American enterprises. Of course, this can only happen if all protectionist barriers are removed and Europe remains broadly accessible to international competition. World-America needs a united free-trade Europe, but not a European Union forming a bloc that might be tempted to assert some sort of autonomy from the world market.

The White House responded to the process of European political unification by launching the idea of a "new Atlanticism". This concept covered not only defence and security matters, but also the bulk of political relations between the two shores of the Atlantic. What it meant, in fact, was adapting the Euro-American alliance to the new international situation, while preventing the emergence of a competing power centre in the Old World. After the fall of the Berlin wall, therefore, George Bush invited the main continental power, reunified Germany, to join a "partnership in leadership". This hint of a Bonn-Washington axis was an antidote to any possible leanings towards autonomy on the part of the Europeans (the French in particular).

In practice, the Bush-Baker duo conducted a virulent campaign against the dangers of a "fortress Europe". Their aim was to mobilize the northern EU countries traditionally favourable to free trade (Britain, Holland, Denmark and Germany) against the Euro-nationalist ideas propagated by France. Washington's arguments were partly endorsed by the process of European economic unification, which includes relinquishing a range of national economic prerogatives in the interests of greater market freedom. In any case, with the costs of German reunification weighing heavily on European internal growth, access to export markets outside Europe had become essential to all the countries of the Old World.

Like Japan, therefore, most members of the EU could only hope that the Uruguay Round negotiations would be crowned with rapid success. And the United States used this fact – as it did with Tokyo – to demand a radical liberalization of private and public markets, as well as trade and financial flows. This was so successful that some countries have been forced – like America itself – to sacrifice local sectoral interests to the integration of the world market as a whole: agriculture in France is one example. By these means the Bush and Clinton administrations have managed to curb and then to isolate the French autonomist positions. This early victory over the idea of forming a European economic bloc also owed a good deal to Britain. London views Europe simply as a free trade zone needing to be properly regulated and extended to the former East European countries, and has played a pioneering role in reducing state power over the economy and opening the market to trade and capital flows.

DEVELOPMENT AID FOR MARKETS

The America/Europe/Japan triangle represents nearly two-thirds of world trade. But the biggest growth potential is to be found in the "emergent", more advanced developing economies: the new Asian "dragons", the middle-income industrialized countries of Latin America, the former Communist states of central Europe. Integrating these economies harmoniously into World-America is thus an important objective. Especially as the biggest challenge awaiting Washington at the turn of the century is the task of easing two giants, China and Russia, into its international network of politico-economic institutions.

Priority to the Private Sector

Here, too, the Bush administration acted with the utmost speed and decision. It was quick to see what the collapse of Soviet power entailed: Third World governments, suddenly deprived of political choice, could no longer raise the bidding on development aid by playing the Communist world off against the West. In the last decade of the twentieth century even the most stubborn Third-Worldists are being forced to give up fantasies of planned or self-sufficient economies. The market and openness to the outside world now seem to offer the only realistic path. Seizing this opportunity, the White House has launched a vigorous campaign to reform the philosophy of development aid organizations in general: recipient countries would now have to undertake to liberalize their economies, and their societies.

Edward Perkins, former American ambassador to the UN, made a clear statement of the American view. Prosperity, he told the UN General Assembly in November 1992, depends on a growth-oriented "international economic order", but one that "safeguards the environment" and in which the private sector is the "engine of expansion" in "emergent and developing economies". Involvement of the private sector across frontiers would help establish "economic fraternity" instead of just continuing the "charity" of "traditional government-to-government aid".[3] Henceforth, in other words, aid will go primarily to private concerns and to countries that promise to encourage privatization, lift barriers to foreign capital, open their markets to trade and reform their laws and regulations generally to ease their integration into the world economic concert. While the very poorest countries will still be able to get aid to develop their infrastructures, the economic viability of every project will have to be carefully evaluated.

In 1991, the White House supported the candidature of Lewis Preston, a former director of the New York bank J.P. Morgan, for the post of president of the World Bank. Once elected, Preston, who already favoured reform of the Bank, started by abolishing the posts of the senior vice-presidents, who had established fiefdoms around themselves within the Bank and were accused of giving in too easily to pressure from customers. In their place he set up a presidential office, with three executive directors reporting personally to Preston himself (henceforth, so would vice-presidents in charge of operations). Of course, an ocean liner like the World Bank cannot (so to speak) steam full speed astern without slowing down first. But the New York banker's radical centralization of the decision-making process tightened the American hold on the institution, enabling Washington to press even more heavily for the reallocation of funds to the private sector.

The New Loans Strategy

The policy of reforming the World Bank (IBRD) was extended to the regional institutions. A prime example was the negotiation to set up the European Bank for Reconstruction and Development (EBRD) in April 1991, making it responsible for channelling aid to the former eastern bloc countries. The United States in effect blocked any decision until the other (European and Japanese) members had agreed in principle that 60 per cent of funds should be reserved for projects from the private sector. In order to keep a closer eye on an organization that is not under their exclusive control, the Americans supported the creation of a World Bank East Europe office, which, in practice, will duplicate the EBRD's work. In addition to all this, George Bush had suggested creating a free trade zone between the United States and the "Visegrad triangle" countries (Poland, Hungary and former Czechoslovakia).[4] This was a way of putting pressure on the EU to speed up the integration of central Europe, while securing a foothold in the region in case the European project fails.

The United States adopted the same attitude for the annual meeting of the Asian Development Bank (ADB) in June 1992. The American representative again opposed any increase in the Bank's capital, despite insistent Japanese demands, until the Bank agreed to increase its aid to private firms. He suggested, moreover, that loans should be conditional on the beneficiary country opening its financial markets, and that states that had already given proof of economic dynamism – China in particular – should apply to private banks in the first instance when seeking loans.[5]

This drive for radical reform found a perfect outlet in the reshaping, in late 1992, of the Inter-American Development Bank (IADB), responsible for aid in the American hemisphere. The Bush administration suggested in effect that the resources of the IADB should be increased in parallel with the adoption of a new loans policy. Aid for the development of social infrastructures or the fight against poverty would henceforth represent 30 per cent of the total, and be largely reserved for the region's poorest countries; the rest would have to call on private capital flows. Provision of credits to the private sector would be considerably improved by the internal merger of two of the Bank's specialist branches, the InterAmerican Investment Corporation (IIC) and the Multilateral Investment Fund (MIF). The merger served the additional purpose of diluting the influence of European share-holders, who had a stronger presence in these branches than in the IADB proper. And to encourage privatization in the region, the United States would also like the Bank to be able to lend directly and without govern-ment guarantees, for a transitional period, to nationalized enterprises recently sold off to investors.[6]

Cybernetic Dependence

As the twenty-first century approaches, affirmed the former American treasury secretary, Nicholas Brady, "the powerful Bretton Woods institu-tions will again help nations to help themselves".[7] A North American free trade agreement that could be extended to all the Americas; a new trans-Pacific organization under American leadership; a strong position in GATT and in relation to Europe and Japan; a restoration of influence over the economic institutions founded at Bretton Woods and a general reform of development aid: Bill Clinton's political and economic inheritance from George Bush was a considerable one. From the moment he took power, the new president was at the controls of a solid international linkage enabling him to extend and consolidate the great democratic empire of World-America.

To be quite fair, the young tenant of the White House had more to do than just polish his predecessor's great oeuvre. The development of an integrated world economy is somewhat more arduous, in any case, than the power game so skilfully played by the Bush-Baker duo. Both men, despite their "professionalism", subscribed to the classical view of international relations: a mechanistic balance of forces in which size and influence are proportional to political and military power. In this context, the United States is the gear lever, controlling the speed and direction of the component wheels in the international machine.

What mattered in this mechanical universe was the overall balance of major forces. Compelled to adapt to new political or economic upsets, American power was always used prudently – by negotiation if at all possible – to establish, at each stage, new rules to govern the balance of forces. Despite the brilliance with which he managed the transition, George Bush was undoubtedly the last president to be shaped by our iron twentieth century: a time when the American Republic, although firmly established as *primus inter pares*, was not yet faced with its own metamorphosis into an empire covering the entire world.

Bill Clinton inhabits a very different space. Here the metaphor is cybernetic rather than mechanical: a single, complex world network, able permanently to react and adjust to the smallest changes. America – or rather the central government in Washington – functions like an electronic processor or "black box", in which general rules are constantly modified before being issued to ensure the survival of the whole system. Security in any part of the world has now become everyone's business, and the internationalization of economies and production processes has made every region of the world irremediably dependent on all the others. Making fine adjustments within this system, which is literally bionic, calls for something more subtle than the clanking tools used to maintain the balance of power. There is really no other choice than a leap towards global management. Without it, there is a real risk of hostile fragmentation leading to economic collapse and catastrophic wars.

So to anyone who is not tempted by apocalyptic sentiments (so modish these days as the millennium draws near), the emergence of a new imperial form seems almost to impose itself as inevitable. The only entity in the late twentieth century capable of mustering enough power and collective strength to manage this transformation is the democratic *imperator* in the White House. But Bill Clinton and his successors do not have a great deal of time. The centrifugal forces are formidable. If the American president wants the great mutation to succeed, he is compelled, crudely, to throw the whole weight of American power into the balance. Especially in the most sensitive area: the accelerated integration of the world economy.

The urgent nature of the task explains the economic combat team put in place by the baby-boomer president, and the noticeable hardening of United States trade policy from the very beginning of Clinton's administration. The job is not limited to persuading Europe and Japan that joining a democratic empire based on growth and free trade is a better idea than plunging the world into confrontation between rival economic blocs. The hardest challenge will be to extend the global politico-economic network into the two territories still largely outside it: Russia and China.

Clinton had already hardened his tone towards the Chinese leadership during his electoral campaign. The message was a firm one: if China wanted to continue its economic boom and integrate with the world market, it would have to accept the political and economic rules of the game, of which Washington is the referee. This severity was shown during the Sino-American negotiations over Beijing's admission to the World Trade Organization, despite the pragmatic concession made by the Democratic White House in separating "most favoured nation" status from human rights issues (and thus being able to restore MFN status to China). In Russia's case, priority was given to the rapid dismantling of its nuclear arsenal to prevent the reappearance of a rival pole of military power. But it was also important to bolster the position of reformist leaders in Moscow by multiplying the links between the Russian economy and the world economic system. Clinton's hope is to mobilize a coalition of industrialized countries willing to promote foreign investment in Russia and able to advance enough credit to avert the catastrophic collapse of Russian society, leading to the defeat of the pro-Western leadership.

The White House is clearly determined to use its strength overtly for the benefit of World-America. There is no question of blinkered nationalism now. The new president's team reiterated at every opportunity that it was not protectionist, that it sought on the contrary to open the rest of the planet to the benefits of political pluralism and free trade. Similarly, the new leaders of the Republican party have shown that they too are deeply attached to this free trade internationalism, even if it means fighting the strong protectionist tendencies in their own party. It could be said that Bill Clinton represents one pole of the globalizing tendency, Bob Dole and Newt Gingrich the other. Clinton's multilateralist view is that the US should animate and drive a great system of international cooperation, in which the allies might sometimes need, at most, to be jostled into line for their own good. The Republicans incline towards a more unilateral assertion of Washington's power, without much regard for the sensibilities of friends or enemies. Both factions realize, however, that there is no longer an American Republic to defend. The universal democratic empire is up and running.

14

A NEW WORLD SECURITY PACT

Washington wasted no time on celebrating its victory in the Cold War. Action was needed from the moment the Soviet empire collapsed. The whole network of institutions and political and economic relations set up by the United States to hold the "free world" together was in danger of breaking up now that the threat which had made it necessary was gone. When chosen by fate to preside over the disintegration of the Communist bloc, the Bush administration had only one concern: how to adapt the great Western institutional Meccano to its new global role, while maintaining America's central place in the structure.

George Bush has often been accused of lacking a large-scale world vision, what he self-deprecatingly called "the vision thing". As the president during the transition from a codified world of bipolar confrontation to the uncertainties of the post-Cold War situation, he was thought at most to possess ability and extensive international experience. But by the time Ronald Reagan's successor relinquished power, on 20 January 1993, he and his friend and adviser James Baker could pride themselves on having established the main outlines of a new White House foreign policy. The two men, both "pragmatic" to say the least, had not just effected a very rapid reform of all the institutions inherited from the great East–West confrontation. They had also, paradoxically, left their successors a conceptual heritage signposting an international course of action for the American presidency into the dawn of the twenty-first century.

A POST-NUCLEAR POWER

The action of the Bush-Baker tandem can only be properly evaluated in terms of the stakes involved. It was concerned with nothing less than managing one of the century's greatest revolutions – the crumbling of communism and its statist avatars – while preserving the overall equilibrium of World-America against the forces of disintegration inside and outside the United States. Their objective, the establishment of a "new world order", sounds both pompous and ambitious, aiming to do nothing less than lay the foundations of an institutional edifice that would have to preside over the world's organization in the decades to come.

Dismantling the Nuclear Arsenals

Since the end of the Second World War, the United States had always advocated policies in the political and military fields that paralleled its policies on the international economy. Pursuit of this double leadership, the one reinforcing the other, was clearly apparent in the pattern of Western institutions created under American influence from 1945 onwards. The International Monetary Fund (IMF), the Marshall Plan, the Organization for European Economic Cooperation (OEEC) and the General Agreement on Tariffs and Trade (GATT) came in a package with the Organization of American States (OAS), the North Atlantic Treaty Organization (NATO), the Pacific Pact and so on. Even when the White House was sacrificing short-term economic interests to some strategic political objective, it always made a point of linking the two aspects of its leadership.

In following this tradition, George Bush showed considerable prudence and restraint. Faced with a sudden and brutal upset in the rules of the planetary game, he resisted the temptation to flounder into a morass of new institutional engineering. His gamble was somewhat more economical: to base the new world order on the ready-made platform provided by the network of international organizations which had ensured Western cohesion for most of the previous half-century.

The dissolution of the Warsaw Pact in 1989, and then the USSR itself in 1991, upset all the world strategic balances. It also emasculated the ultimate symbol of hierarchy between the powers in the second half of the twentieth century: nuclear weapons. Since codification of the balance of terror ("mutually assured destruction") at the beginning of the 1960s, the two great powers had based their pre-eminence in their respective camps on their formidable nuclear arsenals. But with Moscow no longer posing a direct and permanent threat, what use were the thousands of American missiles and warheads? American leadership was based essentially on the role of protector of European and Asian allies against the Soviet threat; might not the leadership be contested, now that the threat had gone? The United States thus had to find solutions to two crucial problems: how to supervise the dismantling of a large part of the former Soviet nuclear arsenal while simultaneously reducing its own strategic forces; and how to maintain its position as sole surviving military superpower in the future.

The first of these was obviously more urgent. The former USSR's strike force is the only one capable of threatening American territory directly. Unfortunately, the single nuclear power with which Washington signed the first effective nuclear arms reduction treaty, START 1, in July 1991 has now become four: Russia, Ukraine, Kazakhstan and Byelorussia. There is clear danger in the confused situation – the possible duplication of chains of command controlling the missiles, bombers and submarines – as well as the risk of proliferation ("embezzlement", perhaps for profit, of short-range weapons, restricted technologies and fissile material; a "brain drain" of scientists and technicians). It was therefore essential to establish some sort of workable authority over the Red Army's stocks of strategic weapons as quickly as possible.

This made implementation of the START 1 treaty, which included a very intrusive programme of *in situ* checks and verifications, a priority of American policy. Some hard negotiations, accompanied by strong White House pressure, persuaded the four nuclear states that succeeded the Soviet Union to agree, in May 1992, to hold to the July 1991 treaty. The Ukrainians, Kazakhs and Byelorussians also undertook to relinquish their nuclear weapons and sign the nuclear non-proliferation treaty; the short-range atomic missiles based on their territory were to be transferred to Russia for dismantling. Given the political tensions already present in the new Community of Independent States (CIS), this was quite a good result. In June 1992, however, George Bush and the Russian president Boris Yeltsin announced their intention to continue the process. A START 2 treaty was accordingly signed in Moscow on 3 January 1993, the two parties promising to effect the biggest reductions of strategic weapons in the history of nuclear strategy.

These agreements opened the way for the deployment of a system of close inspection and supervision of nuclear weapons stationed on former Soviet territory; yet another giant stride to be credited to the Bush administration.[1] The treaties alone, however, did not assuage all the American leadership's fears. Dismantling such a large quantity of atomic weapons is an extremely expensive undertaking, quite beyond the means of the Soviet Union's successor states. In 1992, the White House managed to extract half a billion dollars of credit from Congress to help these countries keep their promises. And the START 2 treaty included specific aid provisions for Russia.

But the programme is far from complete. The risk of nuclear dissemination through the world black market in arms remains as real as ever. Although the technological concentration and relatively small numbers involved make the problem appear containable, there are persistent anxieties about proliferation, caused by the brain drain from the former Soviet military-industrial complex. To stop this process, in February 1992 the United States and Germany announced the foundation of an international science and technology centre in Moscow, intended to absorb and redirect scientists and engineers from the CIS countries' arms industries. How effective this will be remains to be seen. New worries soon began to appear. Early in 1996, voices were still being raised in the Russian parliament against the ratification of START 2.

But despite their limitations, the START 1 and START 2 treaties, which stipulate the destruction of nearly two-thirds of the former ideological adversaries' nuclear forces, have the merit of instituting a framework of legal constraints. Negotiated and signed at breakneck speed by the Bush administration, they provided Bill Clinton with a solid base for further action. While still a presidential candidate, Clinton had affirmed: "No national security issue is more urgent than the question of who will control the nuclear weapons and technology of the former Soviet empire."[2] To counter the danger of a possible "fervently nationalistic and aggressive regime in Russia still in possession of long-range nuclear weapons", Clinton said he was prepared to provide substantial aid to enable the Russians to start destroying their nuclear arsenal right away: ". . . we should shift money from marginal military programmes to this key investment in our future security."[3]

The Electronic Battlefield

The United States alone has the capacity to manage this transition to a world in which atomic weapons will no longer be virtually the sole measure of real power. But would not this downgrading of nuclear weaponry cast doubt on continuing US political leadership among the principal allies in Western Europe and Japan? The protection against the Soviet threat provided by the famous American "nuclear umbrella" had been the cornerstone, in effect, of the network of Western institutions set up by Washington after 1945, NATO in particular. But no sooner had there been mention of a post-nuclear age, and of a reduced US military presence in Europe or Asia, than some of these allies started dreaming aloud about regaining some of their lost autonomy of decision. To maintain its primacy, the surviving superpower was going to have to reformulate the material and symbolic instruments of its authority.

In January 1988, as the disintegration of the Communist world became more evident by the day, a group of American experts and strategists – including Brent Scowcroft, who later became George Bush's national security adviser – launched a new concept, "discriminate deterrence", intended to replace the strategy of "mutually assured destruction".[4] This new paradigm, a sort of synthesis of the discussions held during the 1980s in the Pentagon and among the defence community, postulated the maintenance of a much reduced nuclear capability for the marginal purpose of deterring the adverse use of nuclear weapons, instead of deterring all forms of armed conflict. Politico-military authority would be enforced in future by very mobile conventional forces, rendered invincible by the use of leading-edge organizational and weapons technologies: front-line electronics, smart missiles, satellite battlefield management and communications, stealth technologies, and so on.

This evolution towards a conventional army of intervention, adapted to dominate a battlefield that has become electronic, was extended early in George Bush's presidency by the GPALS project (Global Protection against Accidental Launchings System). This system, the product of a compromise between the White House and a Congress with a Democratic majority, is really no more than a downward revision of the Strategic Defense Initiative (SDI), the notorious Reaganite fantasy of a space-based shield supposedly capable of destroying incoming Soviet missiles in flight. GPALS is also an anti-missile system, but unlike the SDI does not claim to provide total protection against massive nuclear attack, which is somewhat unlikely in any case following the collapse of the USSR. Its purpose is the more modest one of countering the threat of ballistic missile technology falling into the hands of Third World countries believed to be resistant to the logic of deterrence.

In reality, GPALS – combined with electronic management of the conventional battlefield – establishes a new hierarchy of military power. The existence of a global anti-missile system (even a limited one) buttressed by classical forces, all increasingly dependent on up-to-the-minute computing and telecommunications gadgets, implies the very advanced integration and centralization of chains of command. Overall management is very complex, calling for supervision from a strong decision-making authority to compensate for the relative decentralization of tactical decisions on the ground. It also demands perfect mastery – both technological and financial – of the aerospace industries: surveillance and communications satellites, their associated rocket technology, ground-based relay stations and so forth. At the end of the twentieth century, the Americans alone possess the kind of muscle needed to complete such a project. Even so, the White House wanted its European and Japanese allies, and even the new Russian government, to join the initiative.

Without the means to promote an adventure of this sort for themselves, Japan and Europe were cornered. If they aligned themselves with the new American defence logic, their position would be that of simple industrial and technological subcontractors. Militarily, their armed forces would only have the status of auxiliaries in an organization run and commanded by the United States. But if they refused, their advanced industries and laboratories would be squeezed out of the most "promising" military programme of the 1990s. By keeping aloof from the American setup, and thus losing the chance to make their voices heard within it, they would also be exposing the limitations of their own defence policies. This would further accentuate their ancillary status.

The decisive blow in this battle to "recast" the American leadership was struck on 17 June 1992, when George Bush managed to persuade the Russian president Boris Yeltsin to take part in the GPALS project. The White House, after toying with the idea of stifling the Russian aerospace industry, thus finally chose the path of cooperation. By authorizing (in November 1992) satellite launches using Russian vehicles, and commercial cooperation between American companies and their Russian equivalents, the United States put itself in a position to influence the development of the former Soviet aerospace industry, both civilian and military.[5] An additional benefit was that the prices charged by the Russians (and the Chinese), which are far too low to be matched in Europe or Japan, indirectly but effectively undermined the European company Arianespace, the world's leading launcher of civilian satellites.[6] This strategy has been brilliantly pursued by President Clinton. In May 1995, he negotiated with Boris Yeltsin a new intepretation of the 1972 anti-ballistic missiles (ABM) treaty to enable theatre missile defences (TMD) to be deployed; in July of the same year he presided over the joint space mission by Atlantis and Soyuz.

The Bush administration can thus pride itself on the successful completion – in the space of a single term – of one of the great conceptual revolutions of the nuclear age. Military power no longer resides in a capacity for nuclear destruction and deterrence, coupled with vast armies manning the battlements along the Iron Curtain. It now consists of a combination of a residual nuclear arsenal and a global anti-missile defence system with classical military forces, smaller in numbers but very mobile, protected by theatre anti-missile systems, their superiority guaranteed by their mastery of space and advanced technologies: "leaner and meaner". At the dawn of the twenty-first century, America is once again the only country with the means to make this "triad" work properly. On coming to power, Bill Clinton endorsed this new strategic thinking unambiguously; he also tried to increase the sophistication of the intelligence services, essential if they were to evaluate the various dangers emerging from this "era of unpredictable threats".[7]

REINING IN THE EUROPEAN ALLIES

With American leadership redefined for the post-Cold War era, the relations between Washington and its leading Western allies, and the modalities for maintaining order on the planet, needed to be reformulated. Solutions were needed to three major problems: how to maintain the Atlantic alliance – the only institution giving America formal pre-eminence in Europe – while reconstructing a security system to shield the Old World from the turbulence of the transitions taking place further east; how to consolidate the US presence in Asia-Pacific while bringing home some of the forces based there; and how to deal with regional crises in the Third World.

Rebuilding NATO

In Europe, the Bush administration sought to consolidate NATO's structures, and broaden its applications, to create a minimal institutional framework capable of covering the security needs of the new Central and Eastern European democracies. This strategy soon came up against the determination of some Western European states – France in particular – to secure greater independence for the EU in foreign policy and security matters. In particular, the partisans of European autonomy argued that America was certain, sooner or later, to succumb to its old isolationist demons and withdraw its troops from the Old World, leaving Europe to face the mounting chaos further east with no guarantees of support. It was therefore necessary to create a security system in which Europe could manage its own affairs and deal with Washington as an equal.

After the fall of the Berlin wall in November 1989, though, American leaders began touting the idea of a "new Atlanticism". This was a way of showing clearly that they wanted no truck with an organized European lobby whose positions could be harmonized in private before being put to the Americans. The difference crystallized around the role that would be given to the Western European Union (WEU), the only collective body in which the Europeans can discuss security without the United States being present. Under the circumstances there were two main options. Either the WEU could become an independent military structure, a sort of strong right arm of the European Union, commissioned under the Maastricht treaty of December 1991; or, as the Americans preferred (with British, Dutch and Italian backing), it could be the "European pillar of NATO", subject by definition to the alliance's mechanisms under US management.

In the event, the Bush-Baker team hardly gave partisans of European autonomy enough time to draw breath. In July 1990, under American pressure, the Atlantic alliance proclaimed the end of the Cold War and at once abandoned the whole strategic doctrine – "flexible response" and "forward defence" – that had kept the western organization together. In the resulting vacuum, NATO was compelled to undertake a full re-evaluation of its arrangements. This was hustled through at great speed. An in-depth reform of the alliance's machinery was announced in June 1991: there would be a sharp reduction in troop numbers, especially those of the United States, and multinational units were to be created, including "rapid reaction forces" subject to strict integrated NATO command (and thus under the ultimate orders of the American staff). This choice, coupled with the adoption of a centralizing concept of the "electronic battlefield", trapped the allied forces in an American-run system even more thoroughly than during the Cold War.

The New Atlanticism: Vancouver to Vladivostok

At the same time, on 18 June 1991, Secretary of State James Baker launched the idea of a "Euro-Atlantic community from Vancouver to Vladivostok".[8] This had the effect of depicting the renovated NATO to the former Communist countries, including Russia, as their only credible interlocutor on security matters. The main difficulty would be to establish institutional links with these states without granting them full member-ship (for that would endanger the coherence of NATO as a Western alliance). In November 1991, George Bush managed to persuade his NATO partners to establish the North Atlantic Cooperation Council (NACC), a new structure that would be able to include the Eastern democracies in dialogue and common action on security.

This new institutional Meccano for ensuring American leadership and extending it to the entire Old World was consolidated on 4 June 1992, when NATO announced that it could make its forces and infrastructures available to the Conference on Security and Cooperation in Europe (CSCE) for peacekeeping missions between the Atlantic and the Urals.[9] For the first time in its history, the alliance had given itself permission to intervene outside the zone defined under the 1949 treaty ("out-of-area"), and not only in strict self-defence ("out-of-function"). The Clinton administration completed this new architecture by setting up the Partnership for Peace (PFP), clearing the way for close military cooperation with former members of the Warsaw Pact in Central and Eastern Europe. These were crushing successes for the American administration. France, in particular, did its best to fight for WEU independence and to organize a Franco-German army corps, the "Eurocorps", intended as the nucleus of a possible future European army. But the reform and extension of the Atlantic organization had already occupied all the areas of autonomy: the member countries of the Europe of the Fifteen simply do not have the means to duplicate the new Euro-American politico-military setup merely in order to assert their independence. And all too soon, the European Union's impotence in dealing with the fighting in the Balkans was to deliver a *coup de grâce* to its autonomist pretensions.

But this metamorphosis of NATO does not address all the problems posed by European security. The wars in former Yugoslavia have exposed the limits of both the EU's ability to make decisions and the Atlantic alliance's capacity to intervene. Paradoxically, however, the drama of Bosnia-Herzegovina further consolidated the dominant position of the United States. At first by default as Washington's passivity, based on the belief that the Europeans should deal with the problem, exposed their powerlessness to do so. After that the White House had only to suggest an arms embargo on the warring parties, or mention a possible military intervention, and all the allies would immediately fall into line. The apotheosis of this display of American authority was the 1995 peace agreement signed by the Serbs, the Croats and the Bosnians, under heavy White House pressure, inside a military base in Dayton, Ohio.

The reformulated NATO, the NACC, the PFP, the START treaties and the Russian-American collaboration to deploy an anti-missile defence system are quite obviously transitional structures. Established in record time, they are nevertheless well adapted to the White House's European objectives in the closing decade of the century. So that Bill Clinton, on his inauguration, already possessed a diplomatic and military scaffolding that had preserved Western cohesion and American leadership – both threatened by the collapse of the bipolar world – and would now enable him to look to the future. This is by no means the smallest of Clinton's debts to his predecessor.

AN INTERNATIONAL POLICE

Although a less complex question, the American military presence in Asia is just as delicate in practice. The United States is proud of its status as a Pacific power. But with the exception of the ANZUS military pact with Australia and New Zealand, its relations with states in that region are all founded on bilateral agreements. Hence there is no regional defence organization to reform. Apart from the special case of the large American contingent deployed in South Korea, the main problem is to retain the bases and facilities used by the US Navy. With the Cold War no longer imposing bloc discipline, these bases are permanently at risk from local political mood-swings and the reappearance of old buried animosities.

Floating Airbases in the Pacific

The disappearance of the Soviet threat from Southeast Asia and the Sea of Japan had the effect of creating a strategic vacuum. As in Europe, the idea that the Americans might be thinking of bringing their troops back home made the situation even more unstable. The small states of the Asia-Pacific region and Anglophone Oceania suspected each of the three regional powers – China, Japan and India – of wanting to fill the space left empty by the superpowers. Under the circumstances the scale of these regional giants' rearmament programmes, and the Tokyo government's efforts to break the pacifist taboo inhibiting the use of its military forces, were far from reassuring.

In a zone where disputed frontiers are legion, the multiple claims on the Spratly archipelago in the South China Sea, which theoretically pit China, Taiwan, Vietnam, Malaysia, the Philippines and Brunei against each other, have a sinister aspect. More seriously still, it is feared that a race to acquire weapons of mass destruction is under way in the region. India and China are nuclear powers already; North Korea's clandestine nuclear programme would – were it to succeed – probably induce Japan to acquire weapons of this type in a defensive reflex. So that in Asia-Pacific the end of the Cold War, far from reducing tensions, has started a race for the latest weapons, conventional and other.

This dangerous break-up of the regional balances has paradoxically served the cause of American leadership. Nobody was surprised when in October 1992 Sohei Miyashita, director-general of the Japanese Defence Agency, addressed a pressing appeal to the United States to maintain a "strong presence" in Asia, while one of his subordinates pleaded for Japan to be able to "exercise the right to collective defence".[10] Many similar declarations had already been heard from other leaders in the region. The message was crystal clear: if the Americans did not continue to underwrite regional security, it was going to be every man for himself. America thus took on the appearance of an indispensable, muscular Mr Good Guy, whose position as arbitrator reposed essentially on a formidable capacity for military deterrence.

Here, too, the Bush administration wasted no time. In effect, the Asia-Pacific countries needed to be convinced that the United States had no intention of abandoning the region to its fate; and that the troop reductions would be modest, affecting only a few infantry and logistical support personnel. It was simply a matter of adapting the American military setup to the new era: the dense network of land bases that had kept the USSR at arm's length would give place to more mobile and powerful forces, able to intervene quickly and effectively anywhere in the zone. American carrier groups, which are more or less "floating air bases", were to be the heart of the peacekeeping deployment in the Pacific.

The Pentagon accordingly agreed, without too much arm-twisting, to the closure of the big base at Subic Bay in the Philippines. In exchange, it was able to multiply its agreements on the use of naval and air facilities with Indonesia, Singapore, Malaysia, Thailand and Brunei. It also extended its cooperation arrangements with the region's top military: both Jakarta and Kuala Lumpur now carry out joint exercises with American forces. Even India, the champion of non-alignment, agreed to hold regular joint naval exercises with the US Navy.

Clearly the United States has every reason to rejoice when traditionally non-aligned states seek protection under the umbrella of American naval air power. Just as in Europe, the change of military concept implies an increased role for the allies in the joint defence structures. But the simple proliferation of bilateral treaties makes it more difficult to organize a rational security policy in which everyone would have a place proportionate to his role in the collective system. With this in view, in March 1992 the Pentagon launched a new regional doctrine called "Vigilance in cooperation", a sort of huge integrated network of military relationships and agreements organized around the United States. When Bill Clinton arrived in the White House, this Pacific "mini-NATO" – less constraining, of course, than the Atlantic alliance – was still only a project. Although it had received official endorsement from Japan and Australia, it was still held up by the reservations of states reluctant to cooperate militarily with neighbours they did not trust.

Any such system of security will be difficult to finalize without the participation, or at least the acquiescence, of the Beijing government. Nor will it be specifically designed to contain China. Remember, though, that China is the only major territory still free from American political influence: the last frontier remaining to be conquered by Washington's democratic empire. So it is easy to understand why the new American president, anxious to consolidate the world leadership of the united States, should immediately have adopted a harder line towards a government his predecessor had always treated tactfully. With the Cold War over, in Bill Clinton's view, "it makes no sense to play the China card now." Branding China an extreme case in terms of human rights violations, he proposed the creation of a "Radio Free Asia" to promote democracy there, and suggested that "we should condition favorable trade terms on political liberalization and responsible international conduct".[11] In the event, pressure from giant American corporations, drawn by the possibilities of the immense Chinese market, has so far forced the president to dilute this position somewhat. The integration of China into World-America remains the last major challenge facing the White House in consolidating its planetary leadership for the early twenty-first century.

UN Auxiliaries

As the only superpower left after the Cold War, the United States today has to bear one especially heavy burden: it is perceived, like it or not, as the last resort in serious emergencies. George Bush, even when announcing his new order "for a hundred years", repeated insistently that America did not have the means to become the whole world's policeman. What the Bush-Baker tandem really wanted was to establish a set of flexible intervention techniques, enabling actions decreed and coordinated by America to be carried out by coalitions formed for the occasion with its allies. The 1991 Gulf War and the "humanitarian" landing in Somalia in 1992 are good examples.

The days of the "big stick", when the United States would mount expeditions in the name of its own national interests, seem to be over (at least when those interests are not being directly threatened). Before acting, Washington now tries to obtain a legitimate mandate from the international community, while the countries most concerned are expected – within the limits of their ability – to make political, financial and even military contributions. Of course the White House retains the essential prerogative of the dominant power: the right to decide where and when to intervene, on its own if necessary. This privilege has been underlined in the course of various regional crises arising in the aftermath of the Cold War. Where the American administration has decided to ignore the problem, no action has been possible. But where a decision to act has been taken, and allied participation requested, not one ally has succeeded in withholding support. Nothing better illustrates the transition from imperial American Republic to democratic empire of World-America than the new legitimacy of these international operations to keep order.

The most suitable forum in which to arrive at a consensus is still the United Nations. George Bush was very quick to perceive the extensive advantages offered by the world organization. With the dissolution of the USSR, the United States was left in virtual control of the Security Council. Of the five permanent members possessing the right of veto, the Americans can count on three votes in advance: their own and those of the British and the French. Neither London nor Paris can veto any proposal dear to the Americans without causing a dangerous rift in the Atlantic alliance. Russia, in the throes of democratization, is so militarily enfeebled, and so dependent on the United States for its integration into the world economy, that for the time being it has to accept American leadership in the UN. China alone possesses a narrow margin of manoeuvre. But so long as it, too, is struggling to open up its economy, China cannot really afford to isolate itself by rejecting what the other four have agreed on.

The White House, under both Bush and Clinton, has sought to consolidate this instrument for the collective management of international tensions by supporting German and Japanese applications for permanent membership of the Security Council. Of course these countries will have to be induced to assume the responsibilities – financial, but also military – that accompany their recognition as great powers. Washington knows that the two big losers of the Second World War still lack the means to dispute US power in any serious way: not only are they dependent on America, but both are still viewed with grave suspicion in large areas of the planet.

There is, however, no reason to suppose that this situation is permanent. American leaders have consequently avoided submitting to any form of collective UN command, and retain the option of intervening

– either alone or accompanied by ad hoc regional coalitions – without the UN label. While thus ensuring its own autonomy against any possible future upsets within the world organization, the White House has tried at the same time to make stable arrangements for levying forces to maintain order when necessary. In this context the American hemisphere has played a pioneering political role. In 1991, at its general assembly in Santiago de Chile, the Organization of American States (OAS) approved a historic reform of its charter: for the first time, a regional organization formally accepted collective responsibility for the "defence of democracy". In December 1992, the OAS went a step further when it adopted an amendment enabling it to suspend and isolate any member-state whose government had come to power by force. Admittedly, the idea of collective military intervention was not raised. But the Americas have now acquired a juridical basis on which to decide when sanctions are needed and how they should be enforced.[12]

This institutional policy, inaugurated by George Bush, was the one Bill Clinton intended to apply to the UN. In Clinton's own words, he wanted to "institutionalize the UN's success in mobilizing international participation in Desert Storm". America, he believed, "needs to reach a new agreement with its allies for sharing the costs and risks of maintaining peace". Drawing a lesson from the intervention in the Gulf, whose financial costs were well distributed but where "our forces still did most of the fighting and dying", he added, "We need to shift that burden to a wider coalition of nations of which America will be part" and proposed the innovation of a UN rapid deployment force "that could be used for purposes beyond traditional peacekeeping".[13]

What the Democrat White House really wanted was to institute a division of tasks: the allies and regional organizations would look after day-to-day security in their local zones of influence (sometimes with American logistical help); the United States would be responsible for ordering large-scale military interventions – with or without the allies – either in direct defence of American interests, or to counter threats to the major international balances. America would thus avoid risking the lives of its troops except in the last resort. This vision of a planetary security system headed by the American leader is integral with the idea of a body – the UN – with the legitimacy to authorize military interventions in the name of the "international community" as a whole. It is now apparent in any case that when an operation overflows a strictly local setting, or ceases to be definable as a low-intensity conflict, the massive presence of American troops and logistics offers the best guarantee of deterrence (and if that fails, of an effective intervention). Even if the Washington elite does reject the role of "the world's policeman".

The foundations of a new global political and military organization of the world were thus laid in the three years that followed the dismantling of the Berlin Wall. The White House is no longer simply the leader of a Western coalition locked in struggle with a powerful and stubborn enemy. It now finds itself *nolens volens* in the role of final guarantor – and, literally, *ultima ratio* – of a planet that is henceforth integrated in the area of security. But this deployment of US power and influence has been accompanied by a complete metamorphosis of America's relations with its foreign partners, both old and new.

The days of the hegemonic Republic are over. There is no longer a contract under which the military superpower, deployed in the front line, ensures the protection of allies and clients who accept its leadership in return. Washington now sees itself as the hub of decision-making, co-ordinator of a planetary security system in which everyone must take a measure of responsibility proportional to their means. The nascent world democratic empire requires all the states within it – including the United States of America – to make a large contribution to the organization of collective defence, with the American president as legitimate commander-in-chief.

This new distribution of tasks implies the reformulation of political and military arrangements and a reordering of the whole hierarchy of risks and threats. To those in control of World-America, for example, American territory now only represents a bastion of support. That is where it recruits its most reliable legions, the GIs – American citizens – who are its Praetorian Guard and most effective expeditionary troops. And that is where its arms industries are located, along with the research laboratories that ensure its continuing technological superiority.

Within the most important strategic zones – the American hemisphere, Europe and Asia-Pacific – stable regional security organizations have to be created or consolidated. There is urgent pressure for the OAS, for NATO and its "European pillar", and for the network of military treaties between the United States and the Asia-Pacific countries, to acquire the means to maintain peace in their respective areas. Depending on the scale of the threat and the action being taken, this regional policing can expect more or less lavish support from the central – that is, the American – forces. But in every case, even when there is little or no direct American military participation, policing will be carried out in permanent consultation with the White House under its political supervision.

Crises and tensions in the rest of the world will be evaluated in terms of the threat they pose to the harmonious functioning of the empire. The corollary of this outlook is that conflicts and human dramas without "strategic significance" may simply be ignored. The "new order" does not set out to eliminate disorders that remain strictly local.

Conclusion:

AN "IMPERIALISM OF FREEDOM"

White House authority at the end of the twentieth century is accurately described in the German philosopher Karl Schmitt's well-known dictum: "Sovereign is he who decides on the exception."[1] In the bipolar world of the Cold War the Kremlin shared this power of autonomous decision, the ultimate attribute of command. But since the disappearance of the Soviet Union, no major international action has been possible unless Washington has decreed it to be necessary: we have seen the proof in Kuwait, in the Balkans, in Mogadishu. Whether we like it or not, it is this embryonic world government, based in the capital of the United States, that decides whether crises are serious or not, and that determines the conditions under which an intervention will be legitimate.

Nevertheless, this planetary power of decision – so far unique in human history – is not exercised in autocratic fashion. Triumphant America has neither the means nor the inclination to act as the world's police force. The democratic empire emerging from the American Republic is based not on constraint, but on contractuality. Western Europe, Japan and (for the most part) the other allies, are not "subjects". Their freedom of manoeuvre may be more or less limited by their capacity to take autonomous decisions, but these limits are not imposed on them by brute force. True, the White House has never hesitated to bring pressures to bear. And it keeps permanently in reserve the option of taking unilateral action, as it did in Panama in 1989. But it always tries to persuade its foreign partners to act in concert for the common good, as in the Gulf War or the interventions in Somalia and Haiti.

The American armed forces are the Praetorian Guard of the central decision-making authority, not an instrument for keeping order in coercive fashion within the alliances assembled by the United States. Their role is to serve as a rallying point for the allied forces in facing any threat coming from outside. They also serve, of course, as the ultimate guarantee against possible future tension or hostilities between allies, a function recognized as essential even by those states most allergic to American power. The chorus of those worried by the sight of GIs going back home includes Japan, Korea and Southeast Asia; Germany, Britain, Italy (and even France); Greece and Turkey; ex-Communist Central Europe, Russia included; and even a fair number of Arab countries, which discreetly beg Washington to continue to lead the "peace process" in the Middle East.

The truth is that American political and economic leadership has always been founded on pacts freely signed – and often insistently demanded – by the allies themselves. Moreover these allies have always enjoyed immense freedom of action, both internally and externally, provided they did not incline too far in the direction of the Communist enemy, endanger American primacy or threaten the security and cohesion of the alliances. As with its distant Roman forebear, a *foedus* (treaty) legitimizes the status of *primus inter pares* within a federation of free nations, whose interdependence is managed by a central power.

Since the Second World War, the White House objective has not been to destroy the enemies of the Western alliance, but to transform them into friends and allies, the better to integrate them into the great planetary network of World-America. It has always discriminated between "rogue" foreign governments and leaderships, which it can treat very brutally (Communist regimes, Gaddafi, Noriega, Saddam Hussein and so forth), and the "peoples" who ought to be given aid so that they too may accede to the benefits of "individual liberty, political pluralism and free enterprise".[2] These same values lay behind the launch of the Marshall Plan in 1947, and the massive American aid poured into the reconstruction of Europe and the defeated enemies Germany and Japan.

Unlike the twentieth-century ideologies that sought to "change mankind" and impose well-being on it (if necessary against its will), the nascent new empire suggests only a few rules of social procedure to ensure peace and elementary rights for all, the preconditions for prosperity: what Vice-President Henry A. Wallace was calling a "messianic liberalism of abundance" as early as 1942.[3] The American view is that every individual is free and responsible for earning his own earthly paradise. No glittering images of tomorrow, no "blueprints for society", no big collective mirages; just practical, nuts-and-bolts recipes for a better life here and now, for those who are really prepared to take the trouble. The cornerstone of

World-America was laid in January 1941 by President Franklin Roosevelt, when he defined the "Four Freedoms" for which the United States would fight in the future:

> The first is freedom of speech and expression *everywhere in the world*.

> The second is freedom of every person to worship God in his own way – *everywhere in the world*.

> The third is freedom from want – which, translated into world terms, means economic understanding which will secure to every nation a healthy peacetime life for its inhabitants – *everywhere in the world*.

> The fourth is freedom from fear – which, translated into world terms, means a world-wide reduction of armaments to such a point and in such a thorough fashion that no nation will be in a position to commit an act of physical aggression against any neighbour – *anywhere in the world*.[4]

THE CENTURY OF CROSS-BREEDING

This "imperialism of freedom" emerges as the only social model available de facto to deal with what looks like being the biggest challenge in the early decades of the twenty-first century: the irreversible juxtaposition, mingling or fusion of all the races, religions and cultures of the globe. The civilization of the image, of instant information, of great planetary flows (population, capital, goods, even enterprises), is steadily dissolving the nation-states inherited from the great American and European revolutions of the eighteenth and nineteenth centuries. It is putting everyone in the world in direct contact. The anxiety aroused by this rapid process of integration is causing a stampede of movements purporting to protect "identity", with every community (or imagined community) claiming its place in the sun in the vast multicultural "salad bowl". In such a context, only government capable of administering the coming decades of cultural tension will be able to survive – government that can respect the expression of "differences" while favouring their peaceful cohabitation and even the inevitable cross-breeding.

This adeptness in the domain of cultural syncretism is a strength of all Americans, whether from the North or the South. The New World remains after all – its long list of massacres notwithstanding – the most multicoloured, racially mixed area of the planet. Anyone, of no matter what origin, can dream of one day becoming "American", anyway far more easily than of becoming German, Japanese, Chinese or even French. In the American hemisphere, though, the United States is still unique in being able to combine a broad experience of ethnic mixing with military, economic and mediatic power. Racist violence and exclusion are certainly constants of American life; but another is the federal government's traditional firmness in promoting equal rights and opportunities. By the same token, the state also defends the contribution of all specific expressions to the common American culture. No one can deny that, despite flagrant injustices, the integration of non-white minorities, including Afro-Americans, has made giant strides over the past three decades, before receiving symbolic expression in President Bill Clinton's calculatedly "rainbow" first cabinet.

The extensive British and French colonial empires always recoiled from any idea of recasting the metropolitan national identity in a new mould shaped partly by other hands. London forbade all promiscuity with "natives"; Paris wanted them to become French. The European nation-states are facing an analogous problem at the end of the twentieth century. Some – Germany, for example – base their identity on a mythical ethnic homogeneity. This inhibits their participation in the great movement of planetary integration and makes it difficult for them to manage inter-community tensions – inside or outside the country – through peaceful means. Others, like France, reject the ethno-cultural substrata of their societies in order to exalt the status of individuals as "citizens", all equal under the laws of the Republic. But this model presupposes a normalized "public" culture possessing something like the force of law, and thus relegating other specific expressions to the "private" status of folklore. Its adherents are consequently forced to defend, through fire and flood, the only size of sovereign organization capable of practising this type of "social contract": the nation-state.

But the internationalization of images, economies and decision-making processes is encroaching just as rapidly and profoundly on "state cultures" as it is on national sovereignties. Nations in any case, *nolens volens*, are having to melt themselves down into larger entities, of which the European Union is a good example. To cling to the nation-state framework is to embrace the destiny of a besieged tribe, unable eventually to make its voice heard in a civilization larger or more powerful than its own, and sinking resentfully into the cultural ossification that precedes a long and melancholy deathbed.

In truth, the emergence of World-America is a revolution every bit as profound and violent as the appearance of modern states during the nineteenth century. The modernizers of that era attacked, with varying degrees of success, the multiple, overlapping sovereignties and innumerable hierarchies determined by privilege, by "immunities" linked with corporations, orders, castes, tribes and "races". The world was thus dominated by a balancing act between state entities based on official culture and the governmental monopoly of legitimate violence. That era of unstable constructions, characterized by fierce struggles between states or coalitions of states, classified in order of power and political autonomy, reached its peak with the Cold War. Then the disintegration of the Communist bloc, coinciding with the globalization of economic and population flows, opened the way for the first time to the integrated management of the whole planet.

Washington's democratic empire is thus taking shape at a time when the national states – including the United States of America – are finding that they no longer have the means to retain control of their security, their economic lives, the worldwide demographic and migratory revolution, the impact of cultural conflict, mushrooming environmental problems or the speed of scientific and technological development. To deal with the explosion of claims based on identity, this new variant of the ancient Roman dream advances one simple but very powerful idea: an appeal to every individual's wish to improve his own and his family's material conditions. An absolutely universal aspiration common to both sexes, to black, yellow and white, and to Christian, Jew, Muslim and Buddhist.

THE EROSION OF NATIONAL GOVERNMENTS

The imperial discourse, automatically relayed by the giant American image-diffusion industry, proclaims that material well-being can be achieved by those willing to take control of their own affairs and struggle to succeed; and that only a regime of political and economic freedom can guarantee for all, not just the right, but an actual opportunity to attain it. Everyone knows that "many are called but few are chosen", that fraternity and solidarity can get trampled underfoot in the scrimmage; but facts like these detract not at all from the magnetic force of this model. The vast majority of the world population, after all, knows nothing but poverty, and cannot even begin to imagine life in a country like America, where only 12 per cent of the population is classified below a poverty line set at the enviable annual income level of $12,000.

The dream of rapid personal advancement is profoundly destabilizing to old societies, including those of Europe; societies where social mobility is restricted or non-existent, and where the state, or "tradition", determines the stages that have to be traversed to reach a given place – generally fixed in advance – in the social scale. The glories of "identity" and traditional values have scant appeal to the young unemployed, living in bleak suburbs, suffocating under the weight of obsolete custom, their few amusements including a steady diet of American TV programmes, advertisements and news clips. World-America is thus corrosive to all the informal hierarchies, solidarity networks and cultural references that lie behind the cohesion of states and the power of their elites. It proclaims its impartiality between religions, particularisms and lobbies: all are equally welcome, on condition that they do not infringe on business or individual freedom and do not question the central government's status as ultimate decision-maker.

To the poor and marginalized masses of humanity, this does not seem too high a price to pay for the dream of success and wealth. All that is demanded of them is that they refrain from "tribal" fanaticism, and pay lip service to a sort of civic religion whose observance is more or less limited to the televisual worship of the American president. But the cost is exorbitant for those "local" elites – even in the United States – whose power and privileges depend on the permanence of exclusive cultural identities and of clan, regional or national social organizations. The "imperialism of freedom" facilitates the emergence of a new type of political and economic leader: ambitious, impatient of traditional customs and networks, able to conduct dialogues with all cultures, and quite at ease with the internationalization of their own home communities.

In the early days of the Roman empire, similarly, it was not at all easy to be a Celtiberian warrior, a Macedonian kinglet, an Illyrian pirate captain, an Achaean aristocrat or Egyptian noble (or a Republican senator in the Capitol, for that matter). Alliance with imperial Rome would mean adapting painfully to a "new order", giving up part of the local power of decision and, to guarantee peace, accepting the constraints of an imposed universal law. Nevertheless most of the conquered peoples – the Italiots, Gauls and Illyrians in particular – ended by attaching themselves enthusiastically to the Empire, then acceding to Roman citizenship. The undeniable loss of some once-cherished values and symbols of community was compensated by more freedom and greater security and prosperity.

An analogous development is taking place at the end of the twentieth century. The disappearance of the USSR has ended the ability of the leaders of many countries to profit from their alignment with one great power or the other. The victory of World-America has rushed the poor countries, the newly industrialized countries (NICs) and even some highly developed states into jostling for integration with Washington's democratic empire. Governments everywhere are privatizing, deregulating, liberalizing the exchange of goods and capital flows, accepting the values of free enterprise, fighting for more foreign investment; committing themselves, for good or ill, to the path of individual freedom and democratic institutions. All are hoping to establish a direct connection with that great dynamo of the world economy, the American market. The North American Free Trade Area Treaty looks like becoming a symbol of the new era: it is the first agreement to envisage integrating a developing economy into an industrialized one.

This path is evidently much more painful for those with most to lose: the former European powers and Japan. Since the 1950s they have been financing part of their growth and their generous social security systems by adopting discriminatory measures against the competition: closed domestic markets and captive external ones, technological monopolies, public subsidies, commercial dumping, restrictions on capital movements, exploitable immigrant manpower available at the turn of a tap. Obviously the Europeans and the Japanese have not been alone in behaving like fortresses under siege. Faced with the dynamism of other rich countries and the increasingly effective competition of developing economies, many nations have sought to set up trade barriers (not least, of course, America itself). But no one else has approached the sophistication of the protective shields established in the Old World and the Japanese archipelago.

This nationalist type of protectionism nevertheless now seems an obsolete weapon. At best, it may help to gain the time needed to adapt to a mutating world; at worst, it could be the surest route to closure and decline. The imperial space functions as a great leveller by compelling all markets, whether they belong to emergent countries or industrialized nations, to open themselves to competition. This is a requirement that also applies to the United States itself, explaining the ever-fiercer infighting between an internationalist White House committed to free trade and the numerous domestic protectionist and isolationist lobbies.

A NEW CITIZENSHIP

It is not my purpose here to idealize either the Roman empire or the American democratic empire. The *pax romana* was only established after a century and a half of civil war, bloody repression, punitive expeditions, military conquests, economic crises and terrible social upheavals. The "new world order", too, at the end of our iron century, looks out over a scene of dangerous disorder. Will the *pax americana* be established in time? Only the future will tell. Meanwhile, all power is burdensome to its subjects, even when it happens to be in their best interests. But nothing could be more pointless than to waste breath extolling or reviling the burgeoning power of World-America: like the seasons, like rain and sunshine, it just *is*.

What use is it to fulminate against the invasion of the computers and robots that degrade industrial labour? What good does it do to lament the dethroning of literature by the civilization of the image? Why bother to weep for the "good old days" when the prosperity of nations depended essentially on their own resources, and when conflicts remote from their shores could not threaten their security? For there is no going back. Copyists in mediaeval monasteries may well have regretted the passing of illuminated manuscripts and the warmth of collective readings; but printing arrived all the same to liquidate their tactile relationship with text and inaugurate the era of solitary study. Televisual mass culture, democratic and often vulgar, is not going to shrivel under the disapproving gaze of an elegantly erudite happy few. Industry murdered the trade guilds, and with them the taste for superbly crafted artefacts. Now it is the turn of computer networks to dissolve the modern labour unions and start eroding large-scale mass production. The monarchic or republican state was undoubtedly more impartial than the rule of a petty baron in his fiefdom; but it would also have seemed more abstract and remote, less human. Have we the means today to barricade ourselves into our familiar national spaces and conduct a successful siege against our own international interests, our own multinational companies, the great migrations, the global capital markets, the American military umbrella, and all the rest of it?

The success of Coca-Cola, McDonald's or American TV series is not the result of an American plot to conquer the world; good marketing may have helped, but the real reason for it, quite simply, is that these are things people like. Nor does a taste for these products prevent people from continuing to like Camembert, tequila, couscous or sushi; or from introducing them to the Americans, for that matter. Basic English is not being imposed on the planet by battalions of strap-wielding imperial schoolteachers; it is just that in an era of much foreign travel English is the most practical language, being at least slightly understood almost everywhere. It is high time to dedramatize these symbols of the internationalization of human communities; to reassure ourselves that they are not going to make specific cultures vanish. Indeed they may favour a late flowering of cultures long marginalized or imprisoned by the centralism of modern nation-states.

In a rapidly integrating world, therefore, there is little sense in the preservation of cosily inward-looking identities. Inter-community wars in the Balkans, the Caucasus and parts of Africa are a clear enough illustration of the horrors that lie in wait for defenders of "purity", be it ethnic, religious or cultural. Such actions in any case can only, at best, delay the inevitable: when the war is over the economy will have to be restarted and the country eased back into the orbit of World-America. Witness the Islamic Republic of Iran, which since the early 1990s has been painfully negotiating its re-entry to the world trade system, resolutely ignoring the losses of sovereignty that will inevitably have to be digested sooner or later.

How to influence the nature and speed of planetary integration: that is the real issue of the moment. How to create, on all levels (local, regional, national and transnational), the political and social lobbies and institutions needed to make the democratic empire work. How to put one's two cents' worth into the decision-making processes centred on Washington. In a word, how to *conquer* World-America. Remember that Rome, after all, had great emperors, great traders, great intellectuals of "barbarian" origin. History is only tragic if people turn their backs on innovatory optimism.

World-America should not be confused with the United States. As Washington's democratic empire expands, it is becoming more detached from its territorial base and acquiring increasing autonomy from strictly American policies and interests. American territory is of course still the most secure rear base from which to recruit the central armed forces and maintain technological superiority. But Washington, like the Roman empire, is condemned to widen its definition of citizenship, a process beginning with the slow and prudent integration of America's nearest allies, Mexico and Canada.

A PAN-AMERICAN EMPIRE

America owes its dynamism to its unceasing pursuit of the "frontier". The end of the conquest of the West in the late nineteenth century was experienced as a major national trauma. The American "values" – domineering individualism, an instinct for democracy, willingness to offer the chance of a better life to everyone (except the indigenous "enemy") irrespective of their origins – were closely connected, in fact, to the established, ingrained idea of a boundless virgin territory. To stay true to its principles, the young nation had no choice but to seek new spaces to conquer. Theodore Roosevelt's naval imperialism, and successive waves of American foreign investment, blazed the trail to this "new frontier", which now covers the entire planet. Meanwhile the "American dream" was kept alive by the massive arrival of new citizens, immigrants from all over the world.

Until the fall of the Berlin Wall, "the West" was as far as the American nation-state's influence stretched. But this model of the imperial republic has become too narrow for the planetary responsibilities of the White House, and is gradually giving place to a new type of empire of planetary outlook. So what now becomes of the "frontier"? What happens if World-America becomes the whole universe and there is nothing left to conquer? Of course, the democratic empire has yet to integrate Russia and China. But although this task may provide some years' respite, it should already be considering the question of its own mutation. For Washington cannot continue to base its power on permanent expansion if there are no new horizons, and if the whole world is heading for a sort of imperial citizenship. Similarly, the dream of individual success, which is part and parcel of the frontier mythology, may no longer suffice for the peaceful management of the multitude of tensions around questions of identity in all parts of the globe.

At a time when institutions have to be consolidated and resources conserved (the environment, for example, will be a determining issue in the twenty-first century), good administrators become especially valuable. The president-emperor's private office, governmental agencies and departments will have to be staffed by public servants who are zealous, have good knowledge and understanding of the planet and place the service of the state above their own personal interests. Their ethnic or national origins, their religious affiliations, even their ambitions, are of little significance so long as they worship at the altar of public power and subscribe to the new civic morality it requires of them. This need for what might be called a "neo-stoical" elite is already being addressed by the American administration. Bill Clinton's senior staff are bound by ethical rules that may seem modest compared to the virtue expressed in rhetoric, but are nevertheless among the most severe tried in Washington for at least a century and a half.

Unlike ancient Rome, however, the modern democratic empire is directly confronted with the worldwide fermentation of cultures and the intercommunal tensions engendered by it. In the absence of new territorial outlets to release the pressure, it is left with only two management tools: in the short term, the stick and carrot, repression and gratification as appropriate; in the long term, the constant promotion of intermixing. For despite all the racist exclusions that persist in the United States itself, the bosses of World-America know that their future depends on cultural syncretism. George Bush spelled it out quite unambiguously in his 28 January 1992 State of the Union address: "If you read the papers and watch TV, you know there's been a rise these days in a certain kind of ugliness: racist comments, anti-Semitism, an increased sense of division. Really, this is not us. This is not who we are. And this is not acceptable."[5] Bill Clinton's message is clearer still: "Look now at our immigrant Nation and think of the world toward which we are tending. Look at how diverse and multiethnic and multilingual we are, in a world in which the ability to communicate with all kinds of people from all over the world and to understand them will be critical."[6]

NAFTA and the "Miami process" open an immense and indispensable territorial base for the imperial government, covering the whole American hemisphere from Alaska to Tierra del Fuego. The decision to link the empire's destiny to that of the whole New World is perfectly logical, for Central and South America are areas of great experience in the matter of intermixing. What cannot be predicted is exactly how these American cultures will eventually merge; nor how soon there will be a form of pan-American citizenship, permitting all deserving "Americans" to enter the service of the imperial government.

Early signs of the metamorphosis of the United States under Mexican cultural and linguistic influence are quite encouraging. The American hemisphere possesses another advantage over all other regions of the globe: in it, despite the ordinary racism it shares with the whole planet, foreigners and immigrants are still seen as a valuable asset. Elsewhere – in Europe, Asia and Africa – they are perceived as a problem, at best to be managed and at worst eliminated. The Americans, from North and South alike, seem to be alone in possessing the attitudes and know-how essential for managing the internationalization of the world. Models for social organization in the twenty-first century are thus being worked out almost exclusively in the American hemisphere.

But the engagement between the two Americas is not a guarantee that they will marry and have healthy issue. The Anglo-Saxon and Protestant North, despite its violent racial confrontations and rejection of inter-marriage, has succeeded in avoiding dismemberment and ruin by exalting individualism and sharing the economic prosperity relatively widely. The Luso-Hispanic and Catholic South, although based on the murder of the original native populations, has also managed to avoid generalized inter-communal conflicts, thanks mainly to its great sexual tolerance and the resulting mixing of races; and to its acceptance of a curious synthesis between the egalitarian aspirations specific to pioneer societies and an unequal social hierarchy based on bonds of personal allegiance (to families, clans, regions and so on).[7]

Washington's democratic empire is doomed to short-sighted authoritarianism and eventual failure in the absence of sexual freedom, respect for the State and the networks of personal bonds that nurture devotion and channel the interplay of purely individual interests. It is still not entirely clear that North America will manage to make a place for these "Southern" values. Be that as it may: the fate of the empire also depends on the prosperity and economic dynamism of the whole American hemisphere. So Latin America must do likewise, and assimilate some of the values dear to Northerners: competition between free individuals, laws that apply to everyone no matter what their rank in the social hierarchy, and the transparency of democratic political practice. If this cross-fertilization of ideas, values and practices succeeds, the twenty-first century will be a pan-American era, not just a US promotion.

NOTES

CHAPTER 1: THE OLD GODS OF AMERICA

1. George Bush, Speech to the Detroit Economic Club, 10 September 1992, *Wireless File*, USIS, American Embassy, Paris, 11 September 1992, p. 6.

2. Bill Clinton, Speech to the American University on February 26, 1993, *Wireless File*, USIS, American Embassy, Paris, 1 March 1993, p. 11.

3. For this chapter I am greatly indebted to Elise Marienstras for *Les Mythes fondateurs de la nation américaine*, Paris 1976, and to Samuel Eliot Morison's magnificent book *The Oxford History of the American People*, New York 1972, 3 vols; to Perry Miller, *The New England Mind: The Seventeenth Century*, Cambridge, Mass. 1961; Alan Heimert and Nicholas Delbanco, *Puritans in America: A Narrative Anthology*, Cambridge, Mass. 1985; Reinhold Niemuhr and Alan Heimert, *A Nation So Conceived: Reflections on the History of America from Its Early Visions to Its Present Power*, Westport, Conn. 1983; Gerald R. Cragg, *The Church and the Age of Reason 1648–1789*, Harmondsworth 1979; and Steven Ozment, *The Age of Reform 1250–1550*, New Haven, Conn. 1980.

4. Richard D. Heffner, *A Documentary History of the United States*, New York 1991, p. 36.

5. Ibid., pp. 30, 31 and 35.

6. George Washington, Inaugural address to Congress, 30 April 1789, in John Marshall, *The Life of George Washington*, Philadelphia 1833, vol. 2, p. 147.

7. See Ernst Cassirer, *Le Mythe de l'etat*, Paris 1993, pp. 233 *passim*.

8. Andrew Carnegie, "Wealth", in Heffner, *A Documentary History*, p. 178.

9. Quoted by Morison, *Oxford History of the American People*, vol. 3, p. 259.

10. It is well worth reading Morison's thoughtful and sensitive comments on this subject. Ibid. vol. 3, pp. 223–58.

11. Ibid., vol. 3, p. 225.

12. US Bureau of the Census, *Historical Statistics of the United States, Colonial Times to 1970*, bicentennial edition, Washington, D.C. 1975, part 2, p. 796.

13. Herbert C. Hoover, "Rugged Individualism", in Heffner, *A Documentary History*, p. 260.

14. Marcel Le Glay, *Rome – Grandeur et déclin de la République*, Paris 1990, p. 263.

CHAPTER 2: A CULT FOR THE UNIVERSE

1. For a fuller account of this religious aspect of the atomic age, see Carlos de Sá Rêgo, *Une Nostalgie de grandeur*, Paris 1985, pp. 126–41, and Alfredo G. A. Valladão, "Apocalypse nucléaire et rénovation de l'Eglise", *L'Etat des religions dans le monde*, Paris 1987, p. 51.
2. Richard D. Heffner, *A Documentary History of the United States*, New York 1991, p. 347.
3. J. Gordon Melton, *The Encyclopedia of American Religions*, Detroit, Mich. 1989, pp. 115–25; and *Religious Creeds*, Detroit, Mich. 1988, pp. 695–739.
4. US Bureau of the Census, *Statistical Abstract of the United States: 1991*, Washington, D.C. 1991, pp. 55–7.
5. Ibid., and US Bureau of the Census, *Historical Statistics of the United States, Colonial Times to 1970*, bicentennial edition, Washington, D.C. 1975 part 1, pp. 391 and 392.
6. Norman J. Ornstein et al., *Vital Statistics on Congress 1991–1992*, Washington, D.C. 1992, pp. 34–7. The number of Baptists remained stationary at around 12 per cent in both houses (owing to their restricted taste for power), while the representation of all the Protestant denominations combined (including Baptists) declined over the same period from 61 to 51 per cent in the Senate and from 55 to 44 per cent in the House of Representatives.
7. "Le défi de la paix. Lettre pastorale des évêques américains", *La Documentation catholique*, issue 14, 24 July 1983, pp. 715–762.

CHAPTER 3: AMERICA YIELDED TO THE IMMIGRANTS

1. For the history of immigration in the US see M. Allen-Jones, *American Immigration*, Chicago 1992; and Leonard Dinnerstein et al., *Natives and Strangers*, New York 1990. A very good short summary can be found in the chapter "Peuplements et populations", in A. Lennkh and M.F. Toinet, eds, *L'Etat des Etas-Unis*, Paris 1990.
2. On nativism and opposition to immigration in the US, see John Higham, *Strangers in the Land: Patterns of American Nativism 1860–1925*, New York 1968.
3. Dinnerstein et al., *Natives and Strangers*, p. 257.
4. Ibid., p. 261.
5. Allen-Jones, *American Immigration*, p. 278.
6. Ibid., p. 265.
7. US Bureau of the Census, *Statistical Abstract of the United States: 1991*, Washington, D.C. 1991, p. 9.
8. Allen-Jones, *American Immigration*, p. 289.
9. Paul Malamud, "Hispanics a Rapidly Growing Part of US Populations", *Wireless File*, USIS, American Embassy, Paris, 3 July 1991, p. 13.
10. Paul Malamud, "Census Find Asians Fastest-Growing Group in US", *Wireless File*, USIS, American Embassy, Paris, 16 July 1991, p. 23.
11. John Schaffer, "US Population to Climb 50% in Next 60 Years", *Wireless File*, USIS, American Embassy, Paris, 4 December 1992. By 2050 non-Hispanic whites will only constitute 53% of the population, while Latinos will be 21%, blacks will be 16% and Asians 11%.

12. US Bureau of the Census, *Statistical Abstract of the United States: 1991*, Washington D.C. 1991, p. 14.

CHAPTER 4: MANAGING THE WORLD MOSAIC

1. Leonard Dinnerstein et al., *Natives and Strangers*, New York 1990, p. 306 *passim*.
2. Paul Malamud, "Hispanics a Rapidly Growing Part of US Population", *Wireless File*, USIS, American Embassy, Paris, 3 July 1991, p. 14.
3. On the New Immigration between 1960 and 1980, see David M. Reimers, *Still the Golden Door*, New York 1985.
4. Malamud, "Hispanics a Rapidly Growing Part of US Population", p. 23.
5. For a history of the Hispanic immigrants, see Lester D. Langley, *Mex-America: Two Countries, One Future*, New York 1987; and M.S. Meier and F. Rivera, *A History of Mexican Americans*, New York 1972.
6. Malamud, "Hispanics a Rapidly Growing Part of US Population", p. 14.
7. M. Allen-Jones, *American Immigration*, Chicago 1992, p. 244.
8. US Bureau of the Census, *Statistical Abstract of the United States: 1991*, Washington, D.C. 1991, pp. 19–21.
9. Barbara Vobejda, "Incredible Shrinking US Middle Class", *International Herald Tribune* (Paris), 21 February 1992.

CHAPTER 5: THE FACTORY OF WORLD CULTURE

1. On the history of American culture and manners see the indispensable Samuel Eliot Morison, *The Oxford History of the American People*, New York 1972.
2. US Bureau of the Census, *Historical Statistics of the United States, Colonial Times to 1970*, bicentennial edition, Washington D.C. 1975, part 2, p. 796.
3. Harold W. Stanley et al., *Vital Statistics on American Politics*, 2nd edition, Washington, D.C. 1990, p. 48.
4. John Atherton, "La tradition du mécénat", in *L'Etat des Etats-Unis*, Paris 1990, p. 175.
5. Caroline Dequet, *Evolution de l'économie du cinéma américain depuis 1980*, Paris 1992.
6. Suzanne Cassidy, "Finding a Global Audience for Cosmopolitan Message", *International Herald Tribune* (Paris), 14 October 1992.
7. Dierdre Carmody, "Mother Tongue Speaks to US Readers", *International Herald Tribune* (Paris), 6 October 1992.
8. Bill Clinton, Address before a joint session of Congress on administration goals, 17 February 1993, *Wireless File*, USIS, American Embassy, Paris, 19 February 1993.
9. Adam Clymer, "Democrats Promise a House United", *International Herald Tribune* (Paris), 12 November 1992.

CHAPTER 6: THE IRRESISTIBLE ASCENT OF THE WHITE HOUSE

1. Harold. W. Stanley et al., *Vital Statistics on American Politics*, 2nd edition, Washington, D.C. 1990, pp. 328–9.

2. Senators were elected for a six-year term. Their relative job security compensated them for their dependence on their local "bosses".

3. Quoted by Richard D. Heffner, *A Documentary History of the United States*, New York 1991, p. 299.

4. George F. Kennan (X), "The Sources of Soviet Conduct", *Foreign Affairs*, vol. XXV, no. 4, July 1947, p. 576.

5. Stanley et al., *Vital Statistics on American Politics*, pp. 381–6.

6. Ibid., p. 174. In 1967, at the launch of the big social programmes of Lyndon Johnson's Great Society, this figure was still only 60 per cent.

7. Ibid., pp. 331–2.

8. Ibid., p. 165.

9. Steven Pearlstein, "Togetherness Blooms in Defense Industry", *International Herald Tribune* (Paris), 25 November 1992.

10. Stanley et al., *Vital Statistics on American Politics*, pp. 301–2 and 308–9. In 1955, the central government provided 20.9% of state revenues and 2.5% of the budget of local municipalities. On the eve of Ronald Reagan's arrival in power in 1980, these figures had reached 36.6% and 16.3% respectively. On the fiscal relations between the different institutions in the United States, see the clear and concise summary by David McKay, *American Politics and Society*, Oxford 1991, pp. 54–76.

11. Stanley et al., *Vital Statistics on American Politics*, pp. 48 and 69.

12. Norman J. Ornstein et al., *Vital Statistics on Congress 1991–1992*, Washington, D.C. 1992, pp. 74–9 and 191.

13. Ibid., p. 191.

14. US Senate, *Foreign Influence on the US Political Process*, Washington, D.C., 19 September 1990, pp. 55 *passim*.

15. Stanley et al., *Vital Statistics on American Politics*, pp. 186–7.

16. A very clear description of the legislative reforms carried out in the 1970s is to be found in Richard Maidment and Michael Tappin's excellent introduction to contemporary American public institutions *American Politics Today*, Manchester 1991.

CHAPTER 7: THE END OF THE AMERICAN REPUBLIC

1. Richard Maidment and Michael Tappin, *American Politics Today*, Manchester 1991, p. 78.

2. On this period of transition towards a clientelist system, see Morton Grodzins's study *The American System*, Chicago 1966.

3. Harold W. Stanley et al., *Vital Statistics on American Politics*, 2nd edition, Washington, D. C. 1990, p. 291. There were 83,186 local governments in 1987.

4. In 1949, total government expenditure per head of population in the United States amounted to $1,711 (at constant 1982 values). In 1987 the figure had risen to $5,475. David McKay, *American Politics and Society*, Oxford 1991, p. 63.

5. Stanley et al., *Vital Statistics on American Politics*, p. 291.

6. Ibid.

7. Norman J. Ornstein et al., *Vital Statistics on Congress 1991–1992*, Washington D. C. 1992, pp. 124, 126, 130.

8. Ibid., pp. 128–9.

9. Stanley et al., *Vital Statistics on American Politics*, p. 279.

10. Thus, in September 1992, the number of Americans receiving food stamps from the state exceeded 26 million for the first time. "Away from Politics", *International Herald Tribune* (Paris), 1 December 1992.

11. George Graham, "Top Officials Will Face Tougher Ethics Curbs", *Financial Times*, 12 November 1992.

12. In April 1996 President Clinton signed into law a bipartisan "soft" version of the line-item veto. It will concern only individual appropriations or special tax provisions that benefit fewer than 100 people or fewer than 10 businesses. The constitutionality of this law is already being challenged and will be ruled by the Supreme Court.

13. Bill Clinton, Remarks at Georgetown University, July 6, 1995, *Wireless File*, USIS, American Embassy, Paris, 7 July 1995.

14. Bill Clinton, "A New Covenant for American Security", *Harvard International Review*, Summer 1992. Author's emphasis.

CHAPTER 8: THE BIRTH OF WORLD-AMERICA

1. Samuel Eliot Morison, *The Oxford History of the American People*, New York 1972, vol. 3, p. 147.

2. Harold W. Stanley et al., *Vital Statistics on American Politics*, 2nd edition, Washington, D.C. 1990, p. 320.

3. The total value of exchanges of goods, services and revenues between the United States and the international community increased, at current values, by 132% between 1960 and 1970, by 437% between 1970 and 1980, and by 109% between 1980 and 1991 when it reached nearly $1,500 billion. Ibid., pp. 381–2; Bureau of Economic Analysis, *Survey of Current Business*, no. 6, June 1992, pp. 78–9.

4. Bureau of Economic Analysis, *Survey of Current Business*, no. 6, p. 49.

5. Stanley et al., *Vital Statistics on American Politics*, p. 382.

6. Bureau of Economic Analysis, *Survey of Current Business*, no. 6, p. 49.

7. Ibid.

8. Martin Dickson, "Lopez Leads GM Car Parts Crusade", *Financial Times*, 1 October 1992; "Profile: Jack Smith of GM", *Financial Times*, 20 October 1992. In March 1993, Lopez and his team of Europeans returned to Europe, enticed by Volkswagen with enormous salaries.

9. Christopher Lorenz, "When Head Office Goes Native", *Financial Times*, 2 December 1992.

10. Bureau of the Census, *Statistical Abstract of the United States: 1991*, Washington, D.C., p. 517.

11. Ibid., pp. 324–5.

12. Susan Antilla, "Turmoil Overseas Buffets Individual US Investor", *International Herald Tribune* (Paris), 22 September 1992.

13. Barry Riley, "Portfolio of Uncertainties", *Financial Times*, 26 October 1992.

14. Bureau of Economic Analysis, *Survey of Current Business*, no. 6, p. 49.
15. Ibid.
16. Bureau of the Census, *Statistical Abstract*, p. 795.
17. Bureau of Economic Analysis, *Survey of Current Business*, no. 5, May 1992, p. 53.
18. Office of Trade and Investment Analysis, *US Exports to Mexico: A State-by-State Overview, 1987–89*, Washington D.C., April 1991, p. 13.
19. Stanley et al., *Vital Statistics on American Politics*, pp. 391–2.
20. *Washington Representatives 1990*, Washington D.C., 1990, pp. 765 *passim*.
21. US Senate, *Foreign Influence on the US Political Process*, Washington, D.C., 19 September 1990.

CHAPTER 9: ECONOMIC LEADERSHIP

1. Bill Clinton, Speech to the American University on February 26, 1993, *Wireless File*, USIS, American Embassy, Paris, 1 March 1993, p. 7.
2. Bill Clinton, "A New Covenant for American Security", *Harvard International Review* Summer 1992, p. 19.
3. Paul F. Horvitz, "Clinton Says Only US Can Lead the World", *International Herald Tribune* (Paris), 9 December 1992.
4. Bill Clinton, "A New Covenant for American Security", p. 18.
5. Bill Clinton, Speech to the American University on February 26, 1993, p. 6.
6. Bill Clinton, "A New Covenant for American Security", p. 13.
7. Ibid., p. 19.
8. Ibid., p. 18.
9. Ibid., p. 14.
10. Ibid., p. 14.
11. Council of Economic Advisers, *Economic Report of the President*, Washington, D.C. 1992, p. 298.
12. Richard D. Heffner, *A Documentary History of the United States*, New York 1991, p. 302. For good insight into the attitudes of American leaders immediately after the war, see David W. Elwood, *Rebuilding Europe: Western Europe, America and Postwar Reconstruction*, New York 1992.
13. Council of Economic Advisers, *Economic Report*, p. 340.
14. Ibid., p. 22.
15. Bureau of Economic Analysis, *Survey of Current Business*, no. 6, June 1992, p. 88.
16. Olin L. Wethington, "US Economic Leadership in the Post-Cold War World", *Wireless File*, USIS, American Embassy, Paris, 30 October 1992.
17. Council of Economic Advisers, *Economic Report*, p. 22.
18. Ibid., p. 91.
19. Ibid., pp. 344–5.
20. Michael Prowse, "US Productivity Shows Best Gains in 20 Years Again", *Financial Times*, 5 February 1993.
21. Michael Prowse and Sylvia Nasar, "More Jobs in US Manufacturing? Clinton Unlikely to Beat the Trend", *International Herald Tribune* (Paris), 28 December 1992.
22. Sophie Gherardi, "Export: Better Than Ever", *Dynasteurs*, May 1991.
23. Council of Economic Advisers, *Economic Report*, p. 345.

24. Prowse, "US Productivity Shows Best Gains", and Martin Dickson and Louise Kehoe, "The Dinosaurs Arise Again", *Financial Times*, 21 December 1992.
25. Sylvia Nasar, "US Still No. 1 in Something? Yes, Productivity", *International Herald Tribune* (Paris), 14 October 1992. David Wessel, "US Service-Sector Workers Better Foreign Counterparts", *Wall Street Journal Europe* (London), 13 October 1992.
26. "OECD Lists Top Three Research Spenders", *Financial Times*, 11 March 1992.
27. George Bush, Speech to the Detroit Economic Club, 10 September 1992, *Wireless File*, USIS, American Embassy, Paris, 11 September 1992.
28. John S. Wilson, "The Myth of a Decline in US Technological Capacity", *Wireless File*, USIS, American Embassy, Paris, 1 January 1992.
29. Ibid.
30. Pierre Dommergues, "L'Université: la recherche de l'excellence, l'excellence de la recherche", *L'Etat des Etats-Unis*, Paris 1990, p. 278.
31. Bill Clinton, "Putting People First", *Wireless File*, USIS, American Embassy, Paris 23 October 1992, p. 17.
32. Nicholas F. Brady, "Business Must Think in International Terms", *Wireless File*, USIS, American Embassy, Paris, 29 October 1972, p. 7.
33. Andrew Pollack, "As High-Tech Goes Global, What's a Nation to Do?", *International Herald Tribune* (Paris), 2 January 1992.
34. Ibid.
35. Bill Clinton, Speech to the American University on February 26, 1993, p. 7.
36. Bill Clinton, "Putting People First", p. 17.
37. Bill Clinton, Speech to the American University on February 26, 1993, p. 7.
38. Bill Clinton, "Putting People First", p. 19.
39. Jim Fuller, "Clinton Gives Priority to Advanced Computer Network", *Wireless File*, USIS, American Embassy, Paris, 27 November 1992.
40. Louise Kehoe, "Driving Down a 'Superhighway' ", *Financial Times*, 19 November 1992.
41. Nicholas F. Brady, *Business Must Think in International Terms*, p. 8.
42. Bill Clinton, Speech to the American University on February 26, 1993, p. 9.
43. Ibid., p. 8.
44. Ibid.

CHAPTER 10: MASTERING THE
INFORMATION CIRCUITS

1. Bill Clinton, Speech to the American University on February 26, 1993, *Wireless File*, USIS, American Embassy, Paris, 1 March 1993, p. 7.
2. Alan Cane, "Hard Times for European Hardware", *Financial Times*, 4 October 1991.
3. "The Japanese Juggernaut That Isn't", *Business Week*, 31 August 1992.
4. T. Reyd, "Compaq Deals Itself into Japan", *International Herald Tribune* (Paris), 2 October 1992; Stephen Brull, "Apple Blossoms in Japan", *International Herald Tribune* (Paris), 24 February 1992.
5. "The Japanese Juggernaut That Isn't".
6. Steven Butler, "Importance of Shared Memory", *Financial Times*, 6 February 1992; T. Reyd, "American Firm Flexes High-Tech Muscle", *International Herald Tribune* (Paris), 6 February 1992.

7. Andrew Pollack, "US Tariffs Worry Korean Chipmakers", *International Herald Tribune* (Paris), 18 December 1992.

8. Steven Butler and Robert Thomson, "No Winners in the Chip Race", *Financial Times*, 21 January 1992.

9. Martin Dickson and Louise Kehoe, "The Dinosaurs Arise Again", *Financial Times*, 21 December 1992.

10. In value terms, nearly 50 per cent of the Japanese software market – video games included – is controlled by American companies. See "Japan Software – Open System", *International Herald Tribune* (Paris), 17 July 1992.

11. John Markoff, "Chip Alliance Put Sematech in Limbo", *International Herald Tribune* (Paris), 15 July 1992.

12. Louise Kehoe, "Radical Change of IBM Format", *Financial Times*, 21 November 1991, and "IBM's Global Overhaul Aims at Agility", *Financial Times*, 6 December 1991; John Markoff, "'Battleship IBM' Charts a Course for New Times", *International Herald Tribune* (Paris), 28 November 1991; Abdelaziz Mouline and Jean-Louis Perrault, "Un géant dans le fracas: quelles issues stratégiques pour IBM?", in *CEPII, L'économie mondiale 1993*, Paris 1992.

13. Emiko Terazono, "Focus is on Multimedia", *Financial Times*, 21 December 1992; George Gilder, "Now or Never", *Forbes*, 14 October 1991; Andrew Pollack, "Japanese Electronics Run Out of Steam", *International Herald Tribune* (Paris), 28 December 1992. In 1992, the profits of the biggest players in the sector, Matsushita and Sony, dropped by 65% and 61% respectively. Total production volume of all Japanese electronic equipment makers combined registered a two-digit (10.6%) drop for the first time since the Second World War – a most unpleasant surprise compared with the 5.6% increase they had expected.

14. "IBM-Apple Multimedia Standard", *International Herald Tribune* (Paris), 25 May 1992.

15. Hugo Dixon, "The Sleeping Giants Awaken", *Financial Times*, 7 October 1991.

16. Ibid.

17. Hugo Dixon, "Pace of Expansion Overseas Quickens", *Financial Times*, 7 October 1991.

18. Martin Dickson, "Overhaul of US System Looms", *Financial Times*, 7 October 91.

19. See Bruno Aurelle's excellent study, *Les Télécommunications*, Paris 1986.

20. Denis Gilhooly, "Scramble of the Titans", *Financial Times*, 7 October 1991.

21. Hugo Dixon, "Pace of Expansion Overseas Quickens". This experience with computer manufacturing was not a success, and NCR was put on sale in 1995.

22. Jeff Cole, "GM's Hughes Aircraft Wins $48 Million Pact for Tatarstan Telecommunications System", *The Wall Street Journal Europe* (London), 21 August 1992.

23. Michael Richardson, "Asia Launches Satellite Spending Spree", *International Herald Tribune* (Paris), 29 November 1991; Victoria Griffith, "You'll Never Be Alone Again", *Financial Times*, 4 February 1993.

24. Neil McCartney, "Expansion Rate Slows Down", *Financial Times*, 7 October 1991.

25. Sam Burks, "US Technologies Win Broad Support at ITU Conference", *Wireless File*, USIS, American Embassy, Paris, 14 March 1992.

26. "US Opening Up Competition for Telephone Carriers", *International Herald Tribune* (Paris), 29 November 1991.

CHAPTER 11: CONTROLLING THE STRATEGIC FLOWS

1. Agnès Chevallier, *Le Pétrole*, Paris 1986.
2. Alan Friedman, "Oil Industry Refines its Operations", *Financial Times*, 13 July 1992.
3. "US Economic Policy Objectives at the London Summit", *Wireless File*, USIS, American Embassy, Paris, 9 July 1991, p. 8.
4. "Kazakhstan Reaches Oil Deal", *International Herald Tribune* (Paris), 9 May 1992.
5. With the notable exception of the fabulous $6 billion contract landed by British Gas and Agip for natural gas prospecting around Karachaganak in Kazakhstan. See also Neil Buckley, "Developing the Last Great Oil Frontier", *Financial Times*, 7 August 1992.
6. "France Seeks Change in Oil-Futures Market", *International Herald Tribune* (Paris), 3 July 1992.
7. Floyd Norris, "Wall Street to World Markets: Not So Fast", *International Herald Tribune* (Paris), 8 January 1992.
8. "World's Foreign-Exchange Markets See Volume Soar to $1 Trillion a Day", *The Wall Street Journal Europe* (London), 25 and 26 September 1992; James Blitz, "How Central Banks Ran into the Hedge", *Financial Times*, 30 September 1992.
9. "Stock Issues Heard Round the World", *Business Week*, 31 August 1992.
10. Foreign securities held by American investors were worth $120 billion in 1985 and $275 billion in 1991. Their value is forecast to reach $875 billion by the year 2000. Steven Prokesch, "Foreigners Look to US For Long-Term Finance", *International Herald Tribune* (Paris), 6 July 1992.
11. Tracy Corrigan and Patrick Harverson, "Derivatives: Ever More Complex", *Financial Times* 8 December 1992.
12. Tracie Corrigan and Laurie Morse, "Derivatives: A Global Game for Allies and Rivals", *Financial Times*, 8 December 1992.
13. Martin Dickson, "Biggest US Banking Merger", *Financial Times*, 13 August 1991.
14. Caroline Dequet, *Evolution de l'économie du cinéma américain depuis 1980*, Paris 1992, pp. 2–3.
15. Ibid., pp. 47, 51 and 52.
16. Ibid., p. 19 *passim*.
17. Ibid., p 57 *passim*.
18. Ibid., p. 61.
19. Andrew Pollack, "US Breakthrough Sets TV on a Digital Path", *International Herald Tribune* (Paris), 4 December 1991; Steven Brull, "Japan HDTV: Static Before de Start", *International Herald Tribune* (Paris), 9 October 1991; Andrew Hill and Michiyo Nakamoto, "Troubled Transmission for the Big Picture Show", *Financial Times*, 17 November 1992. In February 1993, the Dutch group Philips, which had invested heavily in the European Mac HDTV technology, decided to postpone indefinitely the production of receivers using the European standard.
20. Damian Fraser, "Televisa in US Satellite Expansion", *Financial Times*, 6 January 1993.
21. Michael Richardson, "BBC and CNN Test Asia's New Tastes", *International Herald Tribune* (Paris), 2 October 1991.

22. Steven Brull, "Japan's Global News Dream Fades", *International Herald Tribune* (Paris), 7 December 1991.

23. Alain Woodrow, "Une riposte européenne à CNN", *Le Monde*, 4 May 1991.

24. George Bush, Speech to the Detroit Economic Club, 10 September 1992, *Wireless File*, USIS, American Embassy, Paris, 11 September 1992, p. 4.

25. Bill Clinton, "A New Covenant for American Security", *Harvard International Review*, Summer 1992, p. 18.

26. Ibid., p. 13.

CHAPTER 12: ORGANIZING PLANETARY TRADE

1. The retention of public subsidies and protectionist policies to prop up various industrial dinosaurs in developed countries is a response to social problems – notably unemployment – in certain regions, and has nothing to do with industrial logic.

2. George Bush, Speech to the Detroit Economic Club, 10 September 1992, *Wireless File*, USIS, American Embassy, Paris, 11 September 1992, p. 6.

3. Ibid. Author's italics.

4. International Trade Commission, "Potential Impact on the US Economy and Selected Industries of the North American Free-Trade Agreement", *Wireless File*, USIS, American Embassy, Paris, 4 February 1993, p. 8.

5. Lawrence Eagleburger, Speech before the Council on Foreign Relations on 7 January 1993, *Wireless File*, USIS, American Embassy, Paris, 11 January 1993.

6. George Bush, "Agenda for American Renewal", *Wireless File*, USIS, American Embassy, Paris, 11 September 1992, p. 11.

7. Lawrence Eagleburger, Speech before the Organization of American States, 3 June 1991, *Wireless File*, USIS, American Embassy, Paris, 5 June 1991.

8. In 1990, the figures were 32% for Japan and Taiwan, 30% for South Korea, 29% for Hong Kong, 27% for Singapore, 23% for Thailand, 17% for Malaysia and 13% for Indonesia.

9. Vietnam became the seventh member of ASEAN in 1995.

10. Don Oberdorfer, "US Lobbies against Asia Trade Bloc", *International Herald Tribune* (Paris), 14 November 1991.

11. Ibid.

12. Jane A. Morse and Robert F. Holden, "1992 Brings Major Change in US–East Asia Relations", *Wireless File*, USIS, American Embassy, Paris, 4 January 1993, p. 15.

13. David Marsh, "EC is Turning Inward – and Falling Behind", *Financial Times*, 22 February 1993.

CHAPTER 13: SHARING THE PROSPERITY

1. Jane A Morse and Robert F. Holden, "1992 Brings Major Change in US–East Asia Relations", *Wireless File*, USIA, American Embassy, Paris, 4 January 1993, p. 16.

2. George Bush, "Agenda for American Renewal", *Wireless File*, USIS, American Embassy, Paris, 11 September 1992.

3. Edward Perkins, Speech before the Second Committee of the 47th General

Assembly of the UN, 7/10/92, *Wireless File*, USIS, American Embassy, Paris, 8 October 1992.

4. George Bush, "Agenda for American Renewal".

5. Alexander Nicoll, "US Stance Rattles Asian Development Bank", *Financial Times*, 6 May 1992.

6. Stephen Fidler, "Washington Seeks Shift in IADB Role", *Financial Times*, 30 September 1992.

7. Nicholas Brady, Speech at the Annual Meeting of the Bretton Woods Committee, 10 July 1991, *Wireless File*, USIS, American Embassy, Paris, 11 July 1991, p. 21.

CHAPTER 14: A NEW WORLD SECURITY PACT

1. The START accords were completed with the signature in Paris, in January 1993, of a treaty banning chemical weapons, negotiated within the United Nations Conference on Disarmament and open to all states. This agreement – whose existence owes a great deal to American will – is similarly characterized by very "intrusive" *in situ* inspections. It is the first treaty to stipulate the verifiable, total interdiction of a whole category of weapons of mass destruction.

2. Bill Clinton, "A New Covenant for American Security", *Harvard International Review*, Summer 1992, p. 17.

3. Ibid., pp. 14, 17.

4. Department of Defence, *Discriminate Deterrence*, Washington, D.C., 1988.

5. Daniel Green, "Flying Start for Russia's Satellite-Launch Industry", *Financial Times*, 18 November 1992; Daniel Green and Leyla Boulton, "Fight for the Final Frontier", *Financial Times*, 2 February 1993. In December 1992, the American aerospace group Lockheed signed a joint venture agreement with the company Khrunichev Enterprise to market the Russian Proton launch vehicle. In February 1993, this firm undertook to launch twenty-one satellites for the American company Motorola's Iridium telecommunications network, in which it was to invest $40 million.

6. Daniel Green, "Ariane Chief Accuses US of Unfair Bias Over Satellite Deals", *Financial Times*, 2 November 1992.

7. Bill Clinton, "A New Covenant for American Security", p. 15.

8. James Baker, "The Euro-Atlantic Architecture: From West to East", *Wireless File*, USIS, American Embassy, Paris, 19 June 1991, p. 5.

9. Created in 1975 after the Helsinki accords, the CSCE is made up of the United States, Canada and all the European countries – including, subsequently, the new states emerging from the breakup of the USSR – situated between the Atlantic and the Urals.

10. "Keep Strong US Presence, Tokyo Says", *International Herald Tribune* (Paris), 20 October 1992.

11. Bill Clinton, "A New Covenant for American Security", pp. 16, 18.

12. Georges Couffignal, "Le système américain après la guerre froide", in Zaki Laïdi, ed., *L'Ordre mondial relâché*, Paris 1992, pp. 209–36.

13. Bill Clinton, "A New Covenant for American Security", p. 16.

CONCLUSION: AN "IMPERIALISM OF FREEDOM"

1. Carl Schmitt, *Political Theology: Four Chapters on the Concept of Sovereignty*, trans. George Schwab, Cambridge, Mass., 1985, p. 5.

2. Bill Clinton, "A New Covenant for American Security", *Harvard International Review*, Summer 1992, p. 13.

3. Richard D. Heffner, *A Documentary History of the United States*, New York 1991, p. 296.

4. Quoted in David W. Ellwood, *Rebuilding Europe: Western Europe, America and Postwar Reconstruction*, London 1992. This short but excellent work gives insight into the Old World's cultural resistances to the American view of the world.

4. Ibid., p. 20. Author's emphasis.

5. George Bush, State of the Union Message, *Wireless File*, USIS, American Embassy, Paris, 29 January 1992.

6. Bill Clinton, Speech to the American University on February 26, 1993, *Wireless File* USIS, American Embassy, Paris, 1 March 1993, p. 11.

7. On this subject, see Roberto da Matta's superb study, *Carnavals, bandits et héros*, Paris 1983.

INDEX